The Village in England

THE VILLAGE IN ENGLAND

HISTORY AND TRADITION

Graham Nicholson and Jane Fawcett

RIZZOLI
NEW YORK

First published in the United States of America in 1988 by
RIZZOLI INTERNATIONAL PUBLICATIONS, INC.
597 Fifth Avenue, New York, NY 10017

First published in 1988 by George Weidenfeld & Nicolson Ltd
91 Clapham High Street, London SW4 7TA,
in association with the National Trust for
Places of Historic Interest or Natural Beauty,
36 Queen Anne's Gate, London, S WIH 9A S

Library of Congress
Library of Congress Cataloging-in-Publication Data

Nicholson, Graham.
  [Village in history]
  The village in England/Graham Nicholson and Jane Fawcett.
    p.   cm.
  Previously published as: The village in history.
  Bibliography: p.
  Includes index.
  ISBN 0-8478-0956-0 : $25.00
  1. Villages—England—History. 2. England—Rural conditions.
I. Fawcett, Jane.   II Title
DA667.N53.1988
942'.009734—dc19   88-4395
                                                          CIP

Printed and bound in Italy.

Contents

Picture Acknowledgments

Illustrations have kindly been supplied by or are reproduced by kind permission of the following:

Aerofilms endpapers, 22
The Beaford Archive 146t
Bedfordshire Record Office 195
Janet and Colin Bord 54, 118, 181
BPCC/Aldus Archives 24(Bodleian Library), 32t(Trinity College, Dublin)
Bridgeman Art Library 73
British Library 6, 25, 26, 27, 44b, 45, 74, 101b, 102
Buckinghamshire County Council 186
Cambridge University, Committee for Aerial Photography 20, 21, 52
J. Allan Cash 100, 106–7
Victor Chinnery 56b, 57br
J. Bailey Denton, *Farm Homesteads of England* (1863) 117t
Robert Estall 171
E. T. Archive 97b, 198r, 150
Jane Fawcett 163, 188
Fine Art Photographic Library title page, 56t, 94–5b
Fortean Picture Library 83t
Fotomas Index 74b, 82, 109
Fox Talbot Museum, Lacock 172
Colin Grant 72
George Hall 96l
Sonia Halliday 46
Herefordshire City Library 121b
Clive Hicks 18r, 19, 29, 30, 32b, 48, 62l, 63tr, 65
Michael Holford 39
Hull Town Docks Museum 98
John Hutchins, *The History and the Antiquities of the Country of Dorset* (1774) 161, 164
Pamla Toler/Impact Photos 116–117b
A. F. Kersting 40t, 41, 61, 64, 77, 114, 152
Landscape Only 47
Lucinda Lambton 63tl
Lever Brothers 134
Lincolnshire Archives 104

Manchester City Art Galleries 139
Mansell Collection 40b, 49b, 87t, 88, 94t, 97t, 116t, 117c, 120, 128, 143, 146b
S. & O. Matthews 69, 168
Richard Muir 17, 35, 42, 63b, 71, 90t, 125, 127
Museum of English Rural Life, Reading 57bl, 121t, 140, 141, 144t
Museum of London 44b
National Trust Photographic Library 60 (Kevin Richardson), 91 (Mike Williams), 115, 130 (Geoff Morgan), 160 (Andy Williams), 169 (Nick Meers), 173 (Tymn Lintell), 180–181 (J. G. Oxborrow), 183 (Mike Williams), 187 (Nick Meers)
Pepys Library, Cambridge 70b
Public Record Office 12
Quarry Bank Mill, Styal 129, 182
Rowntree plc Archives 135
Lord St Levan, John St Aubyn 178
Royal Commission on Historical Monuments 68b, 79
Brian Shuel 149
Edwin Smith 6, 13, 15, 58–9, 62r, 66–7, 78, 81, 93, 99, 111, 112, 113, 133, 138, 142
Somerset Rural Life Museum 122, 151
Sutcliffe Gallery 4–5
Tate Gallery 144b
Ulster Folk and Transport Museum 68t
Victoria and Albert Museum 57t
Warwickshire County Record Office 50–51
Weidenfeld and Nicolson Archives 96r, 198l
West Sussex Record Office 136–7
Derek Widdicombe 83b (Simon Warner), 90b, 131, 177 and 179 (Noel Hapgood)
Andy Williams 158, 176, 185
Timothy Woodcock 80, 154, 165
Yorkshire Archaeological Society 148
ZEFA 166

Authors' Acknowledgments

Graham Nicholson (Part One)
I have acknowledged some of my debts to the research and writings of others in the text. The bibliography records more generally the basis on which the chapters are constructed. Lydia Greeves, Margaret Willes, Susan Denyer, Martin Drury and David Thackray of the National Trust have made many helpful comments and suggestions. Peter Eden and Alan Everitt, both formerly of Leicester University, set me off in the 1970s along what were to me completely new avenues of historical enquiry and interest. I am very grateful to them. None of these people, of course, is responsible for whatever shortcomings and errors the text may contain. Finally my wife Frances and sons Oliver and Leo have had to make all sorts of allowances for me while this book was in the writing. I would like to thank them for their support and encouragement.

Jane Fawcett (Part Two)
I am extremely grateful for the help given by many members of the National Trust staff in compiling this list, both at headquarters and in the regions. Above all, I owe thanks to my husband, Ted Fawcett, without whom these histories would not have been written, to Robert Latham who offered invaluable advice, and to Kate Entwistle for her unfailing support.

Sheep shearing, from a late 15th-century manuscript.

PREVIOUS PAGE *Setting up stooks in a wheat field, c.1880, by Frank Meadow Sutcliffe.*

PART ONE

The History of
the Village

Preface

Our forefathers in this village were no doubt as busy and bustling, and as important as ourselves; yet have their homes and transactions been forgotten from century to century, and have sunk into oblivion.

Gilbert White, The Natural History and Antiquities of Selborne (1789)

A few generations ago, Britain herded its population out of the countryside and into the confines of its new cities. It became the most urban, most industrial nation the world had seen. That exodus brought down the curtain on an older and a very different Britain. Most people had, until then, lived in villages. It is their world that this book attempts to portray. We still have the stage settings – the houses and streets, churches and pastures – but the players have vanished. Can we rediscover those authentic village people? Can we make the society of the village live again, in our mind's eye? Can we make sense of the remaining fabric of the village, through understanding the daily work of its people?

The task is dauntingly huge. Village life *was* life to its inhabitants. It encompassed the home, the family, work and recreation, and some less obvious things: industry, trade and transport. Several important components were intangible: beliefs and superstitions, values and ambitions. The variety of human conditions is enough to doom most generalizations about village people. The outlook of master and servant, rich and poor could not be identical.

My task has been to make sense of all this, without writing an encyclopaedia. I have tried to tell a story, to explain how and why villages began, grew, prospered and in some cases faltered. The story is arranged in five chapters, each of which covers a wide (and rather arbitrary) period of time. In each period I have tried to pick out whatever seemed particularly relevant to the story as a whole. That approach means that each chapter is not a comprehensive description of the age. Much detail has been sacrificed in the pursuit of understanding.

The book focuses on the life of the lower orders. In a perverse way it has been inspired by the illuminating descriptions of aristocratic lifestyles in Mark Girouard's *Life in the English Country House*. I have tried to pursue the same approach, relating the fabric, landscapes and structures of the past to the life of the rural community. I have looked upwards from the foot of the tree, while Mark Girouard described the commanding view from the top. It is the same tree, but the perspective is decidedly different.

One particular omission has been the metropolitan villages, by which I mean those communities which were sucked into the orbit of growing cities. Their story has a different ending, though not necessarily a different beginning, from that of their more rural cousins. I have, however, touched on the creation of suburban or garden villages; they reveal much about the way the modern world perceives its rural past.

The subject of perceptions is important. Historians' understanding of the past is coloured by the present and their view of it. They cannot fully escape from their own hindsight and prejudices. I am perfectly happy to own up to mine. Firstly, I take a rather utilitarian view of the past. On the whole, our ancestors' actions can best be explained, in my view, by economic motives. In other words, they built their homes, or farmed the land, or even brought up their children in a way that secured their standard of living. That was not such a base motivation when hardship or even starvation was always around the corner. I have tried not to forget that people do, sometimes, act for other reasons, be they social, religious, moral or philanthropic.

Secondly, I make an assumption: while the present colours our view of the past, the reverse is also true. Our perceptions of yesterday's world influence our attitudes to present-day society. Our cultural outlook is deeply nostalgic for the rural past. It has never fully come to terms with the reality of the urban present.

CHAPTER ONE

Digging for Roots:
The Village to 1300

Introduction

THERE is a poetic vision of an ancient village, much beloved of calendar manufacturers and advertising men. Venerable cottages crowd around a tree-fringed green; bluish wood smoke rises high above thatched roofs. Church and manor house stand together by a three-arched bridge which spans the limpid brook. At the parish pump village women gossip while their men folk (variously smocked, breeched and waistcoated) complete the day's noble labour in the hedgerowed fields. Soon they will return to quaff copious ale in the welcoming pub. Beyond lie the meadows, rank with cow parsley, the green of the plain and the rustling canopy of the woods.

That romantic image of village life is static and timeless. The characters and the cottages, their values and customs, appear unchanged for generations. Thomas Gray's celebrated 'Elegy written in a Country Church Yard' was among the first to sing this tune in the mid-eighteenth century:

The Curfew tolls the Knell of parting Day,
    The lowing Herd winds slowly o'er the Lea,
The Plow-man homeward plods his weary Way,
    And leaves the World to Darkness and to me . . .

Oft did the Harvest to their sickle yield,
    Their Furrow oft the stubborn Glebe has broke;
How jocund did they drive their Team afield!
    How bow'd the Woods beneath their sturdy
      Stroke!

The vision has grown in vigour and uniformity as we have distanced ourselves from the reality of life in a working village. In the comfort and good health of modern times, we are tempted to imagine our rosy-cheeked forefathers living out simple, unpressured lives in Ann Hathaway cottages. The truth, as we shall see, was at once more complex and more sordid.

Baldwin's Manor, Swaffham Prior, Cambs.:
a perfect village house from Henry VIII's reign.

But let the poetic visionary of the fourteenth century, Piers Plowman, provide an immediate antidote to such delusions of rustic charm:

The poorest folk are our neighbours, . . . the poor in their hovels, overburdened with children, and rack-rented by landlords. For whatever they save by spinning they spend on rent, or on milk and oatmeal to make gruel and to fill the bellies of their children who clamour for food. And they themselves are often famished with hunger, and wretched with the miseries of winter – cold, sleepless nights, when they get up to rock the cradle cramped in a corner, and rise before dawn to card and comb the wool, to wash and scrub and mend, and wind yarn and peel rushes for their rushlights. The miseries of these women who dwell in hovels are too pitiful to read or describe in verse.

Villages have never been uniform. Each one is different, and its shape and fabric reflect its life and struggles over the centuries. Today it is perfectly possible for a developer to plan an estate of houses in, say, Buckinghamshire, identical in every respect with another in Northamptonshire, Yorkshire or Powys. Such houses will be miles from the workplaces of the inhabitants, and will pay little or no regard to the history, economy or geology of the locality. That would have been unthinkable before the onset of the railway age.

Nor has village life ever stood still. Village people have often been highly conservative, bemoaning or denouncing change through the centuries. But the countryside has been evolving continuously. There have been sudden cataclysms: invasions and disease, famine and fire. Political action, such as the dissolution of the monasteries, has overturned time-honoured ways. Personal ties, ancient systems of agriculture, and the very appearance of the countryside have been dissolved. The whole fabric of village life, which appears so secure and ageless, has proved mutable.

Today's village has been built and rebuilt countless times. Its roads have been realigned: the settlement itself may have been resited, leaving the parish church stranded away from its flock. The woodland has been burnt, regenerated and coppiced, the fields extended, enclosed and opened out again. Land has been subdivided and amalgamated, ploughed and put back to meadow. At each remove something of the old remains and something new is added. Change and continuity are two strands of a single thread, from which the fabric of a village is woven.

The antecedents: before Domesday Book

It has been conventional to represent the Norman invasion of 1066 as a watershed of English history. The events of that year overturned a dynasty, undermined a culture and replaced an aristocracy. They reverberate today in the language. William the Conqueror imposed a fierce regime by force. He subdued the north by the sword, plundering and burning on an enormous scale, if contemporary chronicles are to be believed. His troops were billeted on the land. He imposed heavy taxes on his new kingdom. And of course he rewarded his followers, who had overcome King Harold at the Battle of Hastings, with huge tracts of the conquered territory.

Domesday Book: a detailed record of the productive and well-peopled land that William of Normandy had conquered.

The new Norman lords came in time to dominate rural society and to operate its machinery of local government. Yet for all that they changed, William's men left far more intact. The victorious army of 1066 numbered perhaps 6000 men, including mercenaries who returned to the Contintent once the Conquest was achieved. The Normans remained a small but powerful élite, and there were no subsequent waves of colonizing invaders; common men and women were, for the most part, not displaced from their daily livelihood. Though the pattern of land ownership was changed by the Conquest, the pattern of land tenure and usage at the local, parish level was not. Most men and women continued to pursue their livelihoods, little affected by the change of dynasty.

Some twenty years after the Conquest, the king ordered an account of his kingdom to be compiled. The extreme thoroughness with which his commissioners went about their work was a source of some amazement: the contemporary *Anglo-Saxon Chronicle* records that 'there was no hide or yard of land, not even . . . an ox, or a cow, or a pig that was not put down in the record'. The process invited comparison with the Day of Judgement, and the account earned itself the popular name 'Domesday Book'.

The survey was not a comprehensive record, however; the king's commissioners shrank from visiting the remote and hostile north of the country, and the record omits London, some other towns and most of the possessions of the clergy. More important still, though Domesday records over 13,000 place names, the great majority of which are recognizable

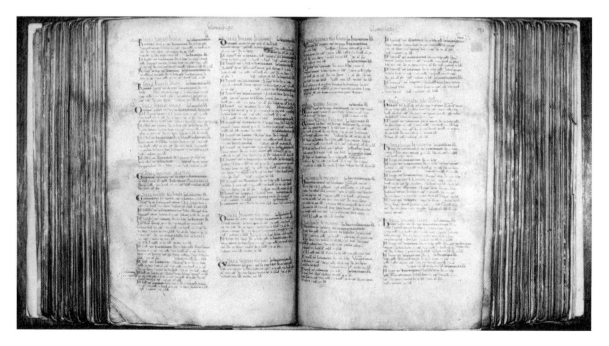

Celtic fields at Morvah, West Cornwall:
a memorial to the efforts of Iron Age farmers.

antecedents of present-day names, it is not a record of settlements. The motive behind Domesday Book was purely financial. The king wanted to know what revenues could be squeezed from his new realm; he required a comprehensive description of the land, and of what was of value, such as the meadows, woods, animals, mills and people. It is a record, therefore, of land holdings, which are identified by name. Those holdings we might call estates: areas of land under a single proprietor who leased portions to men and women who were bound to him by personal ties and obligations.

The traditional view holds Domesday Book to be a list of the villages of England. Where a place name in Domesday is the precursor of a modern name, it is appealing to believe that we are reading of the direct ancestor of a modern village. The difficulty is that large areas of the country, described and named in the survey, had no villages at that date – if ever. This is easiest to see in the so-called highland zone, that is the area roughly north and west of a line from Torquay to Teesside. Though landholdings in that zone are described and named in Domesday, both present-day geography and archaeological investigations show that the population has always been dispersed in isolated farmsteads and small hamlets. 'Nucleated' villages, that is to say settlements of twenty or so dwellings, have never, for instance, been the predominant pattern in Devon and Cornwall. There, as the doyen of English local history studies, Professor W. G. Hoskins, has shown, many still-active farmsteads and hamlets originated well before the Conquest. In Zennor parish, in the Penrith peninsula of west Cornwall, field boundaries were laid out by Celtic farmers using surface boulders to form a pattern of small irregular fields which, once established, became virtually immovable. We can be quite sure that a compact village did not exist here at Domesday, or at any period before or since. As I write this, in the parish of Manley – a Saxon name – in Cheshire, I am aware that there is no village here, no village green, nor even an ancient parish church, just a scatter of houses and farmsteads linked by a tangle of lanes.

But what of the lowland zone, the swath of central and south-eastern England that certainly does have nucleated settlements? An intriguing possibility arises which Christopher Taylor in his impressive study of early rural settlement, *Village and Farmstead*, takes as the basis for a startling reappraisal. If many of the places described by Domesday Book in the highland zone were not villages at all, might it also be that Domesday Book was describing a similar pattern in lowland Britain? Could it be that Domesday Book, so long taken as the clinching proof of the antiquity of present-day villages, is really painting a completely different picture: one of very few substantial villages, and of a profusion of irregular settlements spread across the countryside?

Let us for the moment begin at 1086 and work backwards, trying to find the roots of Domesday Britain. We know that England in 1086 was well peopled. Extrapolating from the Domesday record, we can estimate a population in England and Wales of roughly 2 million. Of these the great majority were rural inhabitants, for the towns were then very small. To support this sizeable population there was vigorous economic activity throughout the land. Mills, weirs, fishponds, ploughs and oxen were seen in abundance. Mixed husbandry of animals and arable was practised everywhere. We know from Domesday Book that there were 71,000 plough teams in action, which suggests an area of 7 or 8 million acres in cultivation; that is a high figure, equalling the amount of land under the plough in 1914. When one adds the exploitation of the poorer soils for grazing and forestry, it would seem that most of the country was being farmed in an active manner in 1086.

Dramatic confirmation has come from aerial photography over the past fifty years, and particularly in the exceptionally dry summer of 1976. In periods of drought, features such as buildings, ditches, field boundaries and roads, which have long disappeared from the surface, stand out clearly from the air in the varying growth of crops and grass. It is clear now that large areas of Britain in most types of terrain had extensive field systems well before the Conquest. Primeval forests had long ago been pushed back; there may have been no more woodland in Britain at Domesday than there is today. The view of an eminent historian only thirty years ago, that 'most areas lay in their natural state, awaiting the sound of a human voice' and of settlements so remote, even in the English Midlands, 'that they betrayed their presence only by the smell of woodsmoke' seems scarcely tenable today.

What manner of people made up this industrious population? Britain, as every schoolchild knows, was subject to conquests and invasions before 1066. Vikings, Saxons and Normans had all settled parts of the country, bringing with them their customs and culture. The Vikings have a harsh reputation as raiders and pillagers. In fact, from the 850s onwards they rapidly established themselves in the eastern part of the country as peaceable tillers of the soil. The Danelaw – the area subject to Danish rather than to English law – is not difficult to perceive even today by its distinctive place names ending in '-thorpe' and '-by'. In the north-west, places such as Stonethwaite, Rossthwaite and Seathwaite in Borrowdale have an Old Norse element, meaning a clearing or meadow, brought in by a slightly later influx of mainly Norwegian settlers. What we know of the Vikings in Scandinavia at the time of the invasion suggests that they farmed from isolated sites in family or kinship groups; not until the late Viking era in Denmark were groups of farmsteads to be found together in a village. Viking armies were composed of free men who held no allegiance to a feudal lord. When in England they defended their free status as 'sokemen' or small proprietors, independently colonizing fen and heath country.

Do we, then, look to the English – the Angles, Saxons and Jutes – for the genesis of the village in Britain? In the fifth century AD these Germanic peoples invaded along the eastern and south-eastern seaboard. The conquest of Kent by the Jutes can, perhaps, illustrate the way the invaders infiltrated and integrated themselves into their new homeland. Settlement in Kent, as elsewhere, has always been much influenced by communications, and Kent is well provided with both rivers and ancient roads. As well as Roman Watling Street, which linked Canterbury and Rochester with London, there were lesser roads leading north and south from Maidstone, and many minor roads, including a spur from Watling Street along the Darent valley. There were a number of Roman villas in that valley, substantial houses at the centre of extensive farmland estates. Older still is the so-called Pilgrim's Way along the foot of the chalk escarpment of the Downs. Another pre-Roman route, the Green Way, follows the spring line below the Pilgrim's Way, and may have begun as a line of travel between settlements. It comes as little surprise to find that the earliest Jutish settlements are near the old routes. The newcomers did not settle *on* the main Roman roads, however, but a mile or so *off* the road,

The Pilgrims' Way above Trottiscliffe, Kent. Along such ancient trackways, which pre-date the Romans, came both traders and invaders.

possibly to avoid the attention of the next marauding troop of invaders. The Jutes settled near the Pilgrim's Way and the Green Way, and along the river valleys and creeks, in the areas in which there had been Roman and pre-Roman farming.

The significance of all this is that the Jutes followed the footsteps of earlier men. They settled on land that had been worked and grazed for centuries. They were not the architects of great change in the countryside; to a large extent they accepted and adopted the status quo. One astonishing survival to the present day is the pattern of Roman fields which the Jutes must have worked. Roman farmers grew cereals in a regular grid of fields, quite unlike the field systems of other cultures in Britain. That pattern appears to survive – though not every scholar agrees – in the alignment of lanes and hedges at Cliffe in Kent and at Ripe, over the Sussex border. It is arguably present also at Rainham and at Ickham, close to the garrison towns of Rochester and Canterbury which would have needed substantial supplies of grain. It seems very likely that the Jutes adopted many of the boundary lines of the old Roman villas and estates, and some of those in turn became parish boundaries after the conversion of Kent. So the invaders took on the patterns of landholdings of their predecessors. The second clear conclusion is that the Jutes did not import from the Continent, nor develop subsequently, the notion of nucleated villages as the main form of settlement. There are, of course, ancient towns in Kent, but they are mostly on the coastal fringe. The centre has always been rural, and has sustained few villages of substance. The population was, and still is, widely spread in hamlets and single farm holdings. It is the garden of England but not the heart of village England.

The question, then, is whether the history of Kent in Saxon times is a good guide to what was happening in other parts of the country. The written evidence suggests it is. From the seventh century onwards we have about 1500 Saxon charters. They are legal documents recording transactions in land, and in particular they set out the terms on which kings granted land to their tenants-in-chief – the Church and nobility. It is striking that many of these earliest written sources refer to estates of immense size. To take just one example, the estate at Malling in Sussex, granted to the archbishops of Canterbury by King Baldred of Kent in the early ninth century, stretched from its centre at South Malling over the South Downs and the Weald of Wadhurst and beyond, a distance of some twenty miles. It included woodland and arable, meadow and pasturage, taking in several parishes and many settlements. The charters are equally impressive in their grasp of detail: when a large estate was granted at Westbury in Gloucester in the eighth century the rent or tribute was precisely stated: two tuns (large casks of 100 or more gallons apiece) of pure ale, large quantities of mild and Welsh ale, six rams and forty cheeses, together with ground and unground corn, payable each year to the royal estates. Such an assessment does not suggest that empty and unexploited lands were being handed over, but rather that the estate was already a going concern and fully productive. There are many similar charters, and the picture that starts to emerge is of well-organized landholdings whose boundaries were clearly known. In the earliest original charter the king of Kent granted lands in Thanet 'by the well-known bounds indicated by me and my reeves'. Other early charters speak of boundaries that are 'ancient and known by the natives'. Such expressions broadly hint that the boundaries, and by implication, the estates, were already old and that the Saxon peoples had taken them intact from their predecessors.

Archaeology confirms that Jutish Kent was similar to other parts of Saxon England. Archaeologists have found settlements of the period in many places, as much by aerial photography as by the excavation of extremely sparse remains. The invaders constructed two kinds of buildings. The less common were rectangular halls, substantially built and as much as 30 feet by 15 feet in plan. They would seem capable of sheltering an extended family. More numerous were small huts of a square or roundish form. They may have been stores for crops, or workplaces, in which case they were probably outbuildings of halls nearby. Whatever their precise purposes, these structures help to reveal a pattern of settlement. Investigations of a Saxon site at New Wintles, Eynsham in Oxfordshire, have shown a scattering of huts and halls over many acres. Similarly at Mucking in Essex, in an area which had been occupied in the Roman era and before, huts of the Saxon age were widely spread in an apparently random fashion. Another pointer to early settlement sites are the fragments of pottery which surface on cultivated land. By careful dating, recording and plotting, those trivial finds gradually compose a picture of where vanished farmsteads or hamlets stood. That exercise has been carefully done over many years at Brixworth, north of Northampton, and has revealed no fewer than nine settlements of the early Saxon period, eight of them at a distance from the present-day village. Allowing for the fact that much of the land is not available for investigation (being under houses, gardens, pasture and a quarry), that single parish might have had thirty or more small settlements – an extreme case, possibly, but a similar pattern has been detected elsewhere.

Peasant huts of the Saxon period, reconstructed near the site of a settlement at West Stow, Suffolk. Such huts were only semi-permanent.

A few larger Saxon settlements have been found, for instance at Catholme in the Trent Valley, and at West Stow in Suffolk. (At West Stow a recent reconstruction of the hamlet gives a flavour of the conditions in which ordinary people lived.) Each settlement had about half a dozen farmsteads, with associated huts. But none of the Saxon settlements so far located possessed the features we would expect in a permanent village. They lack a street plan on which buildings are set with any regularity. There is no recognizable field system. The settlements are transitory, each being rebuilt and shifted a number of times in a lifespan of as little as a hundred years before abandonment. We can picture a rather restless community, exploiting an area of land until the soil was exhausted, before moving, possibly just a mile or two, to a new spot in the same parish.

So we have found old estates continuing into a new era, but individual settlements that were small and transitory. There is no inherent contradiction in that. It is possible to have the continuous exploitation of an area while the individual habitations within it break up and re-form. Equally an estate might change hands, even from one race to another, without any grave disturbance of its existing populace. When a relatively small number of Saxons – in the fifth century there were no more than 10,000 of them – assumed control of a large part of England, they must surely have wanted the Celtic population to stay. Without people, huge estates were worthless. A king, archbishop or nobleman needed a workforce to exploit their lands, and a tenantry able to pay rents in money or kind. Far from the schoolchild's notion of the Angles, Saxons and Jutes driving all the ancient Britons remorselessly into the mountains of the West, we can now see the Saxon settlement as a process of assimilation. There are numerous place names in areas dominated by Saxons which point directly to the co-existence of the two peoples and cultures. Welshpool, Walton, Bretton, Bratton, Bretby and dozens more indicate that Celtic settlements survived in English territory.

Early Churches

In many villages the church is the oldest surviving building, but it is rarely the work of one age. Medieval churches grew over the centuries, and some have shrunk again, as the fortunes of the village rose and fell. Like an archaeological site, the village church may have the stratum of one age overlying the deposits of earlier times, with each providing evidence of the history of the community.

A visit to an old church is best begun with a perambulation of the churchyard; the pattern of building and alteration is more apparent from the exterior than from inside. The forms of window and door openings are the most obvious clues to dates. Saxon work is marked by plain round-headed arches, separated by baluster shafts. Norman masons embellished their work with vigorous carvings, particularly in concentric bands of decoration above round-arched doorways and windows, and in figurative carvings in the *tympanum*, the area immediately above a door. The pointed arch of Gothic architecture percolated down to the level of parish church design by 1200. However, one does have to remember that Victorian architects used medieval forms when building or 'restoring' churches.

Early churches generally contain a mixture of window and door styles, because of numerous enlargements and rebuildings. Saxon churches were narrow; most had only a rectangular nave and a smaller chancel, also rectangular

ABOVE *The fine Saxon tower at Earls Barton, Northamptonshire, topped by later battlements.*

(or, less commonly, a round-ended apse). By no means all had a tower, but some seventy Saxon church towers do remain, particularly in the Eastern counties of England – perhaps they had a defensive aspect in the age of Viking invasions. It is in the tower that Saxon or Norman work is most likely to have survived the remodelling of later ages.

When the population grew in the twelfth and thirteenth centuries, it prompted the widening of the nave – the congregation's part of the church – in many parishes. An aisle or aisles were built, and the additional space increased the opportunities for ritual. It provided a route for processions and a place for side altars and chantry chapels. Something of that medieval ritual can still be discerned in the church furnishings. On entering, a parishioner could moisten his fingers to cross himself with holy water from a stoup set in the wall. Nearby, at the west end of the nave, was the font for baptisms, usually carved of stone with a wooden lid, which was lockable to prevent the theft of holy water. Some font covers of the later medieval period are highly elaborate pieces of Gothic carving.

For centuries the congregation was expected to stand

ABOVE *The superbly carved door-surround of the little 12th-century church at Barfreston, Kent.*

ABOVE *Sedilia for priest, deacon and sub-deacon, with a piscina to the left, at Stapleford, Wiltshire.*

The congregation could only glimpse the ritual of the mass in the chancel, for it was separated from them by a rood screen, so-called because it supported the rood, or representation of Christ on the cross. They peered through the doorway and traceried windows of the gilded and painted screen, which must have been the highlight of most parish churches. To Protestant reformers, however, the screen and the rood were a symbol of superstition, and they swept most of them away. In many churches only a redundant access stair and doorway in the wall at the north side of the chancel arch now mark where the rood screen once was.

In the chancel a *piscina*, or basin, where the priest washed his hands during the mass, may be found set in the south wall. Nearby may be *sedilia*, stone seats under canopies, in which the celebrant priests could sit. Many chancels were extended in the fourteenth and fifteenth centuries, and carved wooden stalls for clergy and choir introduced. The clergy's seats were of the tip-up variety with small ledges underneath known as *misericords* ('compassionate'), since in their tipped-up position the priest could prop himself on these ledges, while appearing to stand, as was required, through lengthy services.

throughout the service. From the fourteenth century the sermon became a more important part of the proceedings, as the Church made an effort to explain the essentials of the faith in the vernacular tongue. Pews were commonplace in the fifteenth century, and in the more prosperous areas, such as East Anglia and the West Country, many churches are enriched by magnificently carved pew-ends, and even by an octagonal pulpit of the same era.

BELOW *The interior of St Nonna's Church, Altarnun, Cornwall, with stone font, vigorously carved pew-ends and rood screen.*

Village and community

This journey through the centuries before Domesday Book has revealed a landscape without the neat villages of popular imagination. It has thereby thrown up more questions than it has answered. If the Saxons did not establish the pattern of our villages, whence did it come, and when? And why did 'traditional' nucleated villages appear in some areas, and not in others?

One important factor was the break-up of the huge estates of Saxon times into much smaller units, the manors. Quite why that occurred is still somewhat obscure, but the old estates must have been unwieldy to administer from a single point. We can surmise that some manors were granted away or sub-let for a rent and in the course of time became effectively autonomous under the lord of the manor. However the process occurred, it is clear that, some large church and royal estates excepted, the manor was becoming the main unit of administration. The timescale of the change was long, but it appears to have been largely complete in the lowland zone by the twelfth century.

Goltho, Lincolnshire, the site of a lost medieval village: its Norman castle mound (left) still guards the outlines of former streets and house plots.

At that juncture there is considerable evidence of villages being newly founded, or extended out of clusters of huts. An example of a new village is Faxton, in Northamptonshire. The site is now deserted, and has therefore been available for close archaeological investigation. The village grew to a substantial size, with many houses, streets and gardens, and substantial open fields. Its origin on this site can be dated from the middle to the end of the twelfth century. Another village to grow was Tatton in Cheshire, the site of which is now within the deer park of Tatton Park in Cheshire, owned by the National Trust. There are signs of some very early settlement here; a large number of small flint tools from about 8000BC has been found. There are traces of Bronze Age settlers, and then from the Saxon period several huts and a large rectangular building have been identified. Finally, in the centuries after the Conquest, a village flourished and at one time had extensive fields, woodland, grazing, a mill and a manor house, Old Tatton Hall (now restored to give a vivid picture of medieval living conditions). The evidence on the ground does not prove the continuous existence of a settlement at Tatton, but it does show a medieval village on a site that had been colonized, temporarily, several times before.

Goltho, east of Lincoln, was a settlement that alternately struggled and thrived for a millenium; only a sad, deserted chapel now marks its site. Once it had a Romano-British farm, but it was deserted in the fourth century and there was a break in occupation of some 400 years. Goltho then acquired a string of timber buildings, each with its own fenced yard – possibly paddocks for cattle. A century later, those houses were being moved away to make room for a timber hall, which after many alterations and rebuilding was to become the village manor house. Having acquired a Norman castle in the interim, Goltho took in its final form around the twelfth century. It superseded, rather than evolved out of, the Saxon settlement. There was a main street and an adjoining side street, each lined with houses and gardens, the manor house and chapel. There was a regularity about the arrangements that suggests a conscious decision to lay out a street plan, on which the houses and gardens were planted. In another excavated medieval village, Wharram Percy in Yorkshire, there was a moment when the manor house was moved out of the clutter of the settlement to a new site at a little distance, and linked to it by a street upon which houses were built on regular plots.

That element of planning could be a critical factor in the emergence of compact villages. Settlements that were growing at this time began to acquire a regularity in layout. The extension of Burwell in

Milburn in Cumbria, a medieval village that was planned and laid out to a regular pattern. Each house plot has a narrow frontage to the green, and a long yard, or croft, to the rear.

Cambridgeshire, for example, included five parallel streets. At Sawston, also in Cambridgeshire, a new, straight street was set out, along which house plots of regular dimensions were formed. There are also medieval villages that were planned from the start. Several have been identified in the north-eastern counties of England. Evenly spaced house plots front either onto a straight road – as at Carlton, County Durham – or else face into a village green of regular proportions – as at Cold Kirby in North Yorkshire, or at Milburn in Cumbria, where the original layout is almost perfectly preserved. It is difficult to escape the conclusion that such villages could be formed or extended only on the initiative, or at least with the co-operation, of the lord on whose land they stood.

If that is the case, what was the motive? We need to bear in mind that new towns and boroughs were being founded, or old towns substantially enlarged, in many parts of the country at this period. For instance the Abbot Baldwin was laying out Bury St Edmunds between 1066 and 1086, while at Stratford-upon-Avon the Bishop of Worcester, the owner of the manor, set out the new town on a gridiron pattern of streets that survives today. The motive for such foundations was largely economic. The proprietor hoped to attract rent-paying tenants to his new town.

Ridge and furrow at Byfield Hill, Northants. This undulating pattern was formed by the ploughs of village farmers cultivating the long strips into which medieval open fields were divided.

The enterprise stood or fell by whether it succeeded in this; Bury and Stratford prospered, while New Winchelsea, laid out by the King in an ambitious manner, failed to develop fully. The new and extended villages of the time also seem to have been examples of medieval property development. The lord of the manor, having marked out the new plots for house and garden, must have hoped either to attract new free tenants, or to move (voluntarily or otherwise) his own serfs into the village, or simply to create tenancies for new families as the population grew. Simple self-interest told him that an expanding village bore the prospects of more rent and of additional hands to farm his own lands.

To attract and hold new tenants, however, he had to assure them a livelihood. That meant letting them use some land for both arable and grazing. In theory each tenant could have rented a compact block of land somewhere in the manor. But there were practical difficulties in that arrangement. The quality of arable land varied considerably, and a simple parcelling-out would have been very unfair. Moreover there were some types of land in which everyone needed a share, particularly the meadow and the heaths. So a system was devised or evolved which gave each cultivator a fair stake in the agricultural resources of the village. It has come to be known as the open-field or common-field system, and it was so important a feature of medieval village life that it deserves describing in some detail.

Most villagers farmed, but some had more land than others. Foxton in Cambridgeshire, in the middle of the thirteenth century, had three or four tenants with up to 72 acres apiece. Some thirty to forty families held between 9 and 18 acres, but a further seventeen had 2 acres or less. Finally, about twenty families whose names are known from local records appear to have had no land at all apart, perhaps, from the house and garden plot on which they lived. In general each family's land was held in strips and was widely scattered about the manor, giving it a share of the good, the bad and the indifferent land. In lowland Britain the landscape was not divided by a network of lanes and neat hedgerows; most of the arable was in open fields. Some villages had two large fields; most had between three and six, all divided into numerous strips. There might also be some smaller, enclosed areas of land, held by the lords of the manor or by a substantial farmer. But even those people had land in the open fields too, and a single farmer could well have fifty or more separate pieces of arable.

In theory there were four strips to an acre; each was a furlong or 220 yards in length, and a rod or $5\frac{1}{2}$ yards in width. In practice dimensions varied, but the strips were always long and narrow, so that the peasant farmer could avoid constantly turning his plough and the ox team that pulled it. As he progressed along the furrows, the mouldboard of the plough continuously turned the earth towards the

Harrowing the land over newly sown seed, from the Luttrell Psalter (1335–40). The man behind is killing crows with stones and sling. Horses were gradually replacing oxen for draught purposes.

centre of the strip; the result was a heaping of the soil into a ridge, which in heavy land could be high and steep. Much of that undulating pattern of ridge and furrow was fossilized when in later years arable was put down to permanent grass. A curious feature of thousands of the preserved strips is an elongated, reverse S shape. Few, if any of the strips are straight, and there is not a single example of an unreversed S. This apparent mystery can be explained, once more, by the process of ploughing. On approaching either end of a strip, the plough team would prepare for a right-handed U turn by swinging out a little to the left, rather as a car driver might do today. This manoeuvre would deflect the alignment of the furrow, while keeping the wasted space of the headland, or turning area, to a minimum. Ridge and furrow can be seen best from the air, but it stands out well when the sun is low, or after a light scattering of snow. It is a conspicuous feature of the landscape in Leicestershire and the East Midlands, and often survives in the parkland of great houses of a later age, whose owners turned former ploughlands into pleasure grounds. There are good examples at the National Trust properties of Erddig in Clwyd, Wimpole in Norfolk and Studley Royal in North Yorkshire. For sheer extent the remnants of open-field ridge and furrow are undoubtedly our major legacy from the medieval peasantry.

The most valuable ground in the village was the meadow. The fertile grassland on alluvial soils was devoted each spring and summer to the making of hay, which was vital for the livestock in winter. The animals in turn were the indispensable source of power for ploughing, of protein from meat and milk, and, not least, of dung. Without manuring, the fertility of the soil could not be retained. So everyone wanted a share of the meadow, and each tenant held strips according to the size of his rent. By custom, the strips in the meadow were periodically redistributed by drawing lots, while strips in the open fields passed from father to son over many generations.

Milking was mostly done outdoors, though this cow is shown in a stall. A Victorian milkmaid would have recognized the coopered wooden pail in this 13th-century English manuscript.

Elsewhere in the parish were commons and wastelands. They were neither cultivated nor parcelled out. Individual villagers shared them as communal resources. Pasturing on the commons was often 'stinted' – that is to say, limited to an agreed number of essential livestock, such as the plough oxen, cows and sheep. Other animals, including pigs and poultry were relegated to the waste, those large tracts of heaths, woods and marsh which separated one village from its neighbours. Rights over the waste were less well defined, and adjacent parishes often 'intercommoned' – that is, their animals shared the waste, and were branded with identifying marks. Commons and waste were the source of many other necessities such as reeds for the roof, wild berries for the kitchen, and wood for the repair of houses and for the fire.

One further type of land ought to be mentioned. The population was growing substantially and may have trebled between Domesday Book and 1300. That in turn increased the pressure on the land to produce more food. Waste and common land was cleared and turned into arable, in a process known as 'assarting'. Some 'assarts' were no doubt the work of the village as a whole. The nearest we come to a written description is from Harlestone in Northamptonshire in 1410, where, by a community agreement, nine good men set out a new field for the benefit of the whole village. Much was also achieved by individuals and families. In the latter case the assarted field remained outside the common-field strip system. Sometimes assarting was done without formal permission, but in general lords of the manor were unlikely to object to the improvement of the land for which they could charge a licence fee or rent. The process of bringing marginal and higher ground into cultivation was an essential safety valve as the pressure of people on the land increased.

There were clear limits, however, to what arable farming could produce. We must assume that the food gap was filled by more cattle, pigs, sheep and poultry. Every year, each of the open fields had a specified purpose. One field would be left fallow to raise a grass crop, and the village animals were free to graze it. The other field or fields were ploughed, either in autumn or spring, and sown with grain crops: wheat, rye, maslin (mixed wheat and rye), oats or barley. The cycle of rotation – two years in some places, three or even four elsewhere – and the type of grain sown, depended on the quality of the soils and the custom of the village. After harvest, the field was again made available for rough grazing. Similarly the hay meadows or Lammas land were temporarily closed to animals, usually from Candlemas (1 February) to the completion of the hay harvest around Lammas Day (1 August), but were then thrown open for pasture. The system nicely balanced the needs of a society of small cultivators. There was always grazing land for the cattle, especially during the winter when foodstuffs were in shortest supply. The cattle in turn fertilized the land, which was then able to bear a further crop of grain. Each family had its hay crop, and each its rights of commons and heath. It is hard to conceive of another system which would give every small farmer access to all the resources he needed.

Common-field agriculture required, of course, a high degree of co-ordination. The villages had to agree which field was to be fallow. They needed to follow a defined order of ploughing and harvesting, otherwise one man's wagon would run over another's newly ploughed land or ripening crops. Animal grazing had to be kept within limits and specified times. The system appears at first sight hopelessly

Haymaking in the 13th century, with a scythe that would scarcely have seemed out of place in the 19th century.

Ploughing with an ox-team, a scene from the Luttrell Psalter. Oxen and plough were major assets shared by several villagers. The ploughmen are wearing 'kirtles', or tunics.

complicated; the dispersion of individual holdings and the common grazing of all manner of animals do have clear drawbacks in terms of efficiency. There can have been little incentive to improve the land if one's neighbour's strip was like an ill-kept allotment, rank with seeding weeds. The agreed timetable prevented any individual experimentation with new methods of husbandry. Yet the system did work because the village maintained a strongly communal outlook. Villagers knew that their land was not private property, and they accepted a high level of regulation in their husbandry.

The mechanism by which that was achieved was the court of the manor. The court was presided over by the lord or by his official, and every serf was bound to attend. It was a mark of his subjection to the lord. The place of assembly was determined by custom. In some villages it was in the hall of the manor house, in others outside, or under a specified tree. The frequency of meetings was also customary: mostly somewhere between once a month and once in six months. The whole court, including the serfs and freemen present, often had the right to make decisions. This is

not too surprising, given that much of what came before them concerned matters of communal interest and regulation. Disputes between neighbours and failures to abide by the agreed pattern of husbandry formed much of the business: one villager brought a suit against another, and had redress. Typical offences were overstepping another man's strip in ploughing, appropriating a neighbour's pig, allowing cattle to trespass on the meadow out of season, and stealing from another man's dungheap (which was normally kept outside his door in the street). Villagers were particularly suspicious of their fellows working in the fields at night, and often banned it at harvest time, when the temptation of sheaf-stealing was strong.

The court had another sort of business, however. It was the lord's court, and he used it to enforce his own rights. Those villagers who were bondsmen, or serfs, were in law the chattels of the lord; they were in theory at his disposal for manual labour. That is how the lord exploited his own land, or 'demesne'. The serfs paid their rent, or part of it, in service. A free tenant, meanwhile, was not personally bound to the lord, and normally paid his rent exclusively in money. The further distinction between freeman and serf was that the former could sell his interest in the land and move elsewhere. The bondman and his heirs were bound to stay on the manor cultivating their holdings.

The burden of service was heavy: three to five 'works' a week was not uncommon over the year as a whole, a work being a period of several hours, but less than a full day. Unfortunately the burden was not evenly spread throughout the year. The lord demanded most at harvest time, for reaping, mowing and carting. But that was also when the peasant farmer needed urgently to attend to his own land. He was also subject to demands for 'boon-work' – extra labour above the normal quota, theoretically given freely to the lord on special occasions, but in practice a source of friction. As a sweetener, the lord might provide ale and food for his workers on a boon day, or a small share of the harvest. There was, none the less, a limit to the service a lord could demand, and it was defined by the body of local precedents, and upheld by the manor court. In many manors the precedents were written down in a document known as a 'custumal'. The decisions of the court, including the terms of tenure, rent and service agreed were entered on the court rolls, or records. The documents could be searched and cited when a dispute arose between one villager and another, or between lord and serf.

The lord's reeve directing the harvest. His staves suggest he will tolerate no slacking, but the horn at his waist may symbolize the ale the lord would provide for his serfs at this season.

Service and rent by no means extinguished the villager's obligations to his lord that the manor court enforced. A lifelong series of exactions emphasized that he was his lord's man. An annual payment was due for his rights to collect wood from the common, whether for the repair of his house or for upkeep of his fire. The marriage of a daughter required a fee to be paid. The proceeds of the sale of a beast might be shared with the lord. Entry into his inheritance of land required him to hand over a valuable 'heriot', commonly his best beast or most valuable chattel. Above all the lord had the right to exact a tax or 'tallage' on his serfs, which in theory could be imposed as often and for as much as he wished.

Such powers of taxation were clearly oppressive, and villagers fought hard to have them defined and limited in the manor custumal, or to buy their freedom from the tallage by a lump-sum payment. Indeed there was a general and steady movement, from the thirteenth to fifteenth centuries particularly, to commute duties of manual service and other obligations into money payments. It often suited both parties to loosen the bonds of the feudal relationship; the peasant was relieved of service and tallage, while the lord found hired labour more manageable than the grudging and half-hearted labour of his villagers.

The manor was the lord's livelihood, the source of his food and income. He was therefore at pains to ensure the prompt collection of rents, the perfor-

A watermill from the Luttrell Psalter. Sluices direct water to an overshoot millwheel which powered the grindstones. Note that basketwork traps for eels have been set in the millrace.

mance of services, and that his own demesne was properly exploited. If he was resident in the manor he could personally supervise activity, but absentee landlords were common. (We need to keep in mind that the lord was not necessarily an individual. Cathedral churches, monastic houses and the Crown itself held major estates of many manors and exploited them with apparently dispassionate efficiency.) A hierarchy of officials executed the lord's business. Those officials impinged on the ordinary family's existence at every turn, and so had an important place in the life of the village. It would be fair to say that they were not the most popular of men (I know of no example of a woman acting in such a capacity). They had a poor press in the literature of the day; duplicity, avarice, fraud, rapacity and indolence were regular complaints. All the same it is difficult not to admire the way they made a complex system work despite the resentment and contrariness they must have encountered among village folk.

The great estates employed a paid steward, or seneschal. He was a powerful figure, the embodiment of the lord's own authority. He was charged with the administration of the lord's affairs, offering business advice, executing deals in land and property, securing the best return on the lord's investment, and enquir-

ing into the performance of the lesser officials. He was a kind of combined solicitor, estate agent and chief executive. But his appearance in the village could only be occasional, such as when he presided over the manor court, or audited the accounts of the manor. The everyday organization of affairs was the province of two local men, the bailiff and the reeve. The bailiff was the land agent, paid by the lord to oversee farming operations on the demesne, and to keep the accounts. As the letter of appointment by the monks of Canterbury puts it, the bailiff is there

to cause the land to be sown, reaped, manured and cultivated, and all the wagons and ploughs and cattle together with the sheep, lambs, hogs and all other head of stock there to be managed and tended as shall seem best for our profit, rendering thereof such an account as it behoves bailiffs to render, and receiving for him and his man, what other bailiffs holding the same office in the past have received.

We might picture the bailiff striding about the manor, checking that ditches had been cleared, that fish traps had not been illicitly set in the river, that the ploughing and harvesting had been done at the due time and without the lord's strips being encroached upon by other cultivators. He was the middle manager of the operation, and as such frequently had responsibility for several manors.

The bailiff required a man on the spot, day in, day out, acting as a foreman or non-commissioned officer. That man was the reeve. He lived on the manor and was both one of the villagers and an official of the lord of the manor. He was elected annually, and though the manner of his election varied from place to place, the villagers usually had some say in the choice, through the manorial court. The rewards of the office were a reduced rent for his land, or the permission to graze his animals on the lord's demesne, and a lightening of his own labour services. Even so, the office was seen as a thankless task. The responsibilities were seemingly endless. We can understand why villagers were most reluctant to accept the job, and why many would willingly pay a fine to avoid it. It was the reeve's duty to make the manor work. He had to coax or coerce his fellow villagers to fulfil their days of service, ensure that the lord's servants were ploughing and manuring the land, see that the harvest was cut, carted and stored, and check that the livestock were being tended. He was collector of fines and enforcer of the decisions of the manor court. He was expected to keep watch on every tree and property of the lord, and to drag offenders and encroachers before the court. It is no surprise that the reeve was generally unpopular. Both lords and villagers seemed to have distrusted him. In the *Canterbury Tales* Chaucer describes the reeve as a man with an eye on everything and everyone. He knew enough about his fellows and their misdemeanours to have a hold over them. Meanwhile he was covertly piling up a tidy fortune at the expense of both his lord and fellows. In reality there was redress against the reeve in the manor court. Reeves were on occasions accused by their fellows of taking bribes or bearing false witness, and fines were sometimes imposed on them for falsifying the manor accounts.

Another important but much-maligned village official was the miller. Domesday Book records an astonishing number of mills in existence in 1086 – around 6000, or perhaps one mill for each 300 of the population. The machinery and upkeep of the mill were very substantial costs by the standards of the day, so that only a lord, and a prosperous lord at that, could afford such an undertaking. For everyday repairs, for dredging the millrace or clearing the sluices, he used the labour of his own servants and serfs. But to make it pay he had to enforce a monopoly of milling within his manor. The peasant cultivator paid in kind for the milling of his grain. A proportion went to the miller for his pains, who in turn rendered a due to the lord, or paid a yearly rent. The opportunities for petty fraud were patent. Everyone suspected the miller of giving short measure, and Chaucer characterized the miller as a noisy, uncouth cheat, who took three times his portion of corn for milling. It is hardly surprising that some villagers tried to circumvent the lord's monopoly and were fined in the manor court for taking grain to another mill, or for grinding with a 'quern' – an age-old device of two small stones that could be hidden at home.

Perhaps it is disappointing that our villages are not quite as ancient as we once thought. The vision of Saxon pioneers hacking a clearing in the primeval forest has a romantic appeal. In reality, compact villages owe their existence to medieval property development. They appeared chiefly, perhaps, between about 1000 and 1200, at a time when the older, huge estates were breaking down into manorial holdings. The lord's self-interest prompted him to acquire a settled workforce. Fortunately the interests of his serfs were not altogether at odds with his own. Only a flourishing community could provide him with a good income, and feed the growing population. Only a communal outlook, enforced by a complex of rights, duties and regulations, made the enterprise work. Now, however, it is time to look beyond the structures of society, to the ordinary people and their daily lives.

CHAPTER TWO

The Making of Village Society:
1300–1500

Village people

WHO were the villagers of medieval Britain? Social commentators of that age – poets, priests and historians – relied on a well-worn formula to describe the sorts and conditions of men. God had ordained three estates. Each had its separate duties and station. The king, the nobility and gentry, those who exercised temporal authority and justice, constituted the first estate. The second estate, the Church and those in holy orders, was said to be spiritual; but we should not forget that the Church wielded power in the spiritual courts over what we would now, perhaps, regard as personal matters, including moral behaviour and belief. The third estate comprised the mass of lay people – the governed.

The first estate was conspicuous in its absence from the village. Great estate holders, be they ecclesiastical or lay, did not maintain a personal presence. Perhaps as few as one in eight or ten manors had a resident lord. His power was, none the less, evident in the manor court. The king's authority must have appeared rather distant, yet it did intrude from time to time. Serious wrongdoers were arraigned before the king's justices at the assizes. Regularly short of money, the Crown extracted taxes (known as subsidies) from both Church and people; on occasions assessors and collectors of taxes for the king were in the village enquiring into each household's affairs with questions about income, disposable goods, numbers living in the house. England had, in fact, the most effective central government in Europe in this period.

The second estate maintained a very visible presence. The church building, though in most instances smaller than today, was the best-built and grandest structure in the village. Its services were recited by a priest, very likely a man of the barest education, and a cultivator of the ground as well as of souls. As a man bound to the Church, he could not be a serf to the lord of the manor, but in many respects he was scarcely distinguishable from his fellow peasant. He was only

A sick child, from 13th-century stained glass in the Trinity Chapel, Canterbury Cathedral. With next to nothing known about the cause of diseases, the death of infants was all too common.

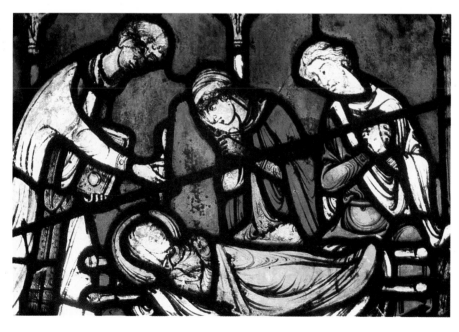

the local representative, however, and the Church impinged on village life in other ways, which we will consider further in a later chapter.

The third estate, the lower orders, was an assorted category. A way of sub-dividing this estate that was favoured in fourteenth- and fifteenth-century literature was between husbandman and labourer. The former was the cultivator of a piece of land big enough to support his family. He was a 'villein' and, though he had obligations to the manor, he was his own man, not an employee. The labourer, by contrast, depended to a greater or lesser extent on paid employment. He might be landless, or be classed as a 'cottar' (cottager) with a small house and garden, and an acre or two of land. At the other end of the scale, above the husbandman, and just below the gentry, were substantial landholders with more than enough to meet the needs of their immediate family. Each manor appears to have had two or three such families, holding 60 to 100 acres of land. They were often termed 'franklins', which denoted their status as freeholders – not in the modern sense that they owned the land, but in that they were not personally bound to the lord and owed him no services.

Another way for us to look at village society is through the composition of households. In the 1960s and 1970s it became fashionable to decry the modern nuclear family. The small household of father, mother, and two or three children is deprived, so the argument ran, of the emotional support provided by an extended family; and that deprivation is at the root of manifold prevailing ills: delinquency, a rising divorce rate, old people uncared for, and so on. The nuclear family was seen as an unfortunate, recent aberration from a traditional pattern of several generations of a family living in close proximity. How far there were ever extended families is beyond the scope of this book to examine. But in rural communities, the nuclear family has been dominant for centuries. Arguably, the Judaeo-Christian tradition has promoted it: 'Therefore shall a man leave his father and his mother, and shall cleave unto his wife: and they shall be one flesh' (Genesis 2 : 24). In a medieval village, marriage was the start of a separate household.

From the thirteenth century at least, and virtually to our own times, most couples have not entered into marriage until they possessed the means to set up home together. Historians have dubbed that convention 'prudential marriage'. In medieval Britain it meant that marriage was delayed until a landholding became available. With the land came a homestead, grazing rights, farming equipment and so on: the apparatus for making an independent living from the land. Most men and women had to wait until the

A couple, dating from the 12th century, placed by a nameless stonemason discreetly out of view on a roof corbel of the Norman church at Studland, Dorset.

death of parents or until some other family arrangement for inheritance was agreed. The wait could be lengthy, and early marriage was unusual. Men married, on average, in their late twenties. Their wives were five or six years younger. By modern standards this may not seem excessively tardy, but we must remember that life expectancy was far lower than it is today. In reality, men and women spent the majority of their lives unwed, either single or widowed, and could expect no more than a dozen or so years of married life.

Manorial authority played a major part in enforcing prudential marriages. Whenever a villein took a wife, he was liable to pay a fine, a 'merchet' or 'gersuma', to his lord. It was a sign of his bond status. When he gave his daughter in marriage, or when a widow remarried, it was only with the licence of the manor, and on payment of a merchet. The customs of the manor gave most lords the right to judge the suitability of matches, particularly as the man was the potential tenant and cultivator of a holding. It was in the interests of the manor to have tenancies filled by vigorous husbandmen. Equally it was undesirable to have a multiplication of families and children without the means (and in particular the land) for support. Such people could become a burden on the local economy and, as outsiders, a threat to the nicely ordered manorial community.

Manorial authority could not force men or women into marriage. The law of the Church demanded that the vows be taken with free will. That left some room for personal choice. Unfortunately we have no records of romantic love or even of affection between man and woman: such things did not interest the manor court or tax assessors – which is not to say they did not exist. What did interest them was extramarital sex and illegitimate children. The court rolls record many fines for fornication – the 'leche-wite' – and for bearing a child out of wedlock – the 'childwite'. The long wait for marriage was evidently too much for some, and the open fields offered manifold opportunities, as Shakespeare later confirmed:

Between the Akers of the rie
 With a hay, with a ho and a hay nonie no,
These prettie Countrie folkes would lie,
 In spring time, the onely prettie ring time
When Birds doe sing, hay ding a ding a ding
 Sweete lovers love the spring.

They cannot have loved the winter so well, once the corn had been reaped and the fields opened to the cattle. The lord's concern in these matters was largely financial and self-interested. A fornicator was liable to a fine at the ecclesiastical court, and money – in theory the lord's money – would go out of the manor. A bastard was also a loss to the manor. Legally a *filius nullius*, no one's child, he could not inherit land and was therefore rather likely to become a burden. He was also a free man, not the lord's serf, and not subject to personal dues or obligations. So the lord condemned such lapses, and thereby both supported a prudential society, and pocketed a useful income.

Widows were another group to cause concern, and more particularly widows in possession of land. Lords of the manor were anxious to see them married off, not for any charitable concern but for economic motives. An unsupported widow was unlikely to fulfil the labour requirements of her land, and was thus something of a liability. Heavy pressure could be brought to bear on reluctant villagers to undertake a marriage in these circumstances. At Hales in Worcestershire, the lord, an abbot, repeatedly tried coercion. In 1274 'John of Romsley and Nicholas Sewal are given till the next court to decide as to the widow offered them'. Three weeks later at the next court, the dithering Nicholas Sewal was given a further week to make up his mind: as the matter then does not reappear in the court records we must assume that he accepted his lot. In Berkshire, at Brightwalton, the manor was troubled by the presence of six widows, all holding land without being able to discharge their obligations of labour; they were ordered, on pain of

forfeiture, to provide themselves with husbands. The sanctions against those who held out against a marriage could include effective expulsion from the manor, as John Cayn of Sedgeberrow found in 1376. He was ordered by the lord (the Prior of Worcester) to marry a widow. He did, in fact, sleep with her, but refused to wed, and left, taking his chattels. Having been offered a pardon he returned, but left once more without accepting the pardon, the price of which was presumably wedlock with the widow. Despite the examples of recalcitrance, widows with land were generally snapped up very readily. When all was weighed and a choice had to be made, defects of face or figure may have counted for less than assets of a material kind.

The size of peasant households is revealed by a number of surveys and tax returns from several parts of the country. In normal times, not adversely affected by famine or plague, a household average of about 4.75 persons was maintained. Two or three surviving children, then, shared their parents' home. How many children did not survive we cannot say; mortality at birth and then from poor nutrition, infection or cold must have been high, though arguably lower than it was in the notoriously unhealthy cities of the Industrial Revolution. Allowing for infant mortality, and for the depressant effect on fertility of lengthy breastfeeding, the number of children to a household was low, and we must assume some conscious limitation. Couples presumably exercised rudimentary forms of contraception and abortion. There is also alarming evidence of the deliberate exposure of infants. Figures from three manors of Spalding Abbey in Lincolnshire of children of marriageable age show a ratio of 118 males to 100 females. Some figures from Essex suggest 120 to 100. While more males than females are born in the course of nature, these Lincolnshire and Essex ratios are disproportionate. The most charitable interpretation we may put on them is that additional care was being lavished on male children.

Why should parents have limited their family? In traditional societies, in many parts of the world, large numbers of children are seen as a source of wealth, and an investment. As long as children contribute their income to the common purse for much of their working lives, they can be self-financing, or even net contributors. In India and Bangladesh, for instance, children are widely regarded as an insurance for old age. But in the ethos of the nuclear family and of prudential marriage there are no clear advantages – from a purely economic point of view – in raising a large family. The cost of upkeep is high and the returns limited. Children helped with the family's work, of course, but it is debatable whether peasant

Masons and carpenters from an Irish manuscript, using, from top left, a level, a plumb-line, and an auger, and, below, a hoist, chisel and axe. Masons worked away from home for long periods.

families farming a few acres and grazing a few animals really had a pressing shortage of labour. Opportunities to earn additional cash income were limited while the major employer, the manorial demesne, depended on customary labour services. Most importantly, the adult child did not want to continue to contribute to the family's income. He or she would seek to marry, to form a household, and to live an independent existence. A further factor was the way land was inherited. Except in Wales, Kent and locally in other counties, the whole of a tenant's holding went to a single heir; it was not split between members of the family. This 'impartible inheritance' effectively disinherited all but one child. It helped to concentrate land in viable holdings, but did not encourage second and third children to stay at home.

The scheme of family life looked after the interests of some sections of the community. But what of the rest, including the elderly and the young disinherited? Manorial custom did not allow a widow to go unprovided on the death of her husband. Her right to hold the family's land, or part of it, for her natural life was secure, subject to good behaviour. One condition was chastity; the manor wanted her remarried, not associating casually with a man who neither paid a merchet nor undertook labour services. She continued to enjoy her property on remarriage. Her spouse did not usually become the new tenant, however. His interests in the land expired on his wife's death and the rights to inherit of the child of the first marriage were upheld.

Arrangements were sometimes made for the older generation to lodge with their children, the details

being recorded in the court rolls. On the manor of Elmley Castle in Worcestershire, one John Bonde surrendered his house and holding to the lord in 1412, for the benefit of his heir Nicholas Bonde. Nicholas thereby entered into his inheritance early, in return for looking after his ageing relative. John was to have space for his bed in the chamber (this was still very much the era of the single, communal bedroom), together with 4 bushels of wheat and a quarter of barley each year, properly winnowed and cleaned, a space for tying up a beast, and other sustenance – presumably food, drink and clothing. By contrast Thomas Brid of Hales in the same county, took over his widowed mother's tenancy in 1281, promising her food, coals and money, but also undertaking to build her at his own expense a separate and suitable house – a sort of medieval granny flat. Perhaps the prospect of a shared bedchamber was too much for Thomas, or perhaps for his wife.

The class of village society holding little land or none is the most shadowy of all. These people flit in and out of manorial records; they have no land transactions to record, no dues of service to fulfil. Only when they are caught trampling the corn or poaching the lord's rabbits does the manor take note of their existence. And yet those smallholders and

Two thieves stealing fruit or grapes, carved on a capital in the south transept of Wells Cathedral in the 13th century.

labourers were as numerous as villeins in the Domesday survey. Afterwards they reappear in the poll tax records of 1377–81. We can distinguish two groups: the dependent labourers – servants working for and living with a tenant farmer – and independent workers, living as cottars or as lodgers, and relying largely on paid employment.

Young men and women without prospects of inheriting a tenancy faced a choice beteen those two groups. They might enter service, at home or in a larger household, forgoing any immediate prospect of marriage. Or they might fall into the uncertain world of labour, with the possibility in good times of earning enough to lead a free, and even a maried life. Some certainly left the manor (with or without the lord's permission) to seek work elsewhere, perhaps in the towns. Some became specialist tradesmen; masons, for example, were itinerant workers who moved from site to site as opportunities arose.

Labourers, especially the wandering kind, were seen as a threat to good order. They were frequently denounced as vagabonds, thieves and begetters of bastards; no doubt they sometimes were. William Langland in the fourteenth century contrasted their laziness and truculence with the honest toil of the ploughman. No one seems to have accepted that such an underclass was the inevitable consequence of the system of prudential marriage and impartible inheritance. Nor did anyone appear to recognize their economic potential. They were a flexible, cash-in-hand workforce. Growing rural industries needed them, and all manner of specialist crafts, developing at the end of the medieval period, depended on them. Their existence eased the transition from the feudal society to a more modern economy of employers and employees.

To sum up, let us glance at the villagers of Church Eaton in Staffordshire, through the eyes of the assessors of the poll tax of 1381. There were two pillars of village society. The lord of the manor was Thomas of Brompton, whose household contained seven servants. The parson, enjoying an unusually rich living, employed thirteen persons, presumably helping him to farm a healthy acreage. After them came thirty or so householders. Just over a half were husbandmen, tenants of the manor with reasonable holdings, though most managed without hired labour. There were then four smallholders or cottagers. That left a group of ten landless labourers, apparently living and working independently, some of them married. And finally there were two artificers, or craftsmen. Church Eaton presents a fairly typical picture, with most of the dependent labour working for the two or three largest landholders, and fully a third of the adult population without land.

Hearth and home

Today, home is for family life: for eating, resting, leisure pursuits, for the raising of children. It is not usually the place where the breadwinning takes place. Members of the family still 'go out to work'. To the medieval villager home was much more than that. It was a shelter not just for his family, but for his animals and his produce too. Home was a workplace; raw commodities such as grain, milk, skin and wool were transformed there into the necessities of life. The house itself, and its back yard, reflected the family's activities. The size and placing of the hearth, the arrangements for sleeping and working, the provision for storage, the garden and the rubbish dump are potentially the best evidence that we have of medieval family life. Yet that evidence, until recently, has been elusive. The homes of ordinary medieval people are literally buried from sight.

In their influential work, *Deserted Medieval Villages*, Maurice Beresford and J. G. Hurst describe how, shortly after the Second World War, they set about excavating medieval peasant houses. It was an entirely novel project; until then medieval archaeology had concerned itself with buildings of the higher levels of society – the abbeys, castles and palaces. Books on the medieval home had focused on the great houses, while authors who had tried to describe the homes of ordinary men and women had relied on scanty literary sources, and on even scantier contemporary illustrations. Some attention had been given to surviving village houses of an early date – to what we have come to call vernacular architecture. But writers generally chose to skate over the date of those houses, few of which are older than the fifteenth or sixteenth century. Most, in any case, were the homes of men of substance. Medieval small houses had simply not survived.

Beresford, a historian rather than an archaeologist, embarked on some trial excavations. He cheerfully dug trenches across the humps and bumps of former settlements, hoping to strike the remains of peasant occupation. To his disappointment and surprise, he found little or nothing. A different and more delicate technique was required. Having enlisted the assistance of Hurst, an archaeologist, he essayed a method of open excavation, which revealed that the traces of medieval occupation did indeed survive. They were, however, wafer-thin. Layer upon layer of shallow deposits and postholes of irregular pattern presented considerable problems of interpretation. It appeared that occupation of the sites consisted of constant rebuilding and realignment of small houses, each of which had lasted only a few years before demolition and replacement.

'Lopping and topping': a peasant cutting small wood from a coppice. March from a 15th-century series of Labours of the Month at Brandiston Hall, Norfolk.

That initial picture has been largely confirmed by the many subsequent excavations of medieval settlement sites. Peasant houses have been revealed as non-permanent structures, which show no signs of the involvement of the skilled craftsmen who were working on the great churches and castles of that period. We can reasonably deduce, from the crude techniques of construction and flimsy materials, that the peasant farmer and his family raised their own home, and that each generation was obliged to repeat the task.

With few exceptions, peasant houses of the period from the end of the Roman period to a century after the Norman Conquest were built of wood. Even where stone was quite freely available, ordinary men preferred timber. Their choice is difficult to explain, for lords of the manor jealously reserved the good wood for their own use, or for sale. So the peasant builder had to work with slender branches, no more than 6 to 9 inches in diameter. Many tenants enjoyed a customary right to 'lopping and topping' in the lord's woods, and after the Conquest, with the pressures of population on the land increasing, materials were secured by coppicing. An ash or oak after felling soon produces new shoots. In fifteen years or so the shoots grow into small timbers that can readily be harvested, to be replaced in turn by a fresh growth. The technique survived into modern times as a way of securing fuel, and overgrown coppices are a not uncommon feature of the landscape.

The peasant farmer set his slender timbers directly into the ground at intervals, and erected between them a fence of wattle. This was no more than an intertwining of twigs and small branches, but the whole structure was daubed with a muddy mixture of earth, straw and dung, with chalk or lime added where available. The mud casing, some 12 to 18 inches thick, kept the wind at bay and gave some protection to the soft sapwood posts which would otherwise have decayed within a very few seasons. The walls of such a house cannot really be called timber-framed: the timbers were there to stabilize an aggregate of other materials, and were not worked into joints or effectively braced into a stable structure. Rarely were the posts set in straight or parallel lines.

Roofing must have been a major difficulty on such flimsy, irregular walls, but so little evidence remains. We can only surmise that light branches were lashed together to form pairs of rafters, and that they were interlaced with smaller, pliable wood to support thatching. The word 'thatch' – or 'thack' in its old English form still in dialect use in Yorkshire – referred originally to whatever local roofing materials were to hand. From travellers' accounts of a later period we can glimpse the expedients that had long been used, including heather, ferns, moss and turf. Straw was preferred, however. At harvest-time, the short medieval sickle left the corn stalks standing unbruised in the field. When the first frosts had made them brittle, they were snapped off, gathered and laid on the roof. A good deal of daubed mud helped keep them in place. Damp was a great enemy of these primitive houses. Even if the roof and walls kept the rain at bay, the unseasoned wood set into the earth would inevitably decay. The ultimate collapse of such a structure could not be long delayed.

In time both peasants and lords had to adjust to the consequences of a rapidly growing population. Britain was running short of trees. Turf was more difficult to find. Forest and waste, the sources of all manner of building supplies, were being farmed and ploughed to produce vital food for more mouths. So necessity drove village builders to use stone. It happened first in the south-west where surface boulders were plentiful. By the thirteenth and early fourteenth centuries it was commonplace elsewhere. Transport problems meant, at least until the railway age, that virtually all village buildings were made with local materials. Ordinary families dug for stones in their 'croft', or back yard. They opened holes to a

The remnants of a deserted village at Wharram Percy, Yorks. Church and millpond are the most visible remains, but years of careful excavation have revealed the traces of peasant homes.

the Norman Conquest, around the twelfth and thirteenth centuries. At that time the climate was worsening markedly – a point to which we will return shortly. It could well be that farmers faced with cold and waterlogged fields chose to winter their cattle indoors, in the family's one substantial building. The survival of longhouses in the west, centuries after they had been abandoned elsewhere, seems simply to point to the region's cultural conservatism and its continuing reliance on animal farming.

At Wharram and elsewhere, a third type of peasant dwelling, superior to both the cot and the longhouses, appeared in the thirteenth century. Such houses may have been the homes of well-to-do villeins, farming 30 or more acres, or else the farmsteads of freeholders. Those more prosperous villagers were building a separate byre for livestock, often at right angles to the house, forming a little farm complex. We find this development first in lowland Britain, where by the fourteenth century the longhouse concept was losing popularity.

In moving the animals out of the house and across the yard, the family gained space for expanded patterns of living and working. The room beyond the cross-passage, the byre in the longhouses, became the area for storage, for the pantry and dairy. Family life could spill over from the central hall into the smaller room at the other end of the house. Names for rooms varied from region to region. The central room was mostly known as the hall, but occasionally in the north as the house, or even the firehouse, for obvious reasons. In southern counties the second room was a bower or a chamber, while in the Midlands and further north we read of parlours in the fifteenth century. Whatever its name, the room off the hall was fitted out with a bed and articles of furniture. It must have been a more private room, somewhat removed from the workaday bustle. One hesitates to ascribe to it any degree of comfort, but from early inventories it was evidently the 'best' room, where the master of the house slept, and where any articles of value were kept.

While villein families were clearing the animals from their houses, lords of the manor were putting a little distance between themselves and their serfs. The manor moved to a new site at Goltho, while at Wharram Percy it migrated twice in the twelfth century, as the village grew. The second move put the manor house at the end of a new street, some way from the mud and congestion at the centre. Meanwhile, manor houses were growing in size and complexity. Excavations at Penhallam Moor in Cornwall and at Wintringham in Cambridgeshire have revealed how a single early hall became a group of buildings. Some such complexes eventually took on a courtyard arrangement, which must have served to emphasize the separateness and superiority of the manorial household. If we look at the earliest surviving manor houses in Britain, at Hemingford Grey in Cambridgeshire, dating from about 1150, we find the River Ouse on one side, and evidence of a moat on three; it was thus physically separated from the village. Many other early manor houses are moated, Boothby Pagnell in Lincolnshire, and Charlestone Manor in East Sussex being examples from around 1200. In fact there are thousands of such sites in Britain. The majority now are no more than a squarish depression in the ground defining the island upon which house, barns and other buildings once stood. A few sites have flourished – Groombridge Place in Kent and Oxburgh Hall, Norfolk, among them – but none more charmingly than Ightham Mote in Kent. There the squires of later generations resisted the temptation to pull down and rebuild the original great hall of the 1330s, but added new wings and a chapel so that the house grew to its present substantial size. The vogue for moats was almost over when Ightham was built, and their function seems to have been largely symbolic. Most were not big enough to afford more than a modicum of security. They were status symbols, and their allusion to fortified castles and the nobility was clear.

Most of the surviving early manor houses have their main rooms – the hall and a smaller private room – on the upper floor. The Boothby Pagnell house had this arrangement, with an external stone staircase for access. Below the hall is a vaulted undercroft, probably used for storage. A similar arrangement is to be found in the old hall at Burton Agnes in Humberside, which stands in the grounds of the Jacobean mansion. (It escaped destruction when the family emigrated to the new house by being turned into a barn.) In this instance, however, access to the upper floor hall is by a newel (a stone spiral staircase). These buildings, few in number and accordingly difficult to interpret, could be the homes of leading families, and closely connected with the Norman dynasty. The massive stone manor house built at Wharram Percy around 1180 certainly speaks eloquently of the resources of a great family of Norman origin, the Percys, Earls of Northumberland. Such houses had some potential for defence, particularly when girded about by a moat. Perhaps they show us how, at a local level, an alien gentry established itself and maintained a slightly uneasy hegemony over an English populace.

Ightham Mote in Kent: a most picturesque, and unusually grand, moated manor house. Mote means not moat but moot, *or meeting of the manor court.*

ABOVE *The manor house (originally moated) at Boothby Pagnell: Norman architecture at its simplest. The square, mullioned window is a later addition which slightly mars the harmony of the design.*
LEFT *A scene from the Bayeux Tapestry (c.1077). The two-storey house, with vaulted undercroft and upper hall reached by an external stair, is much like the Boothby Pagnell house.*

We can detect, as the centuries pass, a gradual improvement in living standards for peasant families. Even the poor were gaining breathing space; one-room cots were very common in 1300, but a century and a half later two rooms was the rule in the lowland zone. Yet the life within those rooms must still have

40

been perilously cold and uncomfortable. Furnishings were sparse. We cannot point to a single surviving example of furniture of the village level from before the sixteenth century. Furniture worthy of the name can only be made from good materials and by skilful carpentry – neither of which were available to village families. Some medieval wooden chests do survive; they are huge, virtually immovable church coffers hollowed from a single tree trunk. Those methods would have been possible on a domestic scale, with the simple woodworking tools, such as chisels and gouges, that have been found in peasant houses. Wooden structures of some kind have been found, uniquely, in an excavated peasant house on Dartmoor but they were too fragmentary to be identified positively as furniture. That is not to say, however, that peasant houses were devoid of all home comforts. Some amenities could be built in. In the south-west, especially in Cornwall, furniture of stone was often built into the thickness of the walls. In that way beds, benches, cupboards, shelves and recesses were provided. In timber houses there were numerous makeshifts which could have been employed – a hanging pole as a clothes-horse, hooks in walls, or simple furniture of staves lashed together, driven into the floor of the house. Unfortunately for historians and their documentation of the past the common end of all peasant attempts at wooden furniture was, undoubtedly, the fire.

Bedding is regularly mentioned in early records. Homes with no other furniture often possessed a bed or 'bed-stocks' and a mattress; warmth and comfort at night were doubly precious when waking hours lacked both. The best mattresses were of feathers; nothing else was half so cosy or so valuable. Poorer men slept on mattresses of flock (a mixture of wool and shredded cloth) or a pallet filled with straw, bracken or rushes. A writer remembering his fifteenth-century childhood recalled how 'we oursleves have lyen full oft upon straw pallettes, covered over with a sheet, under coverlets and a good round logge under our heads, instead of a boulster.' Blankets, coverlets and sheets were in use, but not in ample quantities. Other ways of keeping warm were necessary. Giraldus Cambrensis, writing in the late twelfth century, records:

A bed made of rushes, and covered with a coarse kind of cloth manufactured in the country ... is placed along the side of the room, and they all in common lie down to sleep; their dress at night is no different from that by day, for at all seasons they defend themselves only by a thin cloak and tunic. ... The fire burns all night at their feet and they get much comfort from the natural heat of their bedfellows.

The floor of the village house was of earth. There is no evidence that stone paving was used except, on occasions, around the threshold. As we shall see, earthen floors continued to give good service in modest dwellings for centuries to come. Rushes, straw or bracken laid on the floor afforded some comfort in winter; we can envisage the medieval housewife clearing out the old, rather soiled coverings in the spring. Some excavated peasant homes have quite a smooth earth floor, suggesting some pretty vigorous sweeping. Refuse went out from the house on to the toft, or to be dumped on the edge of the village. However dire their material circumstances may have been, some families were maintaining high standards of housewifery.

While most of the furnishings and wares were drably utilitarian, excavations have thrown up one exception. Fragments of decorated ewers, or jugs, have been found as commonly on the sites of peasant homes as on those of grander dwellings. These marvellous pieces are quite different in character from the rest of the household pottery. The most flamboyant examples belong to the thirteenth and fourteenth centuries, and the range of decorative techniques is very wide. The main design is usually worked out in strips and studs of coloured clay applied to the surface, and patterned further by

The undercroft of the old manor house at Burton Agnes, Humberside. The round pillars, square capitals and ribbed arches are all typical of Norman work.

incised lines, thumbprints and stamped motifs. How were those ewers obtained? And why were they universally popular? They must either have come with itinerant pot-sellers, or through a market. In either event, even obscure English villages must have had contact with a wide pattern of trade. As for the jugs themselves, were they, perhaps, the medieval equivalent of the china dog on every Victorian cottager's mantelpiece, decorative trinkets which became a mark of respectability? Attractive as they are, they were not at the most sophisticated level of taste; by the later Middle Ages, households of substance were preferring vessels of brass, pewter and silver. But the peasant's jug, carried home from the fair, was the summit of his material achievement.

The vital resource for the peasant household was fire. It had the power to transform his produce into edible food, and to lend a little comfort to a flimsy home. In man's keeping, fire has had three homes: the hearth, the fireplace and the stove. Of the three, the hearth has infinitely the longest history. In a peasant's cottage, it was a flat piece of earth or stone. Even much grander houses had an open hearth at the centre of the hall – there are good examples in the restored Tatton Old Hall in Cheshire and at Penshurst Place in Kent. Such households could afford well-dried wood, and louvres in the roof let the smoke drift away. The ordinary family had a fire of brushwood, peat, turf or of whatever could be scavenged from the commons and heath, and the smoke found its way out through the roof or doorway, if at all. Green and smoking fuel was a mark of poverty, so there is a particular point in Chaucer's description of the poor widow's two-room cot, in the 'Nun's Priest's Tale': 'Full sooty was her hall and eke [also] her bower.' An idea of the blackening effect of an open fire can be had from photographs of small houses in the Orkneys which retained their central hearths as late as the nineteenth century.

Fire was a fickle ally. Many cots burned down. At Dinnas Clerk, in Devon, excavation has revealed the charred remains of a house containing a complete storage pot and a ceramic cistern. The inhabitants had evidently made a very rapid exit, abandoning valuable and still usable utensils. The risk of fire was all the greater for the way the peasant family cooked its food. An open fire does not give an even, dependable heat until the fuel has been reduced to glowing embers. To reach this stage the cook had to burn small wood in plenty. His faggots, collected from forest and waste, blazed fiercely for a brief interval. Any misjudgement would drive the flames up to the timber roof and thatch which provided excellent kindling a foot or two above his head.

Fire requires constant tending if it is not to be lost.

ABOVE *The sparse interior of a medieval home. This farmhouse, now at the Weald and Downland Museum, Singleton, Sussex, has an earth floor and open hearth – the source of both warmth and light on winter nights.*
OPPOSITE *'Blackhouses', with open hearth and interior blackened by smoke, were still in use in the Scottish islands a century ago. This example is a reconstruction at Colbost, Skye.*

Domus aaron sperauit in domino:
adiutor eorum et protector eorum est.
Qui timent dominum sperauerunt

ABOVE *Kitchen work (from the Luttrell Psalter): pounding or mixing, cutting and cooking in cauldrons over an open fire. Perhaps the scribe of this manuscript had seen cooking on such a large scale in his monastery kitchen.*

LEFT *Ewer or jug, made around 1300, decorated with applied 'slips' of coloured clay. Such an object would have held a great attraction for a peasant family in a comfortless cot.*

Until very recently it was far easier to maintain a fire than to light one, and, according to tradition, there were homes that kept a fire burning from one generation to the next. In some houses the fire was covered at night by a curfew (i.e. a *couvre-feu*) which dampened down the fire and prevented it burning out. The smouldering ash pile, which was not removed until the winter's end, was a reserve of heat ready to be fanned into life at any time. It might be brought up to cooking temperature with bellows, the primitive form of which is graphically suggested by its etymology: *'blaest bely'* must refer to the intestine of an animal, squeezed vigorously to produce a draught.

Peasant cooking was founded upon the cauldron and the pot. Iron cauldrons – some with three stumpy legs, some without – were in use for centuries, right into Victoria's reign. The large cooking pots of the medieval period were mostly of a coarse, unglazed fabric, crudely made on a wheel. It is some wonder that they served their purpose at all, but a rounded bottom spread the heat of the fire while a pronounced lip may have allowed them to be suspended above the flames. Cauldrons and pottery cooking vessels are found in some quantity in museums; spits for roasting are not. So the material evidence suggests that food was boiled up in a great pot. Similarly, early written mentions of food habitually include pottage (a kind of porridge) and gruel:

Pease porridge hot, pease porridge cold,
Pease porridge in the pot, nine days old.

Scraps of meat, oats, peas, beans, barley, even the seeds of weeds, and a little salt went in the pottage, which was, no doubt, simmered and reheated many times.

The medieval family relied considerably on grain for both protein and carbohydrates. A recent study has suggested that the adult male ate on average 5 pounds of bread a day. Some of the barley, meanwhile, went to make ale. We should not imagine, however, that either the bread or the ale was such as we recognize today. Fermentation of malted grain in water, without hops, makes a thin drink, of low alcohol content by modern standards. It would need to be drunk in volume to cause inebriation. Bread meant different things to different men; there was a hierarchy of colour and textures. Of the poor widow of Chaucer's 'Nun's Priest's Tale' we read:

No wyn ne drank she neither whit ne red;
Hir bord was served most with whit and blak.

In other words she drank milk and ate a coarse 'black' loaf which was a mark of her poverty. At the other end of the scale, white bread of wheaten flour, finely sieved, sometimes called 'manchet', was the preserve of the richer monastic houses and gentry. In between were all manner of shades and textures, deriving from the mix of grains employed. Where wheat would not grow reliably – that is, in the south-west and north-west – barley and oats were the staples. The flour of ground peas and beans, too, was regularly used in bread. The harder the times and the poorer the harvest, the coarser and blacker the bread became.

The village in crisis

Could the land feed the growing population? Domesday England's $1\frac{1}{2}$ to 2 million inhabitants multiplied steadily, until at the end of the thirteenth century their number had grown to perhaps 6 million. That represents about $1\frac{1}{4}$ million households, if an average of 4.75 persons is correct. In turn it suggests about 7

Drinking in a lordly household, with refreshment brought from the cellar to an upper hall. Common men made do without the glass drinking vessels in the less elegant village alehouse.

or 8 acres of arable land per family. Was that enough, with the produce of the commons, fishponds and weirs, to support the people? In a good year it probably was, but everything depended on the productivity of the land. Peasant cultivators have left no records; we have to rely for our ideas of the efficiency of medieval agriculture on the yields achieved by the well-managed and well-documented estates of the Church. On one such, the Winchester estates, yields of 7 bushels of wheat, 10 of barley and 5 of oats per acre sown were achieved between 1209 and 1350. If those yields held good for peasant land (a large assumption), a typical 8-acre family holding might produce 56 bushels of grain. A quarter of that was next year's seed corn. The remainder was about enough to support four adults. Averages easily mislead, however. There was good land and poor.

TOP *Sowing by hand from a basketwork 'seedlip', a technique that had not changed from biblical times: October in a 15th-century series of Labours of the Month from Coslany, Norwich.*
ABOVE *Harvesting grapes illustrates September in the Coslany roundels. A warmer climate in early medieval England allowed farming and population to expand before the Black Death.*
RIGHT *Rievaulx Abbey, North Yorkshire, was a great Cistercian house. Its community of monks and lay brothers controlled huge estates, which generated the wealth to build the abbey.*

The size of the land holdings was not uniform; many households had far less than 8 acres. So an overall sufficiency of grain could leave some farmers seriously short. Even the average producer had to part with some of his crop to pay for milling, tithe, manorial dues, tallage, entry and marriage fines, and for clothing, shoes and farm tackle. The gap had to be filled by the produce of the common: eggs, milk, cheese, the occasional piece of meat and so on.

But the years were not reliably good. By 1300 the climate of the British Isles had taken an appreciable turn for the worse. Conditions had been favourable between 800 and 1000, and the Domesday survey recorded the existence of thirty-eight vineyards other than the king's. Britain's climate was then both drier and warmer than today; winter frosts ended earlier, summer temperatures were higher by 2°–4°F. As the weather worsened in the thirteenth and fourteenth centuries the growing season shortened and yields would correspondingly have lessened. Marginal farming lands were particularly hard hit. The very areas that were the safety valve opened by assarting in the centuries after Domesday proved unprofitable. Upland areas of Dartmoor and the Cheviot Hills, ploughed and worked as arable in the twelfth and thirteenth centuries, were abandoned again to grass in the fourteenth. Even the Winchester estates showed a tendency to declining yields. Early in the fourteenth century the country was hit by a series of poor harvests, culminating in disastrous crops from 1315 to 1317, which sent the price of grain soaring. There was murrain among the cattle. For the first time since the Conquest the population began to decline, its health undermined by the shortage of food.

It was on this debilitated populace that the force of the Black Death broke in 1349. Further though smaller outbreaks occurred up to 1377, by which time perhaps 40 to 50 per cent of the population had succumbed. Here and there whole communities were swept away. In the Oxfordshire village of Tusmore, in 1358, the lord of the manor turned the fields into a park for sheep-grazing as there were no villein tenants left. Many hundreds of villages throughout the country were deserted in the 150 years after the Black Death. As many as a quarter of all Oxfordshire's villages were depopulated. Many more throughout the country shrank from vigorous communities to small hamlets – often no more than two or three farmsteads and a church, sitting by a sea of ridge and furrow fields, fossilized under grass.

Myths, ancient and modern, envelop the fate of those lost villages. An isolated parish church is popularly held to be an infallible signpost to a deserted plague village. But there are other possible

Barns

Barns are popularly thought of as storage places. It is true that they gave shelter to harvested crops and to farm implements. But barns were really workshops, where the harvest was processed for its various uses.

Once the corn had been cut in the field and tied in sheaves, it was brought to the barn. Tall, double doors, usually set in the centre of the side wall of the barn, allowed a fully loaded cart to be drawn inside. The sheaves would be unloaded to one end of the barn, leaving the other for threshed grain.

The threshing floor was in the centre of the barn, and the threshing took place with the tall doors open to allow in some light and air. It was hot, dusty and arduous work, which occupied the farm labourers for much of the winter. They worked with hand-flails – wooden staves from which a short, heavy stick swung on a leather thong. By beating the corn, they separated the ears from the straw, which had its own value and was carted away to be used for animal bedding and feed, and manuring.

Then the winnowing began. Most barns have a second pair of doors opposing the first, and by opening both a good draught of air can usually be contrived. Boards were sometimes set into the jambs at the foot of the doorways to form 'thresholds' which lessened the loss of grain in the winnowing. The threshed corn was repeatedly tossed in the air with a spade or from a basket. The chaff blew away, and the grain itself fell to the floor for collection.

Medieval farming was not noted for the purity of its crops. Indeed farmers often sowed mixed grain such as wheat and rye for preference. To separate the species and eliminate weed seeds, the grain was riddled through different sizes of mesh. Some grain was processed further by malting and brewing; some was saved as seed-corn. The rest was stored until milled, usually in wooden bins or 'hutches' in the barn, the farmhouse or in a separate granary.

The medieval barns that survive today are certainly untypical – they were the best and largest of their age. More modest barns serving the manor demesne have collapsed long ago. Peasant farmers had no barns at all; the storage

Tithe barn at Great Coxwell, Oxfordshire, built by the Cistercians before the Black Death.

and processing of their crops had to be done at home. Yet there were once many hundreds, and possibly thousands of really substantial medieval barns. They were built by monastic orders, priories and cathedral chapters to store the produce of their very large estates and their tithes. The tithe was tax of one tenth of all the produce or profits of the land, and it was payable, usually in kind, to the rector of the parish for his support and that of his church.

In an ordinary village a small barn might suffice for the rector to store both his tithes and whatever he managed to grow on his land – known as his 'glebe'. In many parishes, however, the owner of the rectorship was a monastic house, and the village priest was only a vicar, paid a very modest allowance by the rector. The great monasteries owned many rectorships, and their tithe barns were accordingly huge. The barn at Great Coxwell in Oxfordshire, built for the Cistercian Abbey at Beaulieu in Hampshire in the thirteenth century, is 151 ft long and 42½ ft wide – perhaps the finest surviving example.

RIGHT *Hand-threshing with flails, with the barn's double doors open and the threshold in place.*

LEFT *Light pours in through the open doors of the 14th-century barn at Lacock, Wiltshire, which once served the rich estates of the abbey.*

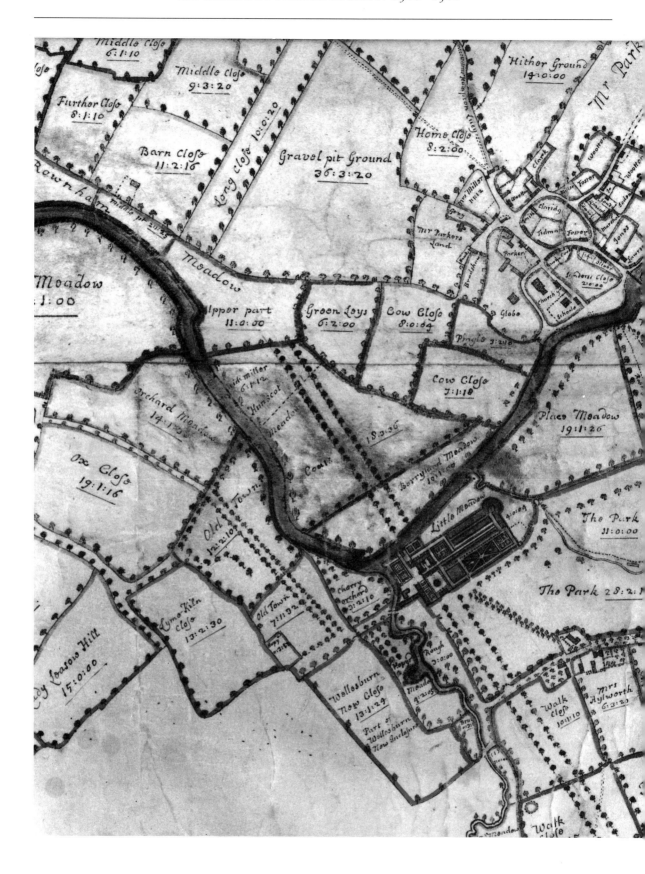

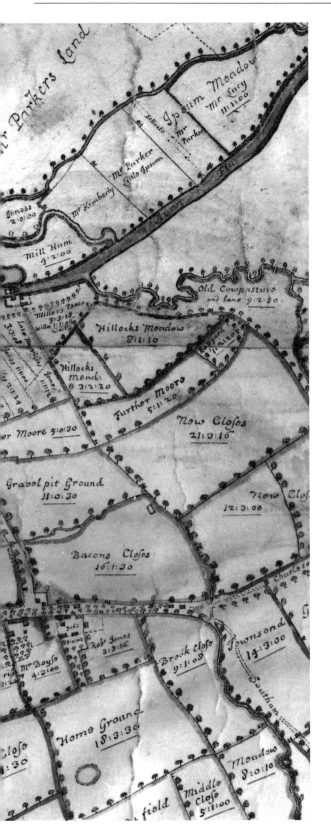

explanations. There may never have been a nucleated settlement there at all, the church serving a dispersed congregation. Or, as quite frequently happened, the population may at some stage have moved to another part of the parish. Desertions have taken place throughout history – including our own century – for reasons which frequently have nothing to do with the plague. The evidence is that the majority of village desertions should not be *directly* attributed to the Black Death. What we can say is that the plague unleashed an irresistible tide of change in the countryside, whose long-term consequence was the disappearance of village communities.

The immediate effect of the Black Death was to appease a great hunger for land. A tragedy for many offered sudden opportunities to others. Men with little or no land stepped into dead men's shoes, to take over vacant plots. They also climbed into their beds, marrying widows and spinster heiresses, enjoying an unexpected prosperity. That sudden upward mobility in village society took up most of the lapsed tenancies. It had another, serious consequence for landholders. It removed the abundance of cheap labour that had made demesne farming highly profitable before the plague. Men and women who had once been willing, indeed desperate, for paid work, now had their own plot, or could be choosy about when and where to work, virtually naming their own price. In something of a panic Parliament legislated to protect the interests of its own, property-owning class. The 1351 Statute of Labourers prohibited workers moving from place to place, and limited the wages they could demand. Further statutes gave the justices power to fix wages locally, in line with the price of bread. But like almost every state attempt at economic management in the Middle Ages, those measures were doomed to fail, being no match for the forces of supply and demand.

Great landholders, the Church included, had to find new ways to manage their estates. Up to around 1300 their policy had generally been to farm the demesnes themselves through their stewards or keepers. In an expanding economy with growing demand, they had been achieving good prices for their grain, wool and other produce. In the case of Leicester Abbey, for instance, income had risen from £286 per annum in 1254 to £1019 in 1341, on the back of much increased returns from grain sales, and good rentals for its tenanted land. Fountains Abbey in North Yorkshire had built up a highly successful

A map of Charlecote Park, Warwickshire, in 1736, which records the site of a deserted medieval village on the left as the 'Old Town'.

system of dependent estates, known as granges, run on its behalf by lay brothers and servants who looked after the Abbey's immense flocks of sheep and cattle. Prosperity of this order, repeated elsewhere, fuelled a colossal building programme of great priories and abbey churches before the Black Death. Yet by 1363 the monks of Fountains were despairing at the ruinous state of many of their granges. They had been hit by the general debility of the economy in the fourteenth century, by stock losses through disease, by Scottish raiding bands and finally by the plague. Leicester Abbey's income had declined, by 1408, to £536 per annum, scarcely more than half its pre-plague level. Prices received for grain had slumped. The crisis prompted landholders almost everywhere to respond with a privatizing policy. As they could find neither reliable men to manage their estates, nor a profitable market for their produce, they increasingly rented out their demesne lands and granges to the highest bidders. That cut expenses sharply and produced a regular rental return. Leicester Abbey's income had recovered to £762 by 1477, and all Fountains's granges were restored to productive use. Renting out of demesne lands, which got under way at the end of the thirteenth century, was almost universal by the close of the fifteenth.

That business decision to abandon demesne farming brought the feudal age virtually to its close. The manor's need for labour services had disappeared. Husbandmen rented land simply for money. While the manor court continued to meet, more and more men and women achieved their freedom from serfdom by purchase, by marriage or by simply renegotiating their leases.

Inevitably some villagers proved more adept than their fellows in exploiting the new opportunities. A 'peasant aristocracy' began to emerge in the two centuries after the Black Death. We can see it developing in the manor of Weedon Bec in Northamptonshire. The manorial rolls reveal how the peasantry had been squeezed in the century before 1348. As the population grew, so holdings were divided. Families who had once farmed 15 or 30 acres were down to 7 or 8 – the level of a cottar – before the Black Death. But after the plague, in 1365, there were 40 per cent fewer tenants than before. We might have expected there to have been more land for all. In fact, there were more cottars and smallholders than ever, while a few families had acquired large acreages. By

In 1412 the lord of Elkington, Northants, reported that his tenants had abandoned the fields because of pestilences. Now their houses, streets and arable are just marks on the ground from the air.

the next century the class system had taken a further leap forward; a single family – ordinary villeins in the thirteenth century – was renting the whole demesne.

The scene was thus set for the great age of village depopulation which took place not immediately after the Black Death, but a century later, especially between about 1460 and 1488. Those dates mark a period when the price of wool was particularly attractive; demand for it was growing because the English cloth industry was enjoying an export-led boom. At the same time, good harvests had knocked the bottom out of the grain market, and the population had not recovered sufficiently to create a high demand for foodstuffs. As Sir John Hales's *Discourse of the Commonweal* put it in 1549, farmers had found 'profits were but small by the plowes' and had accordingly 'turned part or all their arable groundes into pasture, and thereby have waxed very riche men'.

A number of Tudor moralists, Sir Thomas More among them, were to claim that avaricious farmers had turned honest husbandmen off the land to extend their grazing runs, and that sheep were eating men's livelihood. That image of poor families' houses being pulled down, with destitute persons evicted to a life of beggary, was most powerful. It prompted the government repeatedly to legislate, largely in vain, against the laying down of arable to pasture. Yet in the majority of cases examined under the 1517 legislation against graziers, the enclosure of the arable land in a village had involved the eviction of a single household only. Many villages were already much reduced by plague deaths; then the buying-out of the smaller men by the peasant aristocrats or the lord of the manor had reduced numbers further. With empty tenancies available elsewhere, the displacement of the last one or two cultivators may not have been a great disturbance.

The old order of village life was dissolving. It is sometimes said that the Middle Ages ended in England and Wales with the accession of the Tudors in 1485. Certainly on that day at Bosworth Field, Henry VII won a kingdom that was already much changed. Feudal ties and obligations no longer bound men to their lords with any strength. The manorial system had grown rapidly and flowered briefly, but its decay was swift. Common-field farming, which had given most families a share of the land, survived for the moment but was greatly weakened by the polarization of rich and poor among the peasantry, and by the movement out of arable into grazing. The pace of change was not to slacken in the coming century of Tudor rule, and the Crown was itself preparing to demolish the remaining pillars of medieval society.

CHAPTER THREE

A New Order:
1500–1688

The village in view

As we shift our gaze on to the Tudor and Stuart age, the picture of the village and its people becomes more focused. There are houses to see; here and there a whole street survives, and with it a little of the atmosphere of the period. Household goods, and even a certain amount of furniture, are preserved in our museums. That physical evidence mostly reflects life at the top of the tree, socially speaking. A more balanced view can be gained from the documentary evidence, and in particular from an invaluable source of information, the inventories *post mortem*. By decree of Henry VIII's government, an inventory of the goods of every deceased householder had to be made. 'Four honest persons' were to list everything of value in the house, so that his property could be settled. The legal side of proving the will fell to the church courts and their officials, who fulfilled their duties punctiliously. Inventories were checked, endorsed and, after the settlement was made, stored. Fortunately for later generations, the regulations gave no guidance as to when the old records could be discarded. As a result, from the 1520s onwards, there is a very large body of information on the worldly goods of obscure men and women, and on how they arranged them. In reading those documents we see the man and his house as his fellows saw them. We move with the neighbours from room to room, from the hall to the chamber, from the kitchen to the brewhouse. We find that this man kept flitches of bacon in his parlour, that the next had two doublets in his chest, and that the third slept on a mattress of feathers with an old coverlet. All this we read in the semi-literate hand of the deceased man's friends or parish priest.

Cottages at Cropthorne, Hereford and Worcester, the nearest with a 'catslide' roof. The square-panelled framing is typical of the west, but the timbers are thin, suggesting that this was the house of a relatively poor family.

A typical early inventory, that of Robert Frere of Wigston, Leicestershire, who died in 1529, draws for us a picture not of ease, nor of spacious accommodation, but of an industrious life that had yielded some modest rewards. Frere had a two-roomed house of hall and parlour, with a 'spence' (that is, a dispensary or larder) probably built as an extension to the rear of his dwelling. He was one of the prosperous men of the village. His goods show that his activities went a little beyond the normal run of farming. He possessed hemp and hemp yarn and a number of carpenters' tools. Pride of place in the parlour went to a bed and an old mattress. In his chest were some old clothes – very few by today's standards, just jackets, hose, leather doublets and bonnets. What set Frere apart from most of his village contemporaries were his furniture and soft furnishings. On the wall of the parlour, his best and private room, was a painted cloth; he also had one in the hall. They were a modest substitute for the needlework tapestries of greater houses, and in their day were a prized investment, bought in the town; some bore classical scenes, others flowers, trees or animals, and some a simple text. In his hall, Robert Frere had a table with forms, four chairs and stools. Quite a number could have sat at his table for supper. Frere could evidently put on a show to impress. He had a cupboard – quite literally a board for cups, supported on testles – and shelves for the display of ware. Tucked away in the spence he had a garnish of pewter, while cushions were provided for the stools in the hall. All this would have suggested pretensions to gentility, were it not for the pen for capons which he kept in the hall.

Frere was one of the new class of farmers profiting from the opportunities of late-medieval England, a class that was coming to be known as the yeomanry. In Frere's case, disposable income was going into household goods. In the south-east and East Anglia by this time, growing prosperity was funding a housing revolution. Yeomen in Kent, for instance, had access to the London markets; their profits were

Victorian cottage scene, Waiting for May Day *by James Hayllar, with a Windsor chair (right) and an earlier dresser.*

Country furniture

The restoration of the monarchy in 1660 marks (rather approximately) the divergence of 'country' and 'town' furniture. An influx of foreign craftsmen introduced new styles and ways of construction. In London and the larger provincial towns, cabinet-makers began to produce fashionable, highly finished furniture for the court, the aristocracy and the middle classes. Many of these designs were

Small chest of riven boards, perhaps of early Tudor date.

published in copybooks by men who are now household names, such as Thomas Chippendale (1718–79), George Hepplewhite (d. 1786) and Thomas Sheraton (1751–1806).

Country furniture is a much older tradition, and one that made use of whatever woods were locally to hand. Predominantly that was oak, but country furniture can also be found in elm, yew, beech, birch and other woods. The making of country furniture survived into the nineteenth century, in competition with town furniture and often greatly influenced by it. In the end it succumbed (with one or two exceptions) when factory-production of cheap furniture made hand-production uneconomic.

Little medieval furniture survives, but there are enough examples to give us an idea of methods. Chests are the most common items, and the earliest type was dug-out with axe and adze from a solid tree trunk, roughly squared and fitted with a hinged lid. Those that survive are huge, and mostly associated with churches, but it is quite possible that smaller versions were in domestic use. Small chests of a slightly later era were made of planks or boards of oak, fastened together at the corners by wooden pins or iron nails. By the sixteenth century, carpenters were constructing chests based on a frame joined by mortises and tenons, and with inset panels.

This gradual progression to more advanced methods can be seen in other types of furniture. Chairs and stools, for example, progressed from the dug-out method,

Early 17th-century joined chairs, known as Yorkshire and Derbyshire types.

'hutches' or 'aumbrys'. By the eighteenth century, dressers had come to combine the storage and display functions, having a superstructure of open shelves above the dresser-top, with drawers and cupboards below.

One commonly comes across furniture described as Country Chippendale, Country Hepplewhite and Country Sheraton. They are pieces created by local craftsmen in imitation of the fashionable styles of the day, or of a generation earlier. They tend to be simplified versions, not so highly finished or expertly embellished, and fashioned in native wood rather than in the expensive, exotic woods available to London cabinet-makers.

A form of country furniture is still made today – the Windsor chair. There are very many versions and variants of the Windsor, some even incorporating details of Chippendale styles. But their nature is aptly described by their early name of 'stickbacks'. The Windsor chair is essentially a seat cut from a solid piece of wood into which all the legs, arms and back-stays are socketed. In fact the Windsor chair was ideally suited to mass-assembly and division of labour. Wood-turners, or 'bodgers', made the legs and back-stays, 'bottomers' made the seats, the curved top-rail was steamed to shape by a 'bender', and the parts assembled by 'framers'. The High Wycombe area in particular was a hive of rural industry in the nineteenth century, turning out thousands of Windsor chairs each year.

through box-like structures, to joinery techniques by the sixteenth and seventeenth centuries. Similarly, joined tables superseded board-tables – heavy planks of wood on trestles – at about the same time. As a general rule, country furniture became progressively lighter in weight and less massive in proportions as time passed.

Dressers and cupboards were important pieces of furniture in village homes. The former were originally side-tables, where food was 'dressed' before serving; the latter were for storage and display of tableware. A Jacobean cupboard was generally a stand of open shelves – literally boards for cups – but some had doors and were intended for the storage of food, in which case they were known as

ABOVE *Dug-out chair, made from a tree stump and intended for a child's use.*

LEFT *A 'bodger' at work turning legs for chairs on his treadle lathe.*

going into sound timber and good carpentry. Similar progress was made a century later in the north-west and in the Midlands where Frere had lived. There the surviving yeomen's houses suggest a wave of new building between 1620 and 1680. In the stone-built areas of the Cotswolds, Rutland and Northampton-shire, many of the village houses are of the late seventeenth century. Meanwhile the northernmost counties, including the Lake District, were slow to follow the changes elsewhere, with much of the progress in housing postponed until the late seventeenth and eighteenth centuries.

The housing revolution spread in two ways. It moved northwards and westwards from the lowlands to the uplands. And it spread downwards from the leaders of society to the lower orders, as a measure of prosperity was achieved. In the end it affected all sorts and conditions of men, in every part of England. However, it took fully four hundred years for the sound building methods of a medieval manor house to be reflected in the ordinary man's cottage. The divide between peasant dwellings of the distant past, and village houses of a kind that we recognize today, was that of permanence. Crossing that threshold was the crucial advance that was to transform standards of living. The yeomanry had reached that threshold at the end of the Middle Ages. Their Tudor and Stuart houses, probably mistaken today for cottages, are the earliest village houses to survive in appreciable numbers.

They were the products of a well-organized building trade. Much of the carpentry was done away from the building site. The main framework of posts and rafters was prepared and numbered in the yard. (Those carved Roman numerals can often be seen in old houses.) Details such as windows, panelling and doors were prefabricated, providing indoor work for the craftsmen in poor weather. Then the framework was transported to the site, assembled and erected, according to tradition, in a single day. No architect or surveyor was involved. Nor were plans committed to paper. The details were held in the builder's head, and he repeated the form of building that he knew. He copied the houses that he saw locally, and used the techniques his father had taught him. That goes some way to explain why village housing changed so slowly, and why regional styles of building flourished. While a builder could happily tailor the scale of the house to his client's purse, add a room here or subtract one there, real innovation required a re-

A cruck-framed house in the foreground, and beyond it a post- and truss-framed building in the northern tradition with a jetty, or overhang, at Weobley, Hereford and Worcester.

markable leap of imagination. There was much conservatism about vernacular architecture. The medieval three-room plan of hall, chamber and service area was still dominating the layout of village houses in the Tudor and Stuart ages.

It was vernacular architecture that gave the distinctive character to village streets in every part of England. Its simplest and most ancient form was 'cruck' building. Cruck construction was a way of framing a house on two or more pairs of naturally curving tree trunks. The crucks (sometimes called forks) were tied or jointed, and then raised on to a low sill of stone or brick. Once stabilized by tie beams, they became the frame around which walls of timber, wattle and daub were erected. The technique is akin to modern steel-framed building. Both rely for their strength upon a skeleton; the walls and roof are simply a cladding to keep the elements at bay. Structural details such as these are much better seen than described, and a glance at the gable end of a cruck house reveals the builder's secrets. The village of Weobley in Hereford and Worcester is a parti-

cularly good place to see exposed crucks. It used to be said that this type of building was confined to the north and west. The greatest concentration of crucks visible from the exterior is in Shropshire, Cheshire and Staffordshire, in parts of the west Midlands, and above all in Hereford and Worcester. But crucks have now been found elsewhere in the country, the southeast excepted, though they are rarely apparent from the outside because of later plastering. Cruck building proved to be a cul-de-sac in house design, however. Elizabethan and Jacobean families valued good upstairs chambers for their extra space and privacy. When builders attempted to insert a ceiling and an upper floor, the result was cramped rooms constricted by the curved timbers of the frame. Headroom was low and ceilings sloped.

In time, therefore, different forms of timber framing were preferred. They used straight timbers – or as straight as the adze and saw-pit could make them. The frame was morticed and tenoned together, and secured by wooden pegs. Northern builders relied on some really solid corner posts to bear the load of walls and roof; the walls are infilling only, rather as in a cruck building. But in the south, the strength of the building derived from a rigid lattice of timber which made up the walls. That was a true box frame. The difference between the two techniques is often not

Little Moreton Hall, Cheshire, perhaps the most exuberant of all the north-western timber-framed houses, where no opportunity to embellish the square panels of the framing is missed.

Paycocke's House, Great Goggeshall, Essex. Close-studding (narrowly spaced uprights) is typical of the east, but the profusion of glass is a mark of his extraordinary wealth.

apparent from the outside, and it takes some clambering about in the attic to be sure. In the southern technique, multiple rafters spread the weight of the roof evenly along the walls. In the northern tradition substantial trusses brought the load to bear only on the structural corner posts. Sometimes those trusses took the form of the upper, curved portions of crucks – a technique known as raised-cruck construction.

Yet there are some more visible differences between the timber framing of the regions. In the north

and west, most of the surviving examples are large: they are the houses of families high in the social order. There are fewer small houses of Tudor and Stuart date, because wealth was less evenly spread, and many families were still living in impermanent housing. The framed panels of northern and western houses are mostly square. The shape lent itself to embellishment, and builders delighted to add lesser timbers and carved fillets of wood to create diamonds, quatrefoils, chevrons and other exuberant shapes. Another idiosyncracy of the region are the purely decorative, rounded coves under the overhang or 'jetty' of upper floors. Perhaps the most obvious characteristic today is the 'magpie' effect of blackened timber and white panels. The colour scheme is

The Fabric of the Village

ABOVE *Cottage built of coursed flint, with brick quoins and window openings, at Rustington, Sussex.*

Much of the character of old villages derives from the materials used in their buildings. Before the canal and railway ages almost all such materials were found, grown, or quarried locally, and this gives a particular quality to villages in various parts of England and Wales.

Timber was the material of preference, and above all the choice was oak. In timber-framed buildings a variety of ways was found to fill in between the frame to weatherproof the wall. Wattle and daub was the oldest and commonest technique, the wattle being a weaving of pliable withies or twigs around staves set into the timber frame; daub was a mix of clay, horsehair and dung, which was usually finished on both inside and outside faces with a layer of lime plaster.

The resulting 'half-timbering' was highly picturesque, but not particularly weatherproof. One alternative was 'brick-nogging', or infill of the frame with brickwork. Nogging was becoming popular in the late seventeenth century, but much of it is of Victorian origin. Alternatively, there were several ways to clad the entire wall, covering the frame completely in the interests of dryness and warmth. In eastern England, a skim coat of plaster over wooden laths nailed to the wooden frame was popular. It afforded opportunities for ornamental work, known as pargeting. Another approach, common in the

south-east, was to hang clay roofing-tiles over the timber framing. Plain rectangular tiles were commonly used, but specially shaped or coloured tiles were also employed, to introduce decoration and variety. In East Anglia 'weatherboarding', a cladding of timber planks, was sometimes used, though mainly on mills and farm-buildings, and never as extensively as it was in New England.

Stone has been used in even greater variety. A belt of limestone lies across England from the south coast in Dorset, up through the Cotswolds and the East Midlands to Lincolnshire and the North Yorkshire coast. It contains the best building stone in Britain, varying in texture and colour from place to place, but readily workable to a smooth ashlar finish, handsome and mostly quite durable. Yet many other stones have been used in vernacular building, some as unlikely as flint in the east and south-east, pebbles and cobbles in some seaboard areas, chalk and, in the Lake District and Wales, slate. The majority of such stonework is unfaced and irregular in shape, and therefore not laid in precise courses. It was common, however, for the quoins, or corner-stones, to be squared masonry to give strength to a structure of smaller stones. Window and door frames were also usually of dressed stone.

Even mud was widely employed in house-building. It was a surprisingly durable material when mixed with pebbles and straw, raised in walls a metre or more thick and

ABOVE *Re-thatching the roof of a cottage constructed of mud, or cob, in Sheepwash, Devon.*

62

finished with a good coat of plaster and limewash. Devon has many cottages of mud, or 'cob', and the house in which Sir Walter Raleigh was born in 1554, Hayes Barton, East Budleigh, is built of this material.

The regional variations continue up to the roof. While thatch of one type or another has been common throughout the British Isles, materials have depended on local conditions. Bracken and heather, and even turf, have been used in upland areas, while Norfolk has had the advantage of reed from specially cultivated beds in its wetlands. Generally straw of wheat or rye was used after the harvest. But the spread of threshing machines ruined the straw for thatching.

Tiles were the main alternative. They include stone tiles in the limestone areas, including the Cotswolds, and heavier stone flags in the Pennines and north-east Cheshire. Slate was used where locally available, though water and railway transport made it a popular replacement for thatch in the nineteenth century. As for man-made clay tiles, there are two distinct traditions: in the South-East, South and Midlands of England plain tiles have been employed for many centuries, while in the East and North-East, builders used pantiles with an S-shaped profile.

ABOVE *Brick nogging, replacing wattle and daub between the timbers of a building at Lavenham.*
RIGHT *Pargeting on a timber-framed house at Clare, Suffolk, a place with many examples of the craft.*

BELOW *Wattle infill between the timber framing of a house now at Avoncroft Museum of Buildings.*

so universal in the western counties that it seems churlish to question its origins. Yet until tar, pitch and oil-based paints were developed in the eighteenth century, any blacking of exterior woodwork can hardly have been permanent. Elizabethan and Jacobean houses may have been colour-washed, but the evidence has faded long ago.

Houses of the eastern counties happily demonstrate that sound oak needs neither decorative finish nor protection from the weather. Timbers there are rarely painted or tarred. Left untouched, they season to a magnificent silver-grey, while the passage of years appears to make them harder and stronger than ever. The east used oak with a cheerful profligacy. In place of the square framing of the west, narrowly spaced upright studs formed the walls. In extreme cases, there can be almost as much timber as wattle and daub. Another refinement of the east is the

The Old Clergy House, Alfriston, Sussex. This Wealden house, the first building acquired by the National Trust (in 1896), was one of several small medieval houses it saved in its early days.

regular use of finely carved windows, door heads and corner posts. They can be seen in profusion on one of the finest village houses in England, that which Thomas Paycocke, a wealthy clothier, built at Great Coggeshall in Essex around 1500. The buildings of this part of England – which includes East Anglia as well as the south-eastern counties – lack the bold appeal of the western tradition, but excel in the harmony and subtlety of their design.

The most celebrated of the timber-framed types is the so-called Wealden house. It was certainly not confined to the Weald of Kent; it occurs elsewhere in the south-east of England and even as far afield as Coventry and York. Medieval origins are unmistakable. A hall in the centre is flanked at one end by service rooms, screens and a cross passage, and at the other by private living rooms. The hall is open to the rafters, but the wings have two storeys, with bedrooms on the upper floor. The first floor is jettied 2 or 3 feet beyond the ground floor, creating the illusion that the centre of the house is recessed. The whole sits under a single roof, hipped at both ends. Kent has always been a rather prosperous county, so it is no surprise to find houses of this standard there as early as the later fourteenth century. There are many fine fifteenth- and sixteenth-century examples still standing in Kent, though all have been modified at some stage by the insertion of a floor across the open hall. The fourteenth-century Clergy House at Alfriston, East Sussex, is a small Wealden house owned by the National Trust. It was planned with a peculiarity deriving from its purpose: the servants' quarters in the east bay were inaccessible from the rest of the house where the priests lived, in order to scotch any suspicions of impropriety.

In the limestone areas of Oxfordshire and the Cotswolds, the peak of new building activity occurred after the Civil War. The change to stone building was inevitable, as the region was running out of wood. There is, none the less, every sign that timber-framed building was abandoned slowly and reluctantly. Those who could afford it were still building framed houses in the Tudor period, or tried to have, at least, an upper floor of timber. In a significant dispute the tenants of Sir Lawrence Tanfield, who purchased the manor of Great Tew in Oxfordshire in 1614, complained to the House of Lords that he was refusing their customary rights to cut 'great timbers' while continuing to hold them liable for repairs to their homes. It is some comfort, now, that the subsequent rebuilding of most of the houses in stone and thatch has created one of the most amiable villages in England.

Once the yeomanry grasped the possibilities of building in stone, the flowering of the regional style

The Wealden house at Bignor, West Sussex, is particularly attractive for not having been smartened up. The infill of the framing is a patchwork of brick, flint and plaster.

was swift and dramatic. The wool trade had put money into the hands of successful graziers and merchants. Nature had endowed the area with arguably the best stone in England: a readily-worked oolitic limestone, which weathers to handsome hues of buff to silver-grey. Its fruits can be seen today in profusion in villages such as Bourton-on-the-Water and Broadway which are not altogether unaware of their charm and attraction to visitors. But there are less self-conscious places – Lower Slaughter, Snowshill, Little Barrington, Stanton and Barnsley among them. The elements of the style are simple indeed: ashlar stone (that is stone dressed to a smooth finish), high quality carving of door surrounds and windows, a multiplicity of gables, carefully graduated stone roof slates, the largest laid at the eaves. In Bibury, one of the less commercialized Cotswold villages, the

National Trust owns a simple but most appealing terrace of cottages, Arlington Row, which shows how this vernacular style was applied to quite modest buildings – in this case homes for weavers. Travelling a little further north, to the Banbury region, we find straight roof lines, often punctuated by dormer windows, around which thatch is laid in a highly picturesque manner.

Much of this style was intensely conservative. We know that some men at work in seventeenth-century Oxfordshire were trained in vernacular styles by craftsmen who had learned their trade in the first part of the sixteenth century. In the Cotswold villages their influence is felt everywhere. Stone-mullioned windows and drip-mouldings are visible medieval antecedents, but, out of sight in attics, medieval traditions lingered even longer. In much of the region, roof structures derive from the old traditions of raised crucks and trusses. But at the same time some village houses of prosperous yeomen and minor gentry were achieving a degree of architectural sophistication. Here and there the influences of the Renaissance were at work, particularly in the proportions of windows and doors, and in the overall symmetry of the façade. The Manor Farm at North-end, Warwickshire, for example, has a centrally placed front door and an elevation to the road which is very nearly symmetrical. So has Medford House, at Mickleton in Gloucestershire (close to Hidcote Manor Gardens): it also sports classical pediments and Ionic pilasters, but with the proportions and roof of a Wealden house. These are perfect examples of a provincial accent modified by the idioms of polite architecture.

For all its conservatism, vernacular building did change gradually to meet the needs of householders. Improvements appeared first in the largest village houses, and were gradually copied in more modest homes. A substantial sixteenth-century house in Goudhurst, Kent, now serves as a Youth Hostel. If one can persuade the warden to open access to the attic, as I once did, one discovers soot-stained rafters; they betray the fact that the hall of the house was once open to the roof, with a central hearth. It became more and more common in the sixteenth and seventeenth centuries to roof over the hall, and sometimes other rooms too. The description 'chamber over the hall' was increasingly cited in inventories, and, being above the one heated room in the house, that chamber was a good dry place to store produce. The

Small 17th-century houses at Great Tew, Oxfordshire. The local limestone is tinged golden-brown by its iron content and tones perfectly with reed-thatched roofs.

insertion of a floor was the prelude to a general improvement in the house of one enterprising Berkshire farmer, Robert Loder of Harwell. He has left us an account of how he transformed his house in 1618. He had a chimney built in his hall (in place of an open hearth), which took two masons and two labourers two days to achieve. It was followed by new floors and ceilings, giving him an upper level. The new upstairs chambers needed windows, with glass. Once the work had been plastered and painted the bill came to £30, a substantial sum.

Chimneys always went hand in hand with the insertion of upper floors: smoke could no longer find its way out through the thatch or louvred roof. Early fireplaces were really open hearths under a smoke hood, there being a preserved example in a fifteenth-century timber-framed house from Bromsgrove, now re-erected at the Avoncroft Museum of Buildings. The hood leads to a shaft of wattle and daub which rises through the house. It took time before people realized that a tall and constricted flue would 'draw' smoke from the fire, and chimneys proper, rising clear of the roof, are a Tudor phenomenon. Really impressive central stacks, almost invariably of brick-work, are a dominant feature of manor houses of the period, and were evidently marks of status. But the advantages of a chimney were soon demanded by men much lower in the social scale. The chimney became a symbol of better living. One of the earliest (and best) topographical authors, Richard Carew, described in the 1580s the homes of husbandmen in 'times not yet past the remembrance':

walls of earth, low thatched roofs, no planchings [i.e. planked upper floors] *or glass windows, and scarcely any chimneys other than a hole in the wall to let out the smoke ... but now ... the Cornish husbandman conformeth himself with a better supplied civility to the eastern fashion.*

Similarly, William Harrison in his *Description of Britain* of 1577 spoke of a 'great amendment of lodging' and recalled that in his youth

there were not above two or three chimnies if so many, in uplandish towns [i.e. country villages], *the religious houses and manor places of their lords always excepted, but each one made his fire against a reredoss* [i.e. a stone fireback] *in the hall where he dined and dressed his meat. ... Now we have many chimnies, and yet our tenderlings complaine of rheumes, catarhs and poses. ... For as the smoke of those daies was supposed to be a sufficient hardening of the timber of the houses, so it was reputed to be far better medicine to keep the good man and his family.*

The charm of Cotswold cottages in Snowshill, Gloucestershire, with mellowing stone walls and roofs, variable roof heights and dormer windows.

Staircases were another consequence of floored-over halls and two-storey houses. They demanded a high proficiency in carpentry, and presented a real challenge to the builder who had to find them a place within a traditional floor plan. A common solution was an external stair turret, jutting out at the front or rear of the house. There are no fewer than ten, semicircular in shape, to be seen in the Oxfordshire village of Hook Norton. Another way, in poorer houses, was a steep ramp of timber on which shallow steps were notched, or to which triangular blocks of wood were added to form a kind of gangway. The pioneer recorder of small English houses, S. O. Addy,

photographed an example of this sort in a house at Penistone, dated 1671. The first five steps of the stair rose vertically, and the remainder inclined slightly towards the top. Thoroughly inconvenient as it must have been, it used a bare minimum of space. There is no doubt, however, that many families used a ladder as their access to the upper floor, well into the eighteenth century.

Lofting-over marks the threshold of permanent housing. A transient medieval cot could not have supported an upper floor. In his classic study, *The Midland Peasant*, W. G. Hoskins cites evidence from Wiltshire which suggests the transition was made there in the seventeenth century. Just over half of the houses he considered had been completely lofted by 1631–2. One in three was partially lofted, and every seventh house was still open to the roof. The partially

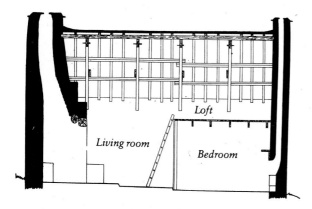

A 'croggloft', or half-lofted cottage, recorded at Llanychaer, Dyfed, earlier this century. The lofting-over provided extra space in simple homes at minimum cost, without the need for a staircase.

lofted homes may have resembled a type of house re-erected at the Folk Museum at Bunratty, County Clare, or found in Wales well into the nineteenth century and known as 'croglofft' cottages. They were two-bedroomed cottages with the master's bedroom on the ground floor at the far end of the living room from the hearth. That bedroom was ceiled at about 7 feet, and above was a loft, a dark and airless triangular space, which was reached by a moveable ladder and constituted the sleeping accommodation for children or servants. Inventories tell us that this first upstairs room was used as frequently for storage as for sleeping. We can imagine a ceiling of beams and planks over part of the hall or parlour where seed-corn, wool, cheese, bacon and saffron were kept, because they were too precious to be left in the yard or barn.

As times prospered, so families of all kinds wanted more room. Farmers of yeomen rank, in particular, needed space. Their growing bands of serving men and women looked for accommodation, and as their numbers increased, so did the need for a kitchen, bakehouse and brewhouse. Their own families, meanwhile, were clamouring for a degree of comfort and privacy. In the village of Troutbeck in Cumbria is a well-preserved example of a yeoman farmer's, or statesman's, house. Known as Townend, it was in the possession of one family, the Brownes, for thirteen generations until 1944, and came into the ownership of the National Trust in 1948. At first, around 1600, Townend had just a hall and parlour on the ground floor. The hall, known in the northern manner as the house 'or firehouse', would have served both as kitchen and living room for the family and servants. There was a bedchamber above (perhaps divided into two), but neither servants nor family can have

enjoyed much privacy. In 1623–6 the Brownes built on a service wing, that is a kitchen on the ground floor and a loft for the servants' bedroom above, served by a separate staircase. Towards the end of that century they added a further extension to the rear, to give themselves better living quarters and an additional large bedchamber. Townend now had a dozen or more rooms, and the domestic quarters were well defined. An inventory of household effects made in 1731 listed the rooms, which included:

The house [i.e. the hall]

The parlour
The little room over the parlour
The great room [the large bedchamber]
My room over the house [another bedchamber]

The low loft [the servants' chamber]
The kitching
The buttery
The skullery
The milkhouse
The cellar [literally the place for salt, alias a pantry]

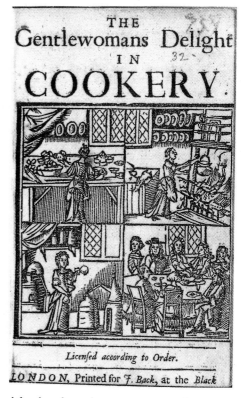

Good food and good company: once the gentry and yeomanry had installed well-furnished dining rooms, they became much more adventurous in their choice and preparation of food.

The 'firehouse' at Townend, Cumbria, furnished much as it was in 1731, if not before, although the oak used for the furniture and panelling would have been light in colour when new.

I have not altered the order in which the rooms were listed, for it helps us to understand which rooms adjoined and interconnected. But I have divided the list into three, in order to emphasize the way the house was used and the extent to which the family had separated itself from the servants. The hall was set out in a fashion which suggests the family still thought of it as a common room. It had robust furniture able to endure some boisterous use by the men of the household. There was a 'long table' (a table of oak boards on a sturdy frame), two forms, four chairs and a settle. Family and servants could still eat together there, in which event the household's pewter plates and flagons, and brass and pewter candlesticks were no doubt brought out of the buttery. For the most part, however, the family and servants had gone their separate ways. Furnishings in the family apartments were rather fashionable. One bedchamber had a bureau and a desk, a clothes press (possibly a wardrobe rather than a press in the literal sense), a round table, a leather-covered chair, an armchair and a 'dressing looking glass'. It is evident, too, that the Brownes normally dined in private, for they had an oval table and ample chairs, together with silver spoons, brandy cup, tankard and 'china ware'. Townend is a particularly interesting house to study since much of the family's belongings have remained there, and it is not difficult to envisage the domestic routines of two and a half centuries ago, or to imagine the Brownes cultivating a civilized lifestyle even in that ruggedly northern environment.

Once families had established the privacy of their rooms, they were free to elaborate the fabric and fittings of their homes. Wainscot (wood panelling to a height of about three feet) appears in houses of yeoman status in the seventeenth century, for warmth as much as for decorative effect. We find mention of a typical improvement undertaken by Robert Furse of Devonshire who, in 1583, 'glaste all the windows'; in

other words he added leaded panels of glass in place of shutters. Another concession to comfort and fashion was the building of a porch, often an ostentatious addition of more than one storey. Ornamental plasterwork, for ceilings and wall friezes, was copied by the yeomanry from the gentry of two or three generations earlier. Plaster was also much used for floors, as John Speed noted in 1611:

Therein [in Nottinghamshire] *groweth a stone softer than Alablaster* [sic] *but being burnt maketh a Plaister harder than that of Paris; wherewith they flower* [i.e. floor] *their upper rooms; for betwixt the ioysts they lay only long Bulrushes, and theron spread this Plaister, which being thoroughly dried becomes most solide and hard, and is troad upon without all danger.*

Many yeomen had at least one ground floor room 'planched' [planked], while service areas were cobbled or flagged, and earthen floors were made by puddling and compacting.

The hall, meanwhile, was ceasing to be an important room. The family had left for their own chambers; the cookery and domestic chores had gone to the kitchens and service wings. It was a rough kind of servant who lived and slept in the hall, a draughty, inconvenient and uncomfortable place. The hall simply had less and less function to fulfil. It became smaller in houses of every kind, until in the nineteenth century it was no more than an entrace, and a place to hang one's hat and coat.

The major impediment to comfort was heating – or the lack of it. Yeomen farmers no longer relied on the hall fire, as cooking was quartered in a kitchen. But as late as the mid-seventeenth century it was still not unusual to find the parlour unheated: a fine and private place, perhaps, but distinctly chilly. The obstacle to progress seems to have been cultural: the continuing notion that a hearth in the hall was proper. In consequence, Tudor and Stuart houses almost invariably have central chimneys. A compromise was to set hall and parlour fireplaces back to back, on either side of the dividing wall sharing a flue. This is the typical arrangement of upland farmhouses in the north-east. The third room, or service end of the house, remained unheated. It continued so until the eighteenth century, when house design solved the problem by placing chimneys on the two gable-end walls; the hall, much shrunken from its medieval prominence, finally lost its fire.

The porch of the early 16th-century Guildhall at Lavenham, Suffolk. The high quality window frames and door surrounds, and the splendid natural colour of the timber are typical of the east.

By the end of the Stuart period, the society of a village frequently comprised one or two very prosperous yeomen and many labourers, cottagers and servants. The gap between rich and poor was wider than ever, and there were fewer families of middling rank. In Foxton, Cambridgeshire, at the end of the Stuart period, one man, Nathaniel Singleton, was farming about 400 acres, presumably with quite a household of servants. Another, John Rayner, left the large sum of £180 in bills and bonds. He was evidently acting as the village moneylender, an important role in a market economy, with wages to be found between harvests and equipment to be bought. A small farmer, Edmund Osler, had been living out a lonely old age without wife or family, struggling to manage a farm of perhaps 18 acres. He had a few animals and poultry, and an old house; it seems unlikely that he had been able to plough, sow and harvest the land to its full capacity. He was one of the last of a vanishing breed of peasant farmers, growing food for himself at a subsistence level. Will Pink, a labourer, ended his days with a little corn and pulses, a cow and some saffron. He had resided in a cottage of medieval layout – just a hall, chamber and buttery. Elsewhere in the village, a widow, Elizabeth Dunnidge, managed with a bed in her cottage, and very little else. A former servant, she was luckier than many, for she had some savings put by, and her family lived just across the road.

The Will Pinks and the Edmund Oslers of the world were selling out to the Singletons and their like, to become part of the growing band of the landless and the cottagers. Their contemporaries saw them as the social problem of the age. More specifically, legislators and pamphlet-writers had four worries: the proliferation of cottagers, the number of wandering beggars and cutpurses, the difficulty of finding work for the poor and the cost of supporting the needy and aged of the parish.

The Tudor government was dismayed by the numbers of small houses going up with little or no land. There was building on subdivided plots, encroachments on the waste and roadsides in distant parts of the parish, and even on the green or on empty corners in the village. Major landowners stamped it out when they could, but enough families persisted for their covert home-making to have left its mark on the landscape. Little settlements of new houses away from the village and church are common signs of economic (and sometimes religious) necessity. Many a village street and market place is diverted and narrowed where cottage building has encroached. Objections to this activity stemmed from the age-old ideal of prudential marriage, of every family with its plot, and the fear that landless families would become

The Tichborne Dole: a 17th-century painting by G. van Tilborg showing the squire of a Hampshire village giving food to the poor at his door and showing some satisfaction at his own largesse.

a burden on the community. In a desperate attempt to stem the tide, the government enacted a bill of 1589 against 'Erecting and Maintaining Cottages' It inveighed against 'the great inconveniences which are found by experience to grow by the erecting and building of great numbers and multitudes of cottages, which are daily more and more encreased in many parts of this realm'. The building of cottages on plots of less than 4 acres of farmland was banned. The statute also tried to prevent more than one family from sharing a cottage. It was a forlorn effort. Within a few years the government had changed its tune a little. With the population growing back to pre-plague levels, it acknowledged that punitive measures could not abolish poverty. The law of 1601 enjoined the churchwardens to build housing for the poor, on the parish waste if need be. A compulsory rate was to be raised by the Justices of the Peace for the maintenance of the deserving poor. 'Overseers of the poor' were to establish workhouses, and to see that pauper children were placed in service.

Beggars and vagabonds were harshly treated, however. It was popularly supposed, no doubt with a basis in fact, that a floating population of workshy rogues and tricksters drifted about the country, living on charity and crime. A contemporary critic, Thomas Harman, distinguished twenty-three categories; they included 'fresh-water mariners' whose ship was wrecked on Salisbury Plain, 'demanders for glimmer', who claimed to have lost all in a fire, 'hookers' who purloined clothes from windows with a long pole, and various 'bawdy baskets', 'doxies' and harlots. The official line throughout the Tudor and Stuart era was that wanderers should be resettled in their proper place. They were liable to be whipped until bloody and sent back to the place of their birth or last residence. In reality many men and women had left their parish because there was no work, and bringing them back was not likely to solve their problems.

Contemporaries saw much aimless drifting, but that was only part of the picture. There was emigration from 'closed' villages – those in which one or two landholders controlled both employment and housing – to 'open' villages and the towns. Major landholders wanted enough village families to fill their tenancies and to labour on their fields but they did not welcome the return of the wandering poor, whose presence would only serve to increase the parish poor rate. They refused to build new cottages or poorhouses, and restricted the practice of rural crafts and other employment on their land, thereby controlling immigration rather tightly. Open villages, by contrast, had a larger number of small landholders, many of whom supplemented their farming income with craft or industrial work. Such places were predominantly in the highland zone, or in newer settlements in the forest, wastes and fens, where gentry control had not been established. Immigration was tolerated, and there was freedom for landless families to establish themselves in some trade or employment. We shall see in the next chapter that these mobile workers were crucial to the growth of the economy. In the meantime they were a problem – one of many – for the Church, as it tried to adapt its ministry to a rapidly changing world.

Beliefs and superstitions

Some years ago, I had the privilege of access to the library of an old Cambridge college. I spent an absorbing afternoon browsing among the volumes that the Fellows had acquired in the sixteenth century: marvellous leather-bound books that were the products of the new technology of the age, the printing press. It was readily apparent to me that a single subject dominated the intellectual agenda. That burning issue was reform of the Church. It was not only the size of the literature that impressed – the shelf upon shelf of weighty tomes which examined every line of creed and ritual in minute detail – but the animation of the language. The finest minds of the age, in Europe as well as in England, were trading blows and calling names. Opponents were never merely mistaken, they were servants of Antichrist, lechers, deceivers, conjurers, apostates and so on. Some very deep-seated animosities, which had been building up for a century and a half, were coming out into the open. The shockwaves of that violent clash were to take a further century and a half at least to subside. In some places, Northern Ireland being one, they are still felt today. At the village level, niceties of dogma must have mattered little. The ordinary parishioner could not read, let alone comprehend all the arguments of the scholars. He must have been aware, however, that momentous events were afoot. Surely everyone, even in the remotest hamlet, must have heard the gossip that King Henry VIII was divorcing Queen Catherine to marry Anne Boleyn, and in so doing had denied that the Pope was head of the Church in England. Later, he must have heard, and possibly comprehended, that Queen Mary was taking the Church back to the Roman allegiance, and then that her half-sister Elizabeth had once more rejected the supremacy of the Pope.

Of more immediate concern to the parishioner was the fact that the services of the Church were no longer said in Latin, that the village priest was not required to be celibate or to hear confession, and that the monasteries and convents had been suddenly suppressed. Their abbeys and priories were left to

The public whipping of a vagabond or convict, the cat o'five tails drawing blood from his bare back, while respectable householders look on with approval as he is led to the gallows.

become quarries of stone or homes of the gentry. Those were changes that went to the heart of religious feeling in the countryside. Before the Reformation, a reservoir of popular resentment had been filling. One source of the ill-will was the wealth of the Church. Some were comparing it unfavourably

The English Reformation celebrated in Foxe's Book of Martyrs, 1563. The king, on receiving the English Bible, treads on the Pope, toppling his crown and, by implication, his authority.

with the poverty of Christ and of His apostles. Ploughmen maintain the world, wrote the author of a fifteenth-century poem, 'God spede the plowe', but the fruits of their labour go to those that rule, including the parson and the friars. Another well of dissatisfaction was the Church's tolerance of superstitions, miraculous relics and pilgrimages. How many were disaffected is impossible to say, but among them were a few who caught the authorities' eye as open dissidents. The Lollards, condemned as heretics, attracted to their number ordinary folk who wanted the Bible in English and a simpler religion based on it. Many more, perhaps, felt aggrieved by the payment of their tithe (the tenth of their income or produce due to the rector), and sceptical of the often unintelligible rites performed by the priest. The strength of those resentments was such that when the state imposed a reformation on the Church, there was widespread, though not universal, support among the people.

There is no doubt that the medieval church was compromised by its acceptance of superstition. Its difficulty went back to those Christian missionaries who first preached the faith in Anglo-Saxon Britain. They had confronted a pagan religion with its own spirits and deities, credited with power to control the natural world. Depending on their somewhat capricious mood, those gods would send good luck or ill, full harvests or bad, health or sickness. Religion and its observances were thus a means of placating the gods and of harnessing their powers to one's own interest, and against one's rivals. The early Christian preachers were in exactly the position of the prophet Elijah in the Bible when he confronted the priests of the god Baal (1 Kings 18); they needed to prove that the Christian God was stronger than any rivals. For that reason early Christian teaching stressed the miraculous: the success of the saints in performing cures, in preserving from dangers or in warding off evil spirits. Christianity proved its worth, to the popular mind, by having access to supernatural influence. The intercession of saints, the healing touch of kings or the sight of holy relics were but a few of the channels of divine power.

Officially, the Church taught that observance and ritual had no power of themselves, and drew their strength only from the faith of the participants. That was too subtle a distinction for ordinary believers. The Church's stance was weakened further by its absorption of pagan elements into its own religion. The celebration of Christmas, for example, took over the festive character of the midwinter feast of Saturn, when holly and other greenery were cut as symbols of rebirth, to decorate the temples. That association with paganism was not lost on Puritan reformers of

the seventeenth century, who would have suppressed the festivities. Some Christian saints are recognizably the characterization of pagan gods: St Michael, often portrayed as a winged warrior, is evidently the reincarnation of Woden and Mercury, the messenger gods of Anglo-Saxon and Classical mythology. Holy places of the old religion (many remembered in the place-name elements 'Stow' and 'Stoke') were taken for the site of churches. Woodnesborough in Kent was 'Wodan's burgh', and the church was founded on a temple site within an Iron Age hill fort. Holy springs and wells continued to be revered, blessed and popularly held to have magical powers. (Even today a surprising number of people will cast a coin into a well or fountain, as though to purchase good luck.) The medieval priest was expected to lead processions through the fields, carrying the gospels, bells and banners, thereby exorcizing any malignant spirits that might harm the growing crops. At Rogation he walked the parish bounds, praying or reading the scriptures at wayside shrines or crosses, in order to protect the village from encroachment by evil influences.

The fabric of our village churches reflects this semi-magical aspect of medieval religion. Virtually every church and chapel has its bell tower or steeple, the tallest structure in the village. There was some competition between villages for the highest tower, and not a few collapsed as a consequence. But the height of the tower also had a ritual significance. In traditional cosmology heaven, where God dwelt, was above the earth. Between them in the air an army of evil spirits, the henchmen of Beelzebub the prince of demons, and Lucifer the fallen angel, held sway. The steeple pierced that dangerous territory, pointing the way to heaven. At critical moments the bells were swung, and their clamour cleared the atmosphere of those malevolent forces, opening a channel to God. Before each service and mass a peal rang out. In a violent storm – the work of the demons – the bells were sounded to quell the mischief. The bell tolled for the dying, for the soul was released from the body at the moment of death, and then the demons might seize it. That ringing in the steeple secured the soul's safe passage to heavenly paradise. Each bell was consecrated for its purpose, and inscribed with ritual words and a cross.

Inside the church there were once many vivid reminders of the spirit realm, but such things were often swept away at the Reformation. Favoured saints, who would intercede with God on man's behalf, were represented in wall paintings. Tradition placed St Christopher's image on the wall opposite the main entrance of the church, to be seen by the arriving and departing congregation. So potent was

The 'doom', or painting of the Last Judgement, in Wenhaston Church, Suffolk. Originally displayed on the wall above the chancel arch, it would be highly visible throughout the service.

his influence that sight of his image gave a day's protection from harm. The world of spirits and demons has survived here and there in pre-Reformation carvings – the bench ends of rich East Anglian churches, and the intricate chancel screens of the West Country.

An essential part in church ritual was played by holy water. Baptism signified a cleansing and, through the marking of the child with the sign of the cross, a protection against evil. It was widely believed that a child's physical, as much as his spiritual health, depended on the christening. By extension of the symbolism, the sprinkling of water by a priest, together with the sign of the cross, became the way of blessing sick men and animals, ships (now launched with a sprinkling of champagne), and buildings and crops. Ancient baptismal fonts have been preserved and are frequently the oldest furnishings of the village

church. Holy water stoups, built into the wall, have also sometimes survived the reformers' zeal.

The churchyard acted as an outer defence against the forces of evil. Its burial ground was consecrated by the sprinkling of water and salt (the latter being symbolic of preservation). Part of the churchyard, usually to the shaded north of the church, was sometimes left unconsecrated, and that was the final resting place of suicides and of others who died in mortal sin. Protecting the churchyard were walls and gates, and within were yew trees, evergreen and living to an immense age – symbols, perhaps, of resurrection and immortality.

The mass was central in the Church's ritual, but little of the ceremony can have been understood by the average parishioner. The priest stood at the east end of the chancel, separated from the congregation in the nave by a rood screen. He recited his prayers and formulas in Latin, ringing his bell, raising the bread and wine heavenward, and mysteriously changing its substance into the body and blood of Christ. Yet the Church taught that the mass had a beneficial power of itself, whether or not the congreg-

ABOVE *Well-preserved Victorian and Georgian tombstones in the enchanting churchyard at Bibury, Gloucestershire.*

ation understood it; consequently masses were said for all manner of objectives such as the recovery of the sick, the safe gathering of the harvest, or for the souls of the dead. Many believed the consecrated elements to contain magical powers. Communicants were known to carry away bread in their mouths, hoping to use it as a charm to cure illness or to scatter on the fields for their fertility.

At the Reformation the most vehement critics argued that the whole fabric of church buildings was irredeemably associated with superstition. Thus the Elizabethan Puritan Henry Barrow condemned the reverencing of the ancient structures:

The first stone must be laid by the hands of the bishop or his suffragan, with certain magical prayers, and holy water. ... They have at the west end their hallowed bells, which are also baptised, sprinkled, etc. ... They have in the body of their church their hallowed font, to keep the holy water wherewith they baptise .... They have also their holiest of all, or chancel, which peculiarly belongeth to the priest .... This church, thus reared up is ... dedicated and baptised into the name of some especial saint or angel, as to the patron and defender thereof, against all enemies, spirits, storms, tempests etc. Yet hath it within also the holy army of saints and angels in their windows and walls, to keep it. Thus I think can no doubt be made but that the very erections of these synagogues (whether they were by heathens or papists) were idolatrous. ...

Barrow went on to call for actual demolition of existing churches. That was an extreme view. Official Anglicanism prohibited the use of holy water (except for baptism), turned the mass into the communion celebrated in the English language, suppressed most of the perambulations and processions, closed the pilgrim shrines, and forbade prayers to the saints.

The second great preoccupation of the reformers, after superstitions, was the wealth of the Church. Many of its lands and possessions were appropriated – some would say stolen – by the state in the sixteenth century. At the Reformation allegations were made about the avarice of the clergy, but in fact most of the Church's wealth came from the bequests of lay people. The medieval Church taught that, after the death of the body, the soul migrated to purgatory, an intermediate resting place. There, by the passage of time and by suffering, the soul was made ready for reunion with God. That period in purgatory could be shortened by prayers and masses recited by the faithful on earth. Understandably men and women

contemplating their eternal fate wished to enlist the prayers of the most effective intercessors. To that end they left generous bequests to the Church, and in particular to the monastic orders. There was a certain irony in this, as some of those orders, the Cistercians and the Cluniacs among them, had deliberately sought out inhospitable locations for their English houses, in order to escape the temptations of secular life. Their poverty and saintliness gained them an unmatched spiritual prestige, which in turn attracted a flood of endowments and bequests. When their estates grew, a small army of lay brothers undertook the manual labour, leaving the monks free to pray and sing in their great churches. Inevitably the very success of the monasteries provoked a reaction. Alarmed by the growth of a rival in wealth and influence, the Crown tried, through the Statute of Mortmain of 1279, to prohibit any further bequests to the Church. Lay sympathy for the monks turned to jealousy and to malicious tittle-tattle about easy living and doubtful morals. The flow of bequests to the monasteries declined markedly after the Black Death.

With the experience of the plague and its sudden slaughter vividly in mind, believers became obsessed with death and with divine retribution. One parti-

Almshouses at Ewelme, Oxfordshire. Together with the parish church and nearby grammar school, all built between 1435 and 1445, they testify to the charitable endeavour of the de la Pole family.

cularly affected by morbid thoughts was Henry Williams, the fifteenth-century vicar of Stanford-on-Avon in Northamptonshire; he had himself portrayed in the chancel window of his church with 'the ymage of death shooting at me'. Village churches, such as those at Pickworth in Lincolnshire and Penn in Buckinghamshire, acquired wall paintings of the Last Judgement over the chancel arch, in full view of the congregation throughout divine service. Small wonder, then, that parishioners sought to buy the safety of their souls by appropriate endowments. Parish churches were major beneficiaries. The greater the medieval wealth of the district, the greater its churches. In East Anglia the flourishing cloth trade of the fifteenth century financed the erection and extension of the magnificent 'wool churches'. Competition between the village played its part, as did the personal ostentation of the benefactors. The resulting cathedral-like structures at Long Melford, Clare, Lavenham Cavendish and elsewhere soar majestically above the countryside that nourished them.

Lay patrons had other means of perpetuating their memory. In 1437 the Duke of Suffolk established a hospital for aged and infirm persons at Ewelme, in Oxfordshire, of which he was lord of the manor. Each resident was to have 'a certain place by themself ... that is to sayng, a lityl house, a celle or a chamber with a chemeney and other necessarys in the same, in the whiche any of them may by himself ete and dryncke and rest....' That was in addition to a common hall and the use of a church. Suffolk's foundation at Ewelme, which still stands, is typical of medieval almshouses and hospitals in being the foundation of a single eminent benefactor. As a contrast, however, the people of Saffron Walden jointly provided for the poor of their village. A meeting of parishioners on 5 August 1400 resolved 'for the remedy of their own souls' to establish and maintain almshouses 'for the refuge and upkeep of 13 poor persons ... such as are decrepit, blind, lame'.

The greater part of medieval endowment did not go into such charitable works. The rich established chantries. There, in chapels set apart for the purpose, masses were recited in perpetuity for the benefit of departed souls. Lesser mortals left money for an 'obit', a special mass or masses said after their death, with alms for the poor. In the century before the Reformation, chantries and obits supported a sizeable profession of clerks in minor orders. That clan of unbeneficed clergy, and the great multiplication of

masses, caught the eye of the authorities in the reign of the boy-king Edward VI. Reforming zeal was then running high; the English Church was denying both the existence of purgatory and the efficacy of masses said for the dead. The chantries were dissolved, their endowments confiscated, and the clerks turned out with a meagre pension. Protestantism also took a firm stand against the notion that charitable deeds assisted towards salvation. Faith in Christ, not good works, redeemed the soul. With the general acceptance of Protestant views in the sixteenth and seventeenth centuries, the long tradition of self-interested charity drew to its close. One result was the near drying-up of major charitable foundations for the poor after about

Chantry chapel of the Clopton family at Holy Trinity, Long Melford, Suffolk. The Cloptons' wealth enabled this most splendid of English village churches to be built in 1460–86.

LEFT *These almshouses at Cavendish, Suffolk, were built by the village green and, as was often the case, close to the parish church, which recipients of the charity were expected to attend regularly.*

It would be quite wrong, however, to portray the countryside as having two separate workforces, industrial and agricultural. Most families had a stake in both worlds. The wives and children of closed villages frequently pursued an 'industrial' sideline, such as spinning thread of wool or flax. Once a year, even closed villages welcomed help from outside. The ripening crops in the field were highly vulnerable to the weather and when the moment for harvest came, proprietors were glad to enlist a swarm of temporary workers. Some came in organized teams – reapers and scythers especially – moving from one farm to another. Others were local people who could bind, lift and carry. During the harvest, wages were at their highest to attract people who did not otherwise work the land at all. William Marshall, another great traveller in the late eighteenth and early nineteenth century and a keen observer of agriculture, claimed that in Kent 'whole families, indeed the whole county may be said to live in the field in the busy season of hopping.... Besides the people of the neighbourhood, numbers flock from the metropolis; also from Wales.' The contrast at harvest time between the past, when dozens of men and women would work together in the field, and the present, when a solitary combine harvester drones and sweeps up the grain, could hardly be sharper.

In open parishes many families learned to combine several employments. They might farm a smallholding or garden, and keep a few animals on the common. Now and again, at harvest in particular, they might earn some cash by casual work on the land. At home, meanwhile, they pursued a cottage industry. This combining of employments was recorded in the village of Mellor in Cheshire, in 1770. It had

between 50 and 60 farmers [of whom] there were only 6 or 7 who raised their rents directly from the produce of their farms. All the rest got their rent partly in some branch of trade such as spinning and weaving woollens, linen or cotton. The cottagers were employed entirely in this manner except for a few weeks in the harvest.

This was not an industrial society as we know it today; manufacture and agriculture still co-existed happily and naturally. Nor was it modern manufacturing, with all its connotations of factories and massive machinery. Manufacture was still 'making by hand'. It was carried out largely at home with simple tools and equipment by thousands of domestic craft workers,

Behind them were entrepreneurs who did the buying and selling and co-ordination. In this way trades became highly organized, and none more so

Reapers (1785) by George Stubbs. The master of the farm, or his bailiff, has ridden out to see that the crucial harvest work is pressing ahead. At this season women work alongside the men.

than the woollen industry. It was the largest of the medieval trades, and one of the oldest. Once the making of woollen cloth had been an urban craft; the old cities of York and Salisbury had prospered on its

back. By the fifteenth century, however, the trade had been reorganized by 'clothiers', who had grasped the advantage of mechanizing the fulling of the cloth (the raising of the nap by hammering) through water power, which was most readily available in the countryside. The industry flourished in the wolds of Gloucestershire and Wiltshire in the west, in the Suffolk wool villages in the east and, a little later, in the Pennine areas of Yorkshire in the north –

wherever there were water, wool and plentiful supplies of labour. Unlike the craftsmen of the city guilds, domestic workers were not organized. They could not demand higher wages and better conditions. Those advantages, from the clothiers' point of view, enabled the rural industry first to rout the urban craftsmen and then to capture the export trade. By the end of the Middle Ages, the rural, part-time workforce was producing cloth in such quantity and

quality that the English industry was absolutely dominant in Europe.

Many individuals were involved in the manufacture of a piece of cloth. Some families washed and carded the raw wool, some spun a yarn, others wove. It took as many as six or eight spinners to keep one weaver in thread, so that thousands of children and women passed a large part of their lives at the wheel. The dyeing and fulling tended to be workshop tasks. Then the piece of cloth had to be collected, transported and sold. Each of those who had a hand in the process, from the farmer who supplied the wool onwards, wanted payment. All this was orchestrated by the clothier. The business needed substantial working capital, but the rewards could be large. Clothiers were often the most prosperous members of the community. In the West Country at Bradford-on-Avon, Defoe noted that 'it was not extraordinary to have clothiers worth from ten thousand to forty thousand pounds a man, and many of the great families who now pass for gentry have been originally raised from, and built up by this truly noble manufacture'. Similarly, at Long Melford in Suffolk, he saw 'very good houses', which were the houses of 'masters of the manufacture'.

The industry was to develop a little differently in Yorkshire. Clothiers there were personally involved in both farming and weaving. Woollen manufacture was a family business, with the master of the household employing a number of weavers and dyers in a workshop attached to his house. Defoe expressed astonishment at the scale of the industry. As he began his descent from the head of the moors at Blackstone Edge, towards Halifax, he found the steep hillsides thick with houses, each one set in an enclosure of a few acres. It was 'one continued village' covering several miles, with 'hardly a house standing out of speaking distance of another'. The wide dispersion of the settlement over inhospitable landscapes was for the convenience of the manufacturers; each clothier's house took advantage of a local stream to have 'a little rill or gutter of running water ... running into and through their workhouses'. Inside, the processes of dyeing, scouring and weaving were undertaken by

Two engravings from George Walker's Costumes of Yorkshire, *1814. In the illustration above a woman is spinning wool at home, using a great, or walking, wheel, while the woman by the fire is carding (meaning combing the fibres straight) ready for spinning. The illustration below shows the knitters of Wensleydale, Cumbria. Hand-knitting, like all handcrafts, was slow work and this engraving captures the atmosphere of the constant endeavour to make a living.*

'a house full of lusty fellows ... all hard at work'. Between the weaving 'shops' were

an infinite number of cottages or small dwellings, in which dwell the workmen which are employed, the women and children of whom are always busy carding, spinning, etc. So that no hands being unemployed all can gain their bread, even from the youngest to the oldest, hardly anything above four years but its hands are sufficient to itself

Yorkshire clothiers continued to prosper through the eighteenth century. Technical advances in cloth manufacture increased their profits and encouraged expansion. Weaving was greatly quickened by the flying shuttle, invented by John Kay in 1733. But the flying shuttle also encouraged the Yorkshire industry to produce a fine broadcloth in place of narrow kerseys (a type of woollen cloth). Larger looms were needed for broadcloth and, with demand growing during the Napoleonic wars, many clothiers added new weaving galleries to their houses. Mostly they extended upwards, building another floor on to their solid gritstone houses. For light and air they installed long lines of stone-mullioned windows. Those 'top-shops' stayed in business in the nineteenth century, the handloom weavers competing with mechanized mills by concentrating on high-quality cloth. Today the lofts are silent, but the reminders of the domestic cloth industry – weaving galleries and spinners' cottages – are everywhere to be seen in the scattered villages of the Pennines.

Woollens were just one of many textile crafts, each of which had a strong geographical focus. The Yorkshire Dales and the Lake District were known for their hand-knitting. 'Stockings are the chief manufacture,' wrote Arthur Young of the Kendal district, 'including wool-combers, spinners and knitters.' A relic of that industry, seen for instance on barns in Troutbeck in Cumbria, are external 'spinning galleries' on which the long hours of northern summer daylight could be turned to profitable work. The assiduous knitters of Dent, near Kendal, were known both for their knitting songs and for their knitting sheaths – needle holders that could be tucked under an arm or into a belt to leave one hand free. The knitting could thus continue while the saucepan was being stirred or a cart horse driven. Some of the sheaths, which one can find in folk museum collections, are highly carved, and were given to young women by their suitors as marks of affection.

The Midland counties of Leicestershire, Nottinghamshire and South Yorkshire as far as Doncaster were also a knitting area, but the industry there was quick to adopt a degree of mechanization. Knitting frames, loom-like machines, were worked by hand

ABOVE *The spinning gallery of the barn at Townend in Troutbeck, Cumbria.*
LEFT *A late 19th-century photograph of a spinning gallery in Low Hartsop, Cumbria, with sheep-shearing in progress. Though known in the Lake District as spinning galleries, such structures seem equally likely to have been used for drying fleeces or storage.*

and treadle. Master hosiers added workshops to their houses, well lit by long, mullioned windows, and accommodating a dozen or more frames. The large village of Wigston Magna in Leicestershire had about one in six families dependent on frame knitting by 1700. But its clothing industry was diversified; there were a dozen or more tailors and several shoemakers, all combining their craft with agriculture. Meanwhile Macclesfield in Cheshire was specializing in silk. Lace was the cottage industry in Shepton Mallet in Somerset, Honiton in Devon and in the Bernwood Forest area of Buckinghamshire. Hemp and flax were

RIGHT *The Market House at Winster, Derbyshire. Originally, the arches of the ground floor were open to form a sheltered market for produce.*

being grown in the Fens, to be spun and woven into sacks and sheets for domestic use.

A number of Derbyshire villages specialized in mining and quarrying. Passing through the Peak District, Celia Fiennes saw 'those craggy hills whose bowells are full of mines of all kinds'. The country was producing a variety of stone, including a sort of marble, mostly of a greyish colour, and often patterned with fossils. It found a ready market for country house fireplaces. Fiennes records the extraction of fluorspar, a white, opal-like mineral that was sometimes cut into ornamental vases and urns, but which 'the doctors use . . . in medicine for the Collick' – presumably powdered. Above all it was a lead-mining area. The industry employed techniques which, whether conceived in ignorance or indifference, had dreadful consequences for the miners. They were lowered by rope or pulley down a narrow shaft, to tunnel underground until they found lead ore. Gunpowder was used, sometimes with disastrous effect. In Fiennes's words, 'they generally look very pale and yellow that work underground'. Those are the all-too-recognizable symptoms of lead poisoning. Defoe, too, witnessed a miner here 'lean as a skeleton, pale as a corps'. The industry none the less provided employment in an unwelcoming landscape. Mining villages, such as Elton, Flagg and Taddington, cling to highly exposed hillside and table-land sites. Spoil heaps and disused mines nearby testify to several centuries of activity in places where farming alone could not have supported a population. At nearby Winster, however, are signs of the prosperity that the industry could endow. A prominent market hall was begun in stone in the seventeenth century and finished later in brick. (It was the first property acquired in Derbyshire by the National Trust, which also owns a lead mine near Lose Hills.) There was a short-lived boom in the industry in the middle of the Georgian period, and Winster's population grew temporarily from around 600 to 2000. Some substantial houses and inns were built, before the village's fortunes and population subsided again.

Winster's gain in population was by no means unique. Other villages with an industrial speciality grew quickly. Such places attracted immigrants, but there was also an absolute increase in the population of England and Wales from about 5 million in 1700 to over 9 million by 1801. The growth can only be explained by a higher birth rate or a lower death rate; in fact both were taking place after about 1750. Men and women were marrying earlier, and having more children. Fewer of those offspring were perishing in infancy, a sign a better nutrition, hygiene and midwifery. In effect the two ancient restraints on population had been broken. The principle of prudential marriage did not apply in an industrial village, for couples could make a living without waiting for a landholding. And the direct relationship of village population and the productivity of its land was set aside by the fruits of industry. Defoe had, as usual spotted the essential point. He wrote of the moors above Halifax:

This whole country, however mountainous . . . is yet infinitely full of people; not a beggar, not an idle person to be found . . . it is observable, that the people here, however laborious, generally live to a great age, a certain testimony to the goodness and wholesomeness of the country, which is, without doubt, as healthy as any part of England.

Defoe was no doubt over-sanguine on the health of the population. Rural industry could be hazardous and debilitating, and the lives of many individuals were still cruelly hard. Yet, considered as a whole, the upland and pastoral areas of the country, and many villages within them, were enjoying a prosperity they had not previously tasted.

Trade created traffic, and traffic created trades of its own – road-making, wagon-building, warehousing and river carriage, to name but a few. For those villages that built their fortunes on transport, and there were many, the eighteenth century was a high-water mark. Before then the roads were lamentable, patently incapable of coping with all the wheeled, animal and human traffic that passed along them; in fact they were largely an inheritance of Roman times. Repairs fell on the parish authorities, who merely dumped cartloads of stones in the muddiest places. However, Defoe witnessed the early days of the turnpike system, an early form of privatization which allowed investors – the turnpike trusts – to construct and repair roads in return for a toll on traffic. At the peak of their fortunes, around 1800, the turnpike trusts were managing a system of well-engineered roads which stretched from London to most parts of the country. They bore everything from long-distance mail coaches (London to Edinburgh in under two days) to slow-moving wagons, packhorses and droves of cattle. The roads were without doubt much busier, with this variety of traffic, than they had ever been before.

Travellers required food and shelter; coaches needed horsepower. Villages on the main routes consequently made a handsome living from innkeeping. One such was Somerton in Somerset. It had always been strategically sited on the Fosse Way, on an island in the periodically-flooded Somerset levels. The village acted as a focus for the surrounding countryside, and it has its old market place and cross. The medieval prosperity of the place is evident from

Tollhouse at Sutterton, Lincolnshire, which, being round, faces both ways along the turnpike. The Gothick windows, classical cornice and thatched roof complete the architectural cocktail.

the handsome church and its impressive octagonal tower. But the village's heyday was really the eighteenth century, when it became an important staging post on the cross-country trade route. With a population of no more than 1000, it supported sixteen inns, some of which were rather grand. The Red Lion, which has a classical façade, pedimented windows, and high arch to permit coaches to pass into its courtyard, is typical of the better sort of establishment which flourished in many similar villages at that time. Associated services were needed

ABOVE *Paying tolls on a turnpike: the highest tolls were levied on carts carrying heavy goods and on coaches. They added 3d. or 4d. a mile to the costs of running a coach.*

too – blacksmithing, ostlery, saddlery and harness repair, wheelwrighting and so on.

The coaching age came to an abrupt end when the railways came. Within a few years the roads emptied, and by 1867 George Eliot, the novelist, was looking back wistfully to the days when 'the glory had not yet departed from the old coach-roads: the great road-side inns were still brilliant with well-polished tankards, the smiling glances of pretty barmaids, and the repartees of jocose ostlers; the mail still announced itself by the merry notes of the horn....' The turnpikes have, none the less, left a memento of their great days; all manner of traffic paid for its passage at tollbars which punctuated the route. Those bars or gates have long since gone, but many of the accompanying tollhouses remain. They afforded the toll-keeper modest living accommodation, an office of sorts and, usually, a good view of the road in both directions. The last requirement prompted a certain ingenuity in design; octagons and half-octagons were favoured, with windows on faces angled to the road. Some faintly classical styles were employed elsewhere, and in at least one example, that at Great Rowsley in Derbyshire, the proximity of a medieval great house, Haddon Hall, prompted a touch of Gothic revival in the detailing. Thus tollhouses form a pleasing little architectural sub-group.

While the roads were busy in Defoe's day, it would be wrong to think of them as the only, or even the dominant means of transport. Sometimes the roads were merely feeders of traffic to the waterside. Indeed the very first turnpike, from Huntingdon to Ware,

RIGHT Departure of the Mail, *by Heywood Hardy. The mail coaches were the fastest things on the road and only stopped briefly at their staging posts for new horses and refreshments.*

completed in 1663, served to join up two major river systems: the Ouse, which carried the farming produce of the Fenlands, and the River Lea, which was the main route to London. Water was the best way to carry goods over any distance. Even trifling streams were used as arteries of trade, and places that now seem landlocked were once centres of activity. Defoe was quick to notice such things: Bawtry, in the West Riding of Yorkshire 'on the little but pleasant River Idle ... becomes the centre of all the exportation of the country'. At Bawtry wharf, according to Defoe, all the heavy goods of the region were loaded onto lighters and taken to the staging post of Stockwith on the Trent. Today the wharves of Bawtry are scarcely more than grassy mounds and hollows, their fame long forgotten. Similar, indeed heavier, traffic once plied the River Severn. Bewdley and Bridgnorth were the principal ports, and had extensive wharves and warehouses. But smaller villages and hamlets along the river also secured a modest income from passing trade. They catered for boatmen who used the exceptional tidal surges of the Severn to carry their craft upstream, pausing several hours for the next tide.

Roads and Tracks

The scandalous state of the roads rivalled the weather as a favourite topic of conversation. In the seventeenth century travellers' tales of coaches that disappeared into seas of mud were only mild exaggerations, and there were such scant signposts and way-marking that it was perfectly possible to become lost even, it seems, on the Great North Road from London to Edinburgh.

The major difficulty was that while the Romans had bequeathed a system of main routes (often incorporating even more ancient trackways) few if any new roads were made in the ensuing 1200 years. Road-mending was the responsibility of the parish authorities. A statute of 1555 required householders to work four days a year on the highways, while larger landholders and those who kept a team of horses or plough oxen had to provide a car and two able-bodied men for seasonal work. This 'statute labour' was understandably short of both enthusiasm and skill, and its techniques were limited to carting stones to muddy places and keeping back the undergrowth at the roadside.

Unfortunately some of the worst roads lay on the heavy clays of the Midland counties, across which most of the country's trade had to pass to and from London. In bad winters the capital could go short of food as supplies from the North and Wales became bogged-down. Up to 1700 at least, wheeled traffic was comparatively rare, because it was impractical except in very dry or frosty weather. Old roads tended to become wider and wider as travellers looked for better ground; Defoe records how enterprising farmers at Baldock used to open gates to their fields for a toll, allowing coaches to avoid a notorious stretch of the Great North Road.

In consequence, most of the country's trade by road was carried either by long strings of packhorses or, in the case of meat, driven on the hoof. In upland areas packhorses were still common in the nineteenth century, serving the

ABOVE *Frontispiece of Ogilby's* Britannia, *1675, the first comprehensive atlas of main roads in England.*

industries of the age. Celia Fiennes saw them in her day, carrying cloth at Exeter, loaded with coal in the West Country, and bringing home the harvest in Cornwall. Packhorse 'trains' consisted of as many as forty or fifty horses travelling in single file, each bearing a pair of wicker panniers. In this way each packhorse could carry up to $2\frac{1}{2}$ cwt. Old packhorse ways can be seen still in upland areas, including paved sections, sometimes known as 'causeys', over boggy ground and narrow bridges with low parapets that allowed the horse and its panniers passage. 'Jagger' was the old name for a packhorse driver, and it appears fairly regularly as a street or place-name in such forms as Jaggers Gate or even Jacob's Ladder.

Arguably the most important commodity to be carried over long distances was salt. The main sources were the 'wichs', or brine pits, of Cheshire (Nantwich, Northwich and Middlewich), together with those at Droitwich in

LEFT *Packhorse bridge in Bradford Dale, Derbyshire, just wide and low enough for a loaded packhorse.*

ABOVE *Droving cattle to market.*

Worcester, and Baswich and Shirleywich in Staffordshire. Packhorses distributed the salt far and wide, and their routes are remembered in countless local names – Saltersford, Saltersgate and Salter Hill among them.

The drovers are mainly pictured as a hardy breed of men who drove large herds of sheep and cattle, or even geese, from the north, the Midlands and Wales to the London markets. Here and there their 'drift-ways' and green roads can be identified, usually away from the main routes. But droving also had a more local significance. The back lanes of an agricultural village may well represent the routes by which animals were brought back and forth from fields to farmsteads. Lengths of otherwise unexplained track going off into the fens or moors are likely to be the way that herds were driven to summer pastures.

For the independent traveller, finding one's way was a major challenge. Guidestones and wayside crosses were sometimes erected by local endeavour, and an Act of 1698 directed the Justices to erect guideposts at crossroads. It seems to have been ineffective, however, and it was not until 1773 that another statute required all turnpike trusts to erect both guideposts and milestones on their roads.

Those turnpikes transformed road travel but left few permanent marks on the village scene. They brought some villages a toll-house, though the gates have invariably gone, and to a few the turnpikes ushered in a brief prosperity through hostel-keeping. Their major contribution to village history, however, was to end the isolation of the countryside and to enable villagers to visit the cities.

BELOW *Repairing the highway with broken stones, from George Walker's* Costumes of Yorkshire, *1814.*

ABOVE *St Nicholas Church, Blakeney, Norfolk. Its twin towers guided navigators approaching the medieval port through treacherous channels.*

While river ports were expanding in the eighteenth century, many coastal villages were actually losing their livelihood. We know, for instance, that on the northerly coast of East Anglia there were upwards of a dozen small havens active in Elizabethan times. The Crown's ever-vigilant customs officers made frequent lists of such places. Some of the villages mentioned seem, at first sight, unlikely ports: Dersingham, Snettisham, Heacham, Thornham, Walsingham, Burham, Brancaster, Wells, Cley and several more are now all inland, some by several miles. These little ports lost their trade partly because of the natural silting of their creeks and inlets and partly because

LEFT *A Humber Keel. The shallow draught and tall sails for catching the breeze made these boats ideal for navigating inland waterways.*

man helped it along in a determined fashion. In the seventeenth century the coastal marshes were drained and embanked against the sea, to create new areas of fertile farming land. Meanwhile the 'burden' or tonnage of the boats engaged in coastal shipping was growing larger. Gradually some of the smaller ports gave up the laborious struggle to keep their channels clear, and the boats went to Lynn for its deep-water anchorage. Alternatively, the village population migrated seawards. That is what happened at Wells, where the medieval church and a line of cottages stand on the medieval waterfront. The basin is dry, however, and the channel to the sea long abandoned. Activity moved to the new coastline, and to the village of Wells-next-the-Sea. On the same coast, the village of Cley surrendered its trade to Blakeney when the channel silted up. The shallows and mudbanks are particularly treacherous in that area, so the church at Blakeney has two towers; a ship's master approaching land could line up the towers in his sights to guide his craft along the channel into

The Butter or Market Cross at Swaffham, Norfolk. The large market place and the grandeur of this building mark Swaffham as one of the minority of medieval markets that survived and prospered.

harbour. Parts of Blakeney harbour and its approaches are now preserved by the National Trust.

Before leaving the subject of trade and transport we should perhaps pause to consider how village people bought and sold their produce locally, and acquired such things as pots and pans, pins and buttons. Country folk did not go shopping, at least not until about the middle of the nineteenth century.

Shops were to be found in the towns and cities and they were the preserve of the gentry and well-to-do. The squire's family would have an account with a tailor, a grocer, a draper and so on, and receive a bill for settlement each month or quarter. Lesser mortals relied largely on the markets, though they no doubt also went in for some private bargaining and exchange. There was a time when almost every village of any size had its own market for produce. That was in the century before the Black Death, when local manorial interests found it profitable to promote a market. After 1350 as many as two-thirds of the country's markets disappeared, never to be revived.

In Tudor and Stuart England there were about 750 markets, and the numbers shrank further in the eighteenth and nineteenth centuries, as turnpikes and railways funnelled trade into the larger country towns. Long-lost markets can, none the less, reveal themselves, even today, in street patterns. Villages on a thoroughfare may have a spindle-shaped broadening of the road at, or near their centres, which once would have accommodated market stalls and animal pens; Tenterden in Kent shows the feature well, as does Lacock in Wiltshire. Wedge-shaped or triangular market places are equally common, typically abutting the village church. Some, such as those at Swaffham in Norfolk and Gamlingay in Cambridgeshire were very large, and mark the medieval importance of those markets for the surrounding countryside. While village markets lack the sophisticated market halls of urban centres, many do still have a market cross. Was the cross set up to dissuade traders from false dealing and short measures?

The visit to market, whether on foot or by cart, was likely to be a day's visit. Indeed it was a commonplace of medieval law that the Crown should not allow markets to be chartered at intervals of less than $6\frac{2}{3}$ miles. This generally meant spending about a third of a day travelling there, another third of the day at the market, and the remainder in travelling home. Saturday was the usual market day, though repeated statutes against Sunday markets suggest that trading on the Sabbath did sometimes occur. Having travelled to town, a husbandman might well be tempted to make a night of it. Market places

invariably had a good supply of inns and public houses, such as the Red Lion at Lacock, offering company, drink and accommodation; not infrequently they were attended by a Silver Street in which services of a personal nature were for sale. The church was also nearby, of course, for more sober reflections on Sunday morning.

For certain goods, the packman or pedlar offered a convenient alternative supply. Such men had been regular visitors to villages from the Middle Ages, carrying packs on their backs as they tramped the roads. An Elizabethan ballad, in which a packman sings to attract customers, gives an idea of the range of his wares:

Fine knacks for ladies, cheap, choice, brave and new.
Good penniworths, but money cannot move.
Within this packe pinnes points laces and gloves
And divers toies fitting a country faier.

Other pedlars and tinkers offered to sell and sometimes to repair hardware – the pots, pans and cauldrons of ordinary home use. All such itinerants were treated with a degree of suspicion; they were seen as outsiders who travelled and slept rough, sometimes begging for food. The final chapter of their long history is described by Flora Thompson, who recorded her Oxfordshire childhood in *Lark Rise to Candleford*.

The packman, or pedlar, once a familiar figure in that part of the country, was seldom seen in the [eighteen-] eighties. People had taken to buying their clothes at the shops in the market town, where fashions were newer and prices lower. But one last survivor of the once numerous clan still visited the hamlet at long and irregular intervals. He would turn aside from the turnpike and come plodding down the narrow hamlet road, an old white-headed, white-bearded man, still hale and rosy, although almost bent double under the heavy, black canvas-covered pack he carried strapped on his shoulders. 'Anything out of the pack to-day?' he would ask at each house, and, at the least encouragement, fling down his load and open it on the door-step. He carried a tempting variety of goods: dress-lengths and shirt-lengths and remnants to make up for the children; aprons and pinafores, plain and fancy; corduroys for the men, and coloured scarves and ribbons for Sunday wear. 'That's a bit of right good stuff, ma'am, that is,' he would say, holding up some dress-length to exhibit it. 'A gown made of this piece'd last anybody for ever and then make 'em a good petticoat afterwards.' Few of the hamlet women could afford to test the quality of his piece goods; cottons or tapes, or a paper of pins, were their usual purchases.

A pedlar or packman around 1700. The rabbits, presumably taken illicitly, reflect the prejudice of the age against itinerants.

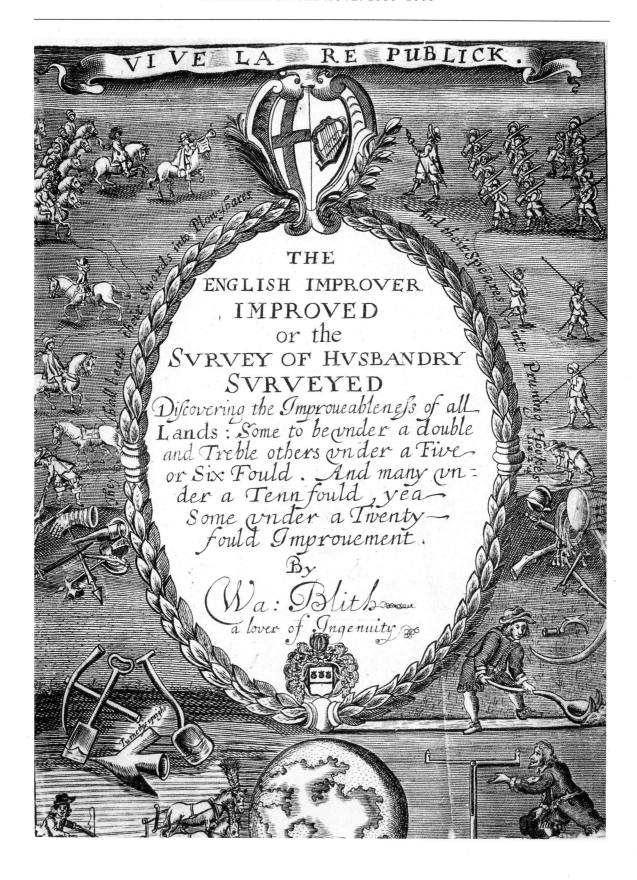

VIVE LA RE PUBLICK.

THE
ENGLISH IMPROVER
IMPROVED
or the
SVRVEY OF HVSBANDRY
SVRVEYED
Discovering the Improveableness of all Lands : Some to be vnder a double and Treble others vnder a Five or Six Fould . And many vn- der a Tenn fould , yea Some vnder a Twenty fould Improvement.
By
*Wa: Blith
a lover of Ingenuity*

A changing landscape

Agriculture was still the main occupation in eighteenth-century Britain, for all the stirrings of industry. Fortunately we possess very detailed accounts of each English county's farming, compiled by the government's Board of Agriculture at the end of the century. One of those responsible for the establishment of the Board, and its first secretary in 1793, was Arthur Young, himself a prolific author and an indefatigable traveller. His published *Tours* through the farming lands of England and Wales gives us a personal but highly informed view of a rapidly changing countryside. Young was writing towards the end of a century of experimentation. New crops and rotations, improved breeds of stock, better farm buildings and equipment were raising the efficiency of the industry. Young also witnessed the movement to enclose open land; it constituted the greatest change to the pattern of property-holding in half a millenium. While Young was in favour of progressive agriculture, he was also alert to its impact on the lives of ordinary men and women. He could be highly critical of the landed classes when, for example, they refused to repair or replace cottages on their land. He warmed most to such as Thomas Coke of Holkham, who combined agricultural improvements (introducing new strains of stock and grain) with a philanthropic concern for the welfare of his tenants. Young sensed at Holkham, where Coke had rebuilt cottages and farm buildings, 'the diffusion of happiness, an overflow of wealth that gilds the whole country and tells the traveller, in a language too expressive to be misunderstood, *we approach the residence of a man who feels for others as well as for himself*'. It is this sense of human values, allied to a grasp of economic necessities, which makes Arthur Young one of the most convincing analysts of the rural scene.

Enclosures had been controversial in the fifteenth and sixteenth century. Those early enclosures had turned arable into sheep walks, and (so its critics alleged) husbandmen into landless vagabonds. The aims and results of Georgian and early Victorian enclosure were different. Arable open fields were converted into arable enclosed fields. At the same time, common grazing in the uplands was enclosed to create consolidated pastoral farms. Of itself, enclosure did not change the balance between arable and pastoral, nor disinherit smallholding farmers. Yet the

LEFT *Improving the land: a treatise of 1652 expressing an eagerness to achieve better returns. The presence of a surveyor (bottom right) hints at a new layout of the land.*

view grew at the time, and has lingered since, that enclosure brought an end to the village as a community of independent farmers, and promoted a class-ridden society. The truth of that we shall weigh in due course. First let us consider the reasons for the enclosure movement, and the progress it made.

Most villages had some 'anciently enclosed' land. At the heart of a village it was normal to find 'closes' of between 1 and 4 acres; they were cottage plots or gardens. In addition the lord of the manor and the rector, and one or two others, had often managed to consolidate some land into compact blocks. This they had achieved by exchanges of strips among themselves without recourse to a thoroughgoing enclosure of the common fields. Such old closes tend to be of irregular shape and stand out readily among the later, more regular enclosures in village maps, or on the ground. Some even retain the reverse S shape of medieval ploughlands in their boundaries.

After the Restoration in 1660, a series of bills was promoted in Parliament to facilitate enclosures. None of them became law, but they expressed the dissatisfaction of landed interests with open-field agriculture. The common fields were preventing proper drainage of the land and encouraging exhaustion of the soil. They gave no incentive to replant timber and led to overgrazing of pastures by commoners' livestock. In short, the fragmentation of land stood in the way of improvements. The critics of the old system were farmers who wanted to specialize in marketable produce and to make a good return from the land. It was a capitalist outlook, in essence, and it was impatient of peasant ways and of the old feudal relationships implied by the common-field system.

Landowners could not unilaterally enclose the farmlands of a village, however. Tenants were protected by customary leases. They had rights to hold land, to graze animals, to collect fuel, and so on. Some seventeenth-century landlords tried to bargain; Thomas Erle of Charborough in Dorset agreed an enclosure with his tenants in 1695 by promising not to raise rents during his lifetime, and to respect their ancient rights to coppice wood. Many enclosures were achieved in this way. In Cheshire, for instance, all common fields (admittedly not so extensive as in the Midlands) were enclosed by agreement, with the exception of two – one of which was an enclosure in an urban context at Chester. Celia Fiennes often noted whether or not the terrain through which she travelled was enclosed, and from her diary we can sense that a great deal had been achieved by 1700.

Enclosure by agreement could be both cheap and speedy – provided that every party agreed. But one or two tenants who would not consent to swap their strips held an effective veto. Even worse, descendants

for common grazing. Occasionally a part would be ploughed and exploited for a few years, as meadow or arable. Then, when its fertility declined, it was abandoned to grazing again, and another area ploughed. The rest was the waste: the poorest land on the upper levels or on mosses and peats. It was common land, used for summer grazing; many such moors remained unenclosed because they were not worth the expense of enclosing. They continued to be 'inter-commoned', that is grazed by the stock of several adjoining parishes. The rest of the land, in-field and out-field, was parcelled out, however. It is easier to say when that process was complete than when it began. A few upland parishes were enclosed by Act of Parliament in the period from 1740 to 1850, but far more had already proceeded by simple agreement of the parties. In Cheshire it is clear that much of the land was enclosed in Tudor times or earlier, forming farms which specialized in sheep-rearing. In Northumberland and Durham enclosures were proceeding apace in the seventeenth and eighteenth centuries. Over much of those upland landscapes dry-stone walls stride for mile upon mile, enclosing rough grazing land, and speaking eloquently of the determination of past generations to win a living from unpromising terrain. Enclosure spawned a new crop of farm buildings. When land and livestock were scattered here and there, farmers chose to live in the village with their fellows. But once their acres were gathered together in some distant part of the parish, it made good sense to build a new farm there. Many new farmhouses, barns and yards were erected after enclosure, but not all immediately. Some farmers had no cash to spare after fencing and improving their land, so it took a generation or two for enclosure to have a full effect on the shape of the village. Typically it was the largest farmers who moved out, and their substantial new farmhouses show a very fair face to the world, sporting façades of classical proportions, sash windows and pedimented doorways. To the rear are the new barns, cattle houses and wagon sheds, arranged, following the best advice of the day, in a square or U-shape around a farmyard. The National Trust owns an example of this kind at Newlands Farm on the Killerton estate. That might leave two or three smaller farmhouses in the village, where they remain to this day. It also left the landless labourers and cottagers in the village, to take over and subdivide the larger village houses and even the manor house as lodgings for several families.

Farndale, North Yorkshire: an upland landscape after enclosure, with hay meadow in the valley bottom, improved and enclosed grazing fields on the hillside, and unenclosed moorland beyond.

What were the social consequences of enclosure? If we accept the view of an arch conservative of the day, William Cobbett, enclosure set a gulf between masters and men, rich and poor. He particularly deprecated 'the pretensions of newly set-up farmers'.

Those [farmhouses] that are now erected are mere painted shells, with a Mistress within, who is stuck up in a place she calls a parlour, with, if she have children, the 'young ladies and gentlemen' about her: some showy chairs and a sofa (a sofa by all means): half a dozen prints in gold frames hanging up: some swinging book-shelves with novels and tracts upon them ...

Similarly he found fault with their mahogany tables and chairs, their decanters and the 'dinner sets of crockery ware', Such domestic trappings meant that the farmworkers had been banished from the farmhouse; the farmer would no longer 'sit at the head of the "oak-table" along with his men, say grace to

BELOW *An enclosure award formalized the share-out of common lands, and set out the new pattern of ownership. Farmers could now begin to instal hedges and walls to enclose their new fields.*

ABOVE *Gillray's cartoon of 1809, satirizing William Cobbett, the farmer's son, and his ferocious verbal tirades against enclosure, amalgamation of holdings and change in general.*

them, and cut up the meat and the pudding'. And in Cobbett's view that system that had enriched farmers and turned them into 'a species of mock-gentlefolk' had also 'ground the labourers down into real slaves'.

Certainly, a generation or so after enclosure, very few village people had a personal stake in the land. It was something they worked for others. In contrast with much of western Europe, England and Wales have no body of smallholders, nor have they had for the past 150 years. It was not enclosure itself that brought this about; indeed there is evidence that the number of village smallholders actually increased on enclosure as parcels of land were allocated in lieu of rights of common. But time after time the small man sold out within a few years. To give just a single example, John Nottingham and his brother of Hessay in North Yorkshire received a plot of rather boggy land for their twenty strips in the open fields, which were enclosed in 1831. They could not afford to fence and improve the land, however, and before long had sold it. Fortunately for John, the Great Northern Railway was making its triumphant progress up the eastern side of the country and he soon found employment as a railway porter. Within sixty years all the freeholders of Hessay had sold out to an absentee landlord.

While small farmers were ready to sell, landlords were happy to consolidate their plots into more substantial farms. They saved themselves the trouble of collecting small amounts of rent, and larger tenants would improve the land. As farms were amalgamated, the cottages which had housed small-holding families became redundant. They, and their erstwhile occupants, could be removed from the scene. From one point of view, this was highly progressive. The *Gentleman's Magazine* in 1790 carried a report that

The rust of poverty and ignorance is now wearing off. Estates are bought into fewer hands; and the poorer sort of people remove into towns, to gain a livelihood by crafts and commerce. Lands increase in value: the houses (or rather huts) of clay, which were small, and ill-built, are mostly thrown down; instead of which, strong and roomy farm-houses are now built, and building . . .

From the labourers' viewpoint, however, the demise of small farms removed their ladder of opportunity. Such was the size and rent of 'engrossed' farms that a landless family had little chance of acquiring land of its own. Arthur Young, though a supporter of enclosure, recognized what the concentration of all

Poachers brought before the magistrate, the evidence of their crime set before him. The wife of one of the accused, to the left, is weeping in anticipation of the harsh sentence to come.

the land, equipment and livestock in a few hands meant to the labouring poor: 'Go to an ale-house kitchen in an enclosed county and there you will see the origin of poverty and the poor rates.' There the labourer might ask, 'If I am diligent shall I have leave to build a cottage? If I am sober shall I have land for a cow? If I am frugal shall I have an acre of potatoes? You offer no motives, you have nothing but a parish officer and a workhouse. Bring me another pot.'

One further corollary of enclosure was the idea of private property. In an unenclosed village a family might hold land, but others had rights over it, such as access and pasturage at certain times of the year. On enclosure, fences and gates went up, and each family's territory was delineated. Old practices, such as gleaning in the fields after harvest, and the collection of small wood, were restricted or suppressed. New game laws confirmed the rights of proprietors to all manner of wild game on their land. An unloved band of guards – gamekeepers – began to patrol the estates of landed proprietors. In the Victorian era the police were given powers to stop and search any person or vehicle for game and poaching equipment; it was a power particularly resented by village people, as it seemed to give the squire and his class the right to intrude in their affairs at will. The poor man's casual picking of a rabbit from the common had long been winked at, and considered 'fair game'. It now became an offence against property, and he was in danger of being hauled before the magistrates and severely punished.

Picturesque enclosures

A peculiar form of enclosure absolutely captivated the minds of the Georgian gentry and aristocracy. It was the fashion for 'emparking' which made its mark on countless village landscapes. The idea was not new. There are great medieval parks such as that at Lyme in Cheshire, given by King Edward III to a supporter in 1388, which was essentially a game reserve cut out of the forest and maintained for the pleasures of the hunt. After about 1630, however, owners were seeing parks less as sporting grounds, and more as ornamental settings for their houses. Fashion then was much influenced by France and Holland, and called for broad walks, avenues of trees, fountains, formal lakes and canals. Something of the effect survives at Bramham Park in Yorkshire, while the National Trust has restored an example of formal gardening at Westbury Court Garden, Westbury-on-Severn in Gloucestershire.

Tastes changed again in the eighteenth century, and the gentry enthusiastically adopted a more naturalistic or 'picturesque' style of landscape gardening. Its best-known exponents were Lancelot 'Capability' Brown and Humphry Repton. This is not the place to go into all its details: the creation of lakes, the clumping of trees, and the positioning of follies and ruins, and cascades and hillocks. Though the initial cost could be high, upkeep was much easier than in a formal landscape. Whether for reasons of economy or taste, almost every gentleman worthy of the name had his grounds, large or small, remodelled in this fashion in the Georgian era. In consequence, the picturesque style gave a distinctive shape to a significant part of the country's landscape.

Most country houses have a village in close association. Up to the seventeenth century, the proximity of cottages and labourers seemed perfectly acceptable to the gentry. But they were clearly inappropriate in a formal landscape, and considered undesirable in an idealized natural countryside. One solution for a gentry family was to move its residence out of the village. Mr William Wrightson of Cusworth in South Yorkshire gave up his old hall on the village street, and its walled gardens of about 3 acres, and in 1740 built himself a fine, new house, Cusworth Hall, on the hill above. From there he had a pleasant view over fields, meadows and pastures, which had been let out to tenant farmers. The family gradually took this land back into its own hands, and by 1760 had created a park of around 100 acres. It was still, however, innocent of any artistic design. At that point, Wrightson called in the aptly named Richard Woods, a gardener in the Capability Brown mould, who surveyed the ground, and drew up a scheme for a naturalistic, partially wooded landscape, with lakes in the middle distance. The scheme, when effected, cost the Wrightsons well over £2000, but it completely shielded the old village from their sight. To complete their privacy, Wrightson had the main road from the village diverted so that it no longer cut across the forecourt of his house. The sweeping lawns before the house, the park walls and the entrance lodge all emphasized the gulf the family had set between itself and its erstwhile neighbours.

The alternative, open only to families of enormous wealth, was to move or to obliterate the village. If such a proposal were made today for the sake of the view of a landed proprietor, it would generate astonishment and outrage. Yet in the early eighteenth century the idea was proposed and the deed enacted on numerous occasions, to the evident self-satisfaction of the proprietors. On the obelisk at Castle Howard, marking the site of the suppressed village of Hinderskelfe, is this inscription:

If to perfection these plantations rise
If they agreeably might earn surprise,
This faithful pillar will their age declare
As long as time these characters shall spare.

ABOVE *New Houghton, Norfolk, built in 1729 when old Houghton, inconveniently within view of the new Houghton Hall, was pulled down.*
RIGHT *The title-page of* The Deserted Village.

Here, then, with kind remembrance read his name
Who for posterity performed the same:
*   Charles, the Third Earl of Carlisle.*
*   Begun 1702. Finished 1731.*

Many grand landscape schemes required a village to be rebuilt outside the park. At Houghton, Norfolk, Sir Robert Walpole built a new village of small whitewashed cottages which line the road leading to his estate. The emparking of Nuneham Courtenay in Oxfordshire led to the demolition of the old village, an act that was probably the inspiration of Oliver Goldsmith's famous poem, *The Deserted Village*. In

The sad historian of the pensive plain

LEFT *Milton Abbas, Dorset, was created in the 1770s by razing an older village.*

its place, Lord Harcourt built pretty roadside cottages of timber and brick in a self-consciously traditional style. He replaced the medieval church with one in the style of a classical temple, and provided a village inn, the Harcourt Arms. Similarly, the first Earl of Dorchester, deciding that the village of Milton Abbas spoiled the view from his house, had Capability Brown build a new one with a deliberately old-fashioned atmosphere. Along the village street were pairs of thatched cottages, each with a chestnut tree growing beside it. An almshouse and a church completed the picturesque scene. At Harewood in West Yorkshire a new village accommodated the estate's 200 workers in a series of grand, stone terraces, more akin to a city than to a rural idyll. It certainly gave the approach to the house and park an air of prestige and solidity, which was no doubt of particular importance to a family which had recently made its money in trade.

The remaking of a village outside the park gates was a practical compromise. The landscape designer Humphry Repton (1752–1818) often warned against

that fatal rage for destroying villages or depopulating a country, under the idea of its being necessary to the importance of a mansion .... As a number of labourers constitutes one of the requisites of grandeur, comfortable habitations for its poor dependants ought to be provided.

Villages added greatly to the convenience of country house life; Repton again:

Notwithstanding the modern fashion of placing a house detach'd from the Haunts of Man, yet there are numerous objects connected with the comforts of habitation for which we must look to the Village ... such as the Church, the Inn, the Shop (the Shop is so essential that I was obliged to build one for a milliner at Harewood, because the ladies complained that there was no place within the reach of a walk, where they could go to purchase penny gauze and two penny ribbons ...), the carpenter, blacksmith, and other Tradesmen to which we may here add the Steward's House and farming buildings.

BELOW *Harewood, West Yorkshire, designed in the 1760s by John Carr.*

So by the later eighteenth century, the sentiment was growing that a village need not be hidden from sight, but could be made an attraction in itself. Repton was the leading advocate, suggesting that

the street might be converted into a neat village green with its benches and a maypole; that almost forgotten emblem of rural happiness and festivity. The cottages belonging to the place might be distinguished by neatness, and deck'd with roses and creeping plants . . . .

Several landowners took the sentiment to heart and erected highly picturesque estate villages. Each reflects an idealized vision of the past. Blaise Hamlet, an adjunct of Blaise Castle in Avon, now owned by the National Trust, was one of the first and most extravagant in style. Its architect was John Nash, the strength of whose imagination can be judged from his work for the Prince Regent at Brighton Pavilion. Nine cottages, each highly individual, were grouped informally around a green. The skyline is punctuated by the most flamboyant chimneys. They were, said Nash, to be of the kind 'frequently seen in old cottages and generally in old Manor Houses and buildings of the reign of Queen Elizabeth, and invariably produce a picturesque effect. Their character requires that they should be very high.'

Some took the recreation of a half-fanciful past even further. Tenants of the 'picturesque' villages of Selworthy and Old Warden were encouraged to dress in red cloaks and tall hats, thereby peopling those carefully contrived stage sets. William Mason, in *The English Garden* of 1772 was advising gentlemen that 'instead of a fence the children of some poor but worthy widow, prettily disguised as Shepherds, might be employed to keep the sheep from straying'. At Nuneham Courtenay, a widow threatened with expulsion from her cottage was allowed to remain on condition that she dressed as an Arcadian shepherdess. Real village characters, of course, poor and dishevelled as they were, were to be kept well out of sight.

Ornamental villages did not lack for critics. William Cobbett and others scoffed. But the style caught a mood of popular nostalgia in an industrializing Britain. The *cottage orné* was a recognized genre in the early nineteenth century, architectural pattern books offering plans and decorative schemes for such bucolic fantasies. One of the surviving examples is at

Blaise Hamlet, near Bristol, built in 1810–11 by John Nash for retired estate workers.
The cottages were a parody of Tudor styles, but they popularized the nostalgic ideal of the cottage orné.

Estate cottages at Wimpole, Cambridgeshire, in Humphry Repton's Red Book. *He proposed to add a trellis arcade to make them more 'picturesque' and suitable to be seen on a great estate.*

Derrymore House, a National Trust property in Northern Ireland. A growing class of urban professionals – bankers, lawyers and physicians – was particularly susceptible to the charms of an idealized out-of-town bolt-hole. Even real farmers succumbed, and were adding verandahs, thatched porches, trellises and dormer roofs to their sturdy old farmhouses.

This episode was really the beginning of the nation's self-conciousness about its history and culture. It has flourished ever since. An unbroken line of nostalgic building can be traced to the present day. The Victorians pursued a vision of the Middle Ages through the Gothic revival, as well as the later Arts and Crafts movement. At the turn of the twentieth century, such leading architects as Voysey and Lutyens were reworking the vernacular building tradition of the fifteenth, sixteenth and seventeenth centuries. That affection for the past (or weakness, depending on one's point of view) has seemed to grow stronger the further our society has moved from its rural origins. There are more 'half-timbered' houses on the bypasses of suburban Britain than ever there were in its medieval villages. And after a disastrous post-war flirtation with modernism and high-rise concrete, popular affections seem to have returned to cottage styles and their human scale.

Model Farms

ABOVE *Mid-19th century model farm at Longleat,
Wiltshire, chiefly for animal husbandry.*

The design of farms evolved through centuries of trial
and error, and it was not until 1747 that an architectural pattern book appeared in print to give some coherent,
practical advice. Its author, Daniel Garrett, and other
Georgian writers who followed, all recommended that the
principal buildings of the farmstead be drawn up in a
square or rectangular plan around a foldyard, in which the
cattle could be herded and their manure collected. Shelters
for animals and hay were to be sited on the south side for
warmth, while houses for carts and equipment were to be
out of the sun, to avoid damage to their woodwork, and
on the outer face of the farmstead for easy access to the
fields. The farmhouse itself was to face south and away
from the muck and stench of the yard, yet close enough for
the farmer's wife and servants to supervise the feeding of
the poultry and pigs, and the milking of the cows.

This sensible, practical approach was well suited to the
needs of post-enclosure farming. Many new farmsteads
had to be built, catering for mixed animal and arable husbandry on a rather larger scale than in the past, but otherwise employing traditional methods and equipment. In the
nineteenth century farm design had to adapt further, to
cope with mechanization and with the higher output required to feed the growing population.

FROM NORTH TO SOUTH, — CENTRE RANGE.

Covered Shed for Stack.

Mill & Machinery

Pitch Hole

Pitch Hole

Straw

Barn

Pitch Hole

Straw Barn

Cattle Stalls

Root & Mixing House

ABOVE *Mechanized threshing and straw-handling on a farm at Uphampton, Hereford and Worcester, in 1863.*

It was the major landowners who had the resources to invest in up-to-the-minute buildings and machinery. They were able to engage surveyors, architects and engineers to create 'model' farms – in which all the human, animal and mechanical systems were integrated within an aesthetically pleasing whole. The most ambitious examples were the home farms of great estates such as at Longleat in Wiltshire, the Duke of Westminster's Cheshire estate at Eccleston, Wimpole in Cambridgeshire and Tatton in Cheshire (the latter two both now preserved by the National Trust).

Improved breeds of stock warranted better housing. Covered foldyards, with individual tethering stalls, protected the health of cattle, but also permitted each beast to have its own controlled ration of food; at Lord Armstrong's farm at Cragside, Northumberland, feed was delivered into the byre by trolleys running on tramlines.

Steam power made considerable demands on the layout and organization of the farm. Engine houses, with their smoking chimneys, became a feature of progressive

ABOVE *Ploughing seven furrows at once in 1907, but steam ploughing proved only moderately successful.*

Victorian farms. The primary task of the engine was to turn machinery, above all the threshing machine. But farmers soon found it other work – pumping water to the stock sheds, powering conveyors and elevators which reduced the labour of transport around the farm, even steaming root crops for cattle fodder. The reign of the stationary engine was brief, however. In the second half of the nineteenth century it was largely superseded by the steam traction engine which farmers found to be more flexible. It could be driven to wherever the work was – to a threshing machine in the fields or even to undertake steam ploughing. This wheezing monster, with its belching chimney and whirring drive belts, could work all day, replacing the muscle power of dozens of farm hands.

The mid-Victorian age of High Farming was a time of expansion. Bigger herds, larger stock houses and more rick-yards were the order of the day. Dairying was highly profitable, once the milk trains began to supply London and other big cities. But one casualty of the age was the barn. Its role as store for unprocessed grain crops and workshop for winter threshing had evaporated with the advent of the steam traction engine. It became a cart shed for fertilizer store. In the hard times that were to follow, in the agricultural depression of the late-nineteenth century, many fine old barns were simply left to decay, while investment in mechanization and renewal of buildings all but disappeared for a generation.

LEFT *Eccleston, Cheshire, built in 1875–80, is one of several model farms on the Duke of Westminster's estates.*

CHAPTER FIVE

Power And Paternalism: 1800–1914

The privileged circle

IN the village there was a circle of people to whom common men touched their hats. It included the parson, who lived in a rather large and draughty vicarage. There was the local squire, or even an earl or baronet at the big house, who exuded all the confidence of a man who not only owned the village but had had a public school education too. And there were the bigger tenant farmers in their sturdy farmhouses, who, with possibly hundreds of acres to tend, employed many of the labouring population. Villagers deferred also to the wives and children of their betters. Young Master John, or Miss Emily, were left in no doubt of their superior position in the world, even in their childhood years.

That privileged circle presumed to control the everyday affairs of the village. Local administration was in the hands of a 'vestry'. In essence it was an assembly of ratepayers who traditionally had met in the church vestry. In practice it was in the pockets of two or three men of substance, the squire and parson among them. Little that went on in the village escaped the vestry's notice. Their appointed eyes and ears, the churchwardens and the constables, watched for every trespass and minor infringement. The constables, who until the mid-century were only part-timers appointed for a year from among the villagers, were none the less expected to take brisk action against disturbers of the peace and suspect strangers. Such persons found themselves as overnight guests in the village lock-up. As in all petty dictatorships, a great deal depended on the character of the local squire and his colleagues. If they were kind-hearted and wise, life in the village might be congenial; but if they were capricious or callous there was little prospect of redress.

Lock-up at Little Walsingham, Norfolk. There were no police stations or cells until modern times, so the village constable needed a place to keep suspects or drunks out of mischief.

The Crown's local representative was the Justice of the Peace. The Lord Lieutenant of the county chose him, on advice from the gentry. All the petty miscreants of the village were called before him for judgement. Now as the Justice was himself probably a squire and farmer who put time and effort into raising pheasants, a poacher brought to book would not expect clemency. Likewise a poor soul seeking relief before the Justices would be surprised to find a wholly sympathetic ear, given that the tribunal members were ratepayers and the relief would come from their pockets. The Justice's powers went far wider than that, however. He was the ruler of his patch; he levied the rates, oversaw the maintenance of roads and bridges, and supervised the prisons and workhouses to which the least fortunate souls were consigned. While many Justices undoubtedly acted in the best interests of their area, as they saw them, they were firmly wedded to the rights of property and of employers.

To make matters worse, village people were tossed about in the wake of world events. At the turn of the century Britain was at war with Napoleonic France and the conflict continued with little respite until 1815. Battles for the trade routes to America, the West Indies, India and South Africa were remote enough to be portrayed officially as glorious endeavours. But every labourer's wife knew the unpalatable consequences. Britain, as an importer of food and raw materials, was vulnerable (as it was in the wars of the twentieth century) to embargoes and blockades. Conflict caused higher prices and a temporary boom for home production. Farmers saw wheat fetching two to three times the pre-war price, and eagerly expanded their production. They ploughed marginal lands, some of which had not been cultivated since before the Black Death. They turned out their living-in workers, since they consumed foodstuffs that could be sold for a good price. But there was farming work for all who wanted it. War brought orders to industry too. The army had to be uniformed, so weavers of broadcloth, spinners and wool farmers, hatters and button-makers were busy. Iron for guns, leather for saddlery, canvas for sails – all were in sudden demand, and countless crafts geared up to the war effort. Village people none the less found that the cost of the war fell on them. Bread shot up in price, some other necessities were in short supply, and though wages also rose it is clear that standards of living fell significantly during the war.

Bust came even more suddenly than boom. With the war ended, the price of foodstuffs halved, reaching a low point in 1823. Farmers who had borrowed heavily to expand production faced ruin. Costs had to be reduced, land taken out of production and hands laid off. The Board of Agriculture's report of 1816 on the *Agricultural State of the Nation* reckoned that a quarter to a third of the rural workforce was underemployed, and reported a great increase in pauperism. While farming recovered in the 1840s, and even enjoyed a high summer of prosperity in the 1850s and 1860s, it slipped back thereafter into a desperate depression. The cause of that slump was in the North American Midwest. Thousands of square miles of fertile land, blessed with reliably warm summers, were able to yield corn in abundance. When railroads opened up the territory and machines

A satire in Punch *on landlords who would sooner spend money on horses than on their tenants.*

got to work on the ideally flat landscape, grain came flooding into Britain. Home producers could not match it for price; hungry city populations could not wait to buy it. At first British farmers reduced their arable, and concentrated on livestock. Within a few years, however, even that market was undermined; new, refrigerated ships began to deliver cheap supplies of beef and lamb from South America and Australia.

The whole farming community was affected. Labourers lost work, while farmers found it hard to pay their rents or to repay their borrowings. Even great landed estates were badly shaken. The Earls of Scarborough, for example, had been buying land and exchanging with neighbours in order to achieve an uninterrupted estate. They were active as improving landlords in the 1860s, amalgamating holdings, draining land, erecting new buildings for their own home farm and cottages for estate workers. But in 1878 their tenants were running into financial difficulties; a quarter of the rentals were left unpaid. In 1879 the arrears reached 50 per cent and the Earl agreed a permanent reduction on the rent roll. Still tenants began to quit, and he was forced to offer inducements to the better farmers to stay. By 1884 his land agent, declining to purchase some land offered to the estate, admitted that 'there are so many difficulties now in letting land that Lord Scarborough does not feel

THE COTTAGE.

Mr. Punch (to Landlord). "YOUR STABLE ARRANGEMENTS ARE EXCELLENT. SUPPOSE YOU TRY SOMETHING OF THE SORT HERE! EH?"

Haymaking: in Britain's capricious climate the whole village helped to bring in the harvest.

inclined at present to increase his acreage'. In other words the land had become an unprofitable investment, and much of it fell out of intensive use until the Great War. With it went the livelihoods of village people.

Meanwhile, farming had become more highly capitalized. Mechanization proceeded in a piecemeal fashion. Where wages were low, there was little to be gained from labour-saving devices. But where competition from industrial employment was forcing up wages, machinery came in more quickly. Nearly all the major tasks of arable husbandry could be done by machines by the 1870s, but, as Flora Thompson observed, man and machine worked side by side:

In some fields a horse-drawn drill would sow the seed in rows, in others a human sower would walk up and down with a basket.... In harvest-time the mechanical reaper was already a familiar sight; but it only did a part of the work; men were still mowing with scythes, and a few women were still reaping with sickles.

ABOVE *By hook and by crook: harvesting with crook stick and reap hook in Hertfordshire about 1900. Hand work gave way slowly to machines because labour was cheap.*

wages and conditions. Matters came to a head in the 1830s. Dorset had the unhappy distinction of offering lower wages to agricultural labourers than any other English county. Ten shillings for a six-day week was normal elsewhere, with as much as fourteen shillings being paid in industrial parts of the north. In Dorset, farmworkers were receiving only seven shillings. Some of the men of the village of Tolpuddle tried to bargain for better pay in an open meeting with their employers. When they made no progress, they prevailed on a sympathetic vicar to intercede on their behalf. At first, the farmers appeared to promise better wages, but later went back on their word. At that juncture a number of the Tolpuddle men formed themselves into a branch of an Agricultural

Salt's School, founded by Sir Titus Salt as part of his great model community at Saltaire, West Yorkshire. It was to provide non-sectarian higher education for the sons of working people.

Labourers' Friendly Society, taking oaths of secrecy and loyalty to each other and to the union. Local landowners became alarmed as the membership grew. They reported its activities to the Lord Lieutenant of the county. Six leaders were arrested, charged and convicted under an old act against administering and taking secret oaths. The sentence – seven years' transportation to Australia – shocked many working people into public protest. There were petitions to the king, and mass marches in London and elsewhere. The government, no doubt conscious of the progress of radical movements in Europe, eventually granted the Tolpuddle Martyrs a pardon, and they returned from exile as heroes of the people. Despite that, the episode can be seen as a triumph for the landed classes. Unionism had been associated in a court judgement with conspiracy, and that was a setback to the nascent movement to organize the workforce. The National Union of the Working Classes collapsed in 1834, and agricultural unions remained very

weak. Trade unionism was not fully rehabilitated in the eyes of the law until legislation in the 1870s removed the taint of conspiracy.

While wages were a focus of dissent, the machines that threatened livelihoods were targets of violent assault. Popular gossip claimed that a series of attacks on industrial machinery was led by a certain Ned Ludd. This shadowy figure, General Ludd to some, reputedly directed operations from Sherwood Forest – a latter-day Robin Hood. He was, presumably, mythical but his name was linked to outrages that were real enough. Rioters smashed a thousand stocking-frames in Nottinghamshire from 1811 to 1812, on the grounds that they were being used to make low-quality, cheap goods. In Yorkshire hand-loom weavers smashed power looms, setting fire to

Somerleyton, Suffolk, purchased in 1844 by a railway magnate, was rebuilt in a flamboyant version of Tudor and Jacobean styles.

their mills. Lancashire men, hit by depression in the cotton industry, broke up spinning machines and demanded cheaper food. In the south, meanwhile, there were sporadic incidents of rick-burning and protests against the high price of bread. But in 1830 rural unrest became really widespread; there were riots throughout the south and south-eastern counties. Marauding bands struck at night against threshing machines and other farm equipment, burning hay-ricks, though rarely causing harm to people. Many of the raids were supposedly the work of a Captain Swing, who left barely literate and threatening messages in the aftermath of his destructive visit.

This was the period in which Marx and Engels were developing their theories of inevitable conflict between the profit motive and workers' conditions, between capitalism and the proletariat. Their evidence was gathered largely from the English scene. And yet while revolutionary uprisings did occur in their native Europe, in Britain the old order was never

STATE OF THE COUNTRY.

Machine wreckers: a satire of 1831 on the country establishment of village squire (on the hayrick), parson (left) and aristocracy (right) and their defence of privilege against reform.

under serious threat. The government reacted to the riots by making frame-breaking a capital offence. Twenty Luddites were hanged. Nine were executed for their part in the Swing riots – one being a young man of nineteen whose crime was to have knocked the hat off a landed gentleman. Several hundred were transported or imprisoned. In reality the Swing raids were led by ordinary labourers. Their demands, beyond the destruction of the offending machines, were simply higher wages and lower rents. Neither they nor their Luddite counterparts had a coherent political programme or revolutionary intent. The draconian measures taken against the Swing and Luddite factions failed to heal relations between employers and workforce, but they did put down the riots before they developed a political significance.

Popular protest in Britain took a different route in consequence. It was channelled into a movement to reform the constitution, and into a parliamentary campaign for improved hours and conditions for workers. The movement was Chartism; it attracted widespread support, and indirectly achieved most of its stated aims – including universal male suffrage.

Supporters of industrial reform did push through a series of factory acts regulating the hours of work, the safety of workplaces and the employment of women and young people, despite the opposition of some manufacturing interests. These were significant advances on a slow road to political and personal rights for working people.

Yet that gradual revolution left the class structure intact. Wealth and the power that comes from it remained in extraordinarily few hands. Nineteenth-century reforms offered a degree of protection against exploitation, and common people eventually gained the right to elect governments. But up to the end of our period, and beyond, the gulf of status, affluence and wealth that separated the squire or factory owner from his workers appeared permanent, unbridgeable and, to many minds, quite natural.

Towards an ideal community

Fortunately, nineteenth-century employers as a whole cannot be characterized as tyrants and oppressors. Most were probably in the mould of the farmer described in *Lark Rise to Candleford*. Neither ungenerous nor avaricious, he tried to do well by his labourers without questioning the hierarchy of society.

On Friday evening, when work was done, the men trooped up to the farmhouse for their wages. These were handed out of a window to them by the farmer himself and acknowledged by a rustic scraping of feet and pulling of forelocks . . . .

He was not a bad-hearted man and had no idea he was sweating his labourers. Did they not get the full standard wage, with no deductions for standing by in bad weather? . . . was there not at least one good blow-out for everybody once a year at his harvest-home dinner, and the joint of beef at Christmas . . . and soup and milk-puddings for anybody who was ill . . . Although they hoodwinked him whenever possible and referred to him behind his back as 'God a' mighty', the farmer was liked by his men. 'Not a bad ole sort,' they said; 'an' does his bit by the land.'

Some Victorian landowners went further than that. There was concern among them about the condition of the poor, which grew deeper as the century

Mill-work: an alarming feature of early factories was the absence of guards around the machines. Accidents were frequent.

progressed. The most enlightened were as willing to invest in the accommodation of their workers as in their barns, roads and equipment. An outstanding example of landed paternalism in action was the Sutherland estate at Lilleshall in Shropshire. It had the services of an exceptional steward, James Loch, for the most of the first half of the nineteenth century. For miles around the landscape was moulded by his progressive approach. He consolidated tenanted farms into larger and more rational units, providing them with planned groups of barns, wagon sheds and cow byres. Roads, boundaries, walls and, not least, the cottages reflect his careful stewardship which equated the interests of the proprietor with those of the tenantry and workforce.

Victorian paternalism was not simply a matter of care for the physical well-being of the lower orders. When Sir Baldwin Leighton of Alberbury in Shropshire set aside allotments for his employees, in a gesture typical of the age he reserved them for those who had shown themselves capable of saving. The rebuilt village of Somerleyton in Suffolk, with attrac-

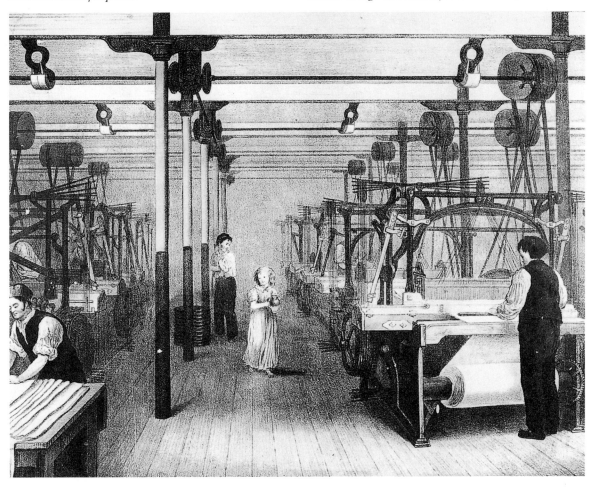

LEFT *Quarry Bank Mill at Styal, near Manchester, was built by Samuel Greg in 1784, as a water-powered mill to spin cotton. It is one of the few such mills to have survived intact.*

tive vernacular-style houses set about a village green, was the creation of Sir Morton Peto, whose avowed aim was to improve the morals of his workforce. The cottages had separate bedrooms for parents and children, which was more than many older small houses could boast. There was, in fact, a widespread assumption that destitution, filth and poor housing went hand in hand with moral laxity and irreligion. The gentry, used to space and personal privacy at home, could not comprehend the different culture of labouring families, who, used to living on top of one another, were quite able to cope with glimpses of a naked ankle without falling prey to carnal desires. Charitable and religious effort rarely lacked a dimension of moral reform. When Hannah More launched a personal mission, in the late eighteenth century, to

BELOW *Cromford, Derbyshire, a community created to serve in Arkwright's revolutionary cotton mill, which with his warehouse, counting house, and canal wharf can be seen today.*

convert the notoriously unruly and ungodly coal-miners of the Mendip hills, she gave over part of her effort to promoting savings clubs and knitting circles, hoping to promote the virtues of thrift and self-reliance.

The most startling attempts at social engineering were made in the new industrial communities. Richard Arkwright based his cotton-spinning factory at Cromford, a tiny hamlet on the River Derwent in Derbyshire. The choice of a place away from areas of domestic textile production seems to have been a deliberate attempt to avoid conflict. Arkwright built a village for his workers at Cromford in the 1770s and 1780s, housing them in long stone-built terraces. (They were solidly constructed and consequently most are still in existence today, protected as a conservation area.) Arkwright's great rivals on the Derwent, the Strutts, created a similar village at Milford. Both places offered schools, chapels and churches, and a more salubrious environment than workers would have experienced either in a burgeoning city or in a farm labourer's cottage.

The most complete factory colony of the period is at Styal in Cheshire, now preserved by the National Trust. Before 1784, when Samuel Greg built Quarry Bank Mill on the swift-flowing River Bollin, Styal

was a small farming community. In the next half century the business expanded greatly, and to accommodate their workforce the Greg family created a spaciously set-out village with an exceptional range of facilities. Conditions were good by the standards of the day: 'The houses in Styal are commodious, clean, white-washed and in every respect superior to the habitations for a similar class of labourers in the town ... [which] are filthy.' Each cottage had an allotment on which vegetables could be grown, and Samuel Greg ran a shop in the village, which sold staple foodstuffs, household goods and clothing. Though it was a 'truck shop' (a shop where the cost of purchases was deducted from wages) its prices appear to have been reasonable, and Greg eventually allowed his workers to run it themselves on a co-operative, profit-sharing basis. The factory had its own compulsory Sick Club; each worker paid a farthing per shilling of his wages, and received in return a sickness benefit of half pay for up to twelve weeks, and a grant towards funeral expenses. Samuel Greg retained a doctor for the factory, one of whose duties was to examine the children taken into employment; each new recruit was given a month's trial to prove his health and strength. Perhaps the most remarkable aspect of Styal was the Apprentice House in the village, where boys and girls were looked after by a superintendant and his wife. As many as a hundred, aged nine to eighteen, lived there at a time.

That the Gregs held themselves in a measure responsible for the well-being of the apprentices, and of the workforce in general, cannot be doubted. 'When there is no natural guardian,' wrote Robert Hyde Greg in 1833, '... the law transfers to a master the privileges of a parent ... [and] it most properly imposes upon him also the duties of a parent, of providing the food, clothing and education of the child and, as far as it can enforce the same, it ought to impose the duty of humanity and kind treatment.' The life of the apprentice was none the less very hard, by the standards of today. Children were bound to their employment for several years. Work began at six or seven in the morning, and continued until around seven in the evening with only a short pause for breakfast and an hour for lunch. The machines dictated a relentless pace of work, and the atmosphere within the factory was always warm and humid. Cotton fibres filled the air, often causing respiratory disease. Apprentices were cheap labour, and even adults were willing to work at Styal for less than the going rate in the cotton mills of nearby Manchester. The Gregs actually opposed the introduction by law of the ten-hour day in the 1840s, on the grounds that it would increase costs, reduce

wages and penalize water-powered mills which needed flexible hours of work to cope with periods of drought.

That philosophy, austere, unsentimental, Nonconformist, but practical and caring, can be seen at work in a second generation of industrial village foundations. Several mid-Victorian industrialists moved their workers out of the city environment, or deliberately established their operations in pleasantly rural situations. The village of Saltaire in Yorkshire was perhaps the earliest and most impressive of such endeavours. Its founder, Titus Salt, was a self-made textile magnate, whose particular success derived from the exploitation of alpaca and mohair fibres. In the 1840s he consolidated his various interests around Bradford in a single new mill, on the banks of the River Aire near Shipley. Salt's Mill was the wonder of the industrial world, the largest and most productive factory of its day. But the lasting fame of Saltaire derives equally from the model settlement that went with it. Salt created all the amenities of a decent life. Besides the school, hospital, chapels and churches, there was an Institute – the Victorian term for a place in which working people could have opportunities for self-improvement. Titus Salt Junior declared, on its opening, that the Institute 'is intended to supply all the advantages of a public-house, without its evils; it will be a place where you can resort for conversation, business, recreation and refreshment, as well as for education – elementary, technical and scientific.' It included a library, a smoking room, a billiard room, a school of art, a gymnasium and a rifle room. In Saltaire much stress was placed on cleanliness – a preoccupation of a period scourged by contagious disease. Public slipper baths and a Turkish bath were complemented by a steam laundry which, as Salt specified, was able to wash, mangle, dry and fold clothes in one hour.

In a sense Saltaire was a cul-de-sac in philanthropic thinking. The village displays a slightly monumental, almost urban character. Its regularly proportioned terraces of workers' houses are constructed in an Italian Renaissance style. Titus Salt, it should be remembered, had been Mayor of Bradford at a moment when the city fathers there, and in similar new industrial cities, were becoming anxious to create a civilized society on the back of industrial success. It was the era of grandiose town halls, public buildings and parks, whose models were the merchant cities of nothern Italy and the Low Countries

Port Sunlight, Merseyside, an image of rural charm created on the outskirts of urban Birkenhead, providing a spacious and airy environment for the factory workers it housed.

where a proud civic identity had long co-existed with commerce. Seen in this light, Saltaire was an attempt to create a community which embraced the values and rewards of industry. In a revealing conversation Lord Harewood once asked Salt why he did not put his capital into land and live the life of a squire – as the Harewood family had. Salt replied, 'As a landed proprietor ... I should be out of my element ... outside of my business I am nothing.' Saltaire is not a rural idyll, for such would not have interested its founder. It is perhaps nearer in spirit to a miniature Italian city-state.

Those who followed Salt reverted to a more picturesque and cottagey style. In the 1850s Price's Patent Candle Company constructed alongside its factory at Bromborough Pool in the Wirral a village of brick and slate cottages, with gardens and a green, which alluded unmistakably to the rural past. Port Sunlight, nearby, which housed William Lever's soap workers, pursued the vernacular idiom with half-timbering and tile-hanging. The concept of a garden village was taken still further by Joseph Rowntree, the Quaker chocolatier of York. He placed his New Earswick village of 1902 well away from the noise and smells of the factory. The cottages are not

In contrast to the village, the Port Sunlight factory, though far superior to many Victorian industrial premises, was crowded and noisy, and pervaded by the smell of carbolic soap.

arranged in terraces, but informally in a pleasantly landscaped setting. New Earswick also broke from the idea of a company village; Rowntree was happy to house employees and others alike. From New Earswick the lineage of the garden cities and new towns can be readily traced. Rowntree's architects at New Earswick were Parker and Unwin, who were also commissioned to create Letchworth Garden City; that led the way to Welwyn Garden City and to the more or less leafy 'overspill' developments of the inter-war years.

With the exception of Saltaire, all the model villages and garden developments have tried to take families out of the context of the factories and mills. It would seem that, culturally, Britain has never accepted its cities as natural or fit places to live. Equally, the reality of country living fails to entice the masses. The suburbs, however, have proved irresistible. Britain's suburbs were the world's first theme parks. They offer a nostalgic, undemanding and often quite tenuous vision of the villages of the past. They contain all manner of visual and social points of reference from dormer windows and half-timbering to the pub with a rustic name – 'The Hare and Hounds' – and the annual village fête. British suburbs are unique in Europe, and a source of some amazement and even ridicule from those whose culture has not thrown up such things. Yet they have succeeded because their character, as idealized villages, is absolutely in tune with popular aspirations.

IVY PLACE - NEW EARSWICK
FOX YORK. 8.

New Earswick, North Yorkshire. This first garden village pioneered the informal grouping of cottages around cul-de-sacs thickly planted with trees, and play areas for children.

Cottage economy

To understand fully the appeal of suburbia in our own century, we should remember that what it represents – a settled and secure life in one's own home and garden – were just the things that nineteenth-century village people aspired to most, but could not always achieve. The Victorian labourer feared unemployment, old age and sickness. If he were unable to cope at home, the workhouse or workhouse hospital was his likely destination. After the Poor Law Amendment Act of 1834, there was less relief for the poor in their own homes; the emphasis was on 'indoor relief' – which is to say accommodation in the workhouse. Several villages would join in a union to build and maintain a workhouse. Life in those austere and barrack-like institutions was deliberately harsh. Families were separated. Meals were taken in silence; gruel, potatoes and boiled bacon figured largely in the diet. Understandably, village

folk did their very best to stay outside (as the Poor Law Guardians hoped), preferring to scrape by than to surrender their independence. Flora Thompson tells the story of an old and sick soldier, known as the Major, who had to be duped into getting into the cart that the doctor had arranged:

As soon as he realised where he was being taken, the old soldier, the independent old bachelor, the kind family friend, collapsed and cried like a child. But not for long. Before six weeks were over he was back in the parish, and all his troubles were over, for he came back in his coffin.

For those who managed to stay at home during sickness or adversity, there was a network of charity. Charitable concern took numerous forms. There were old bequests and endowments in many parishes, which the churchwardens or a lawyer administered. They provided, typically, for the distribution of bread to the poor, for the schooling of destitute children, or for the upkeep of the almshouse. There were disaster and emergency funds, such as the huge one of over a million pounds raised to alleviate the hardship caused in Lancashire when the American

Petworth Union Workhouse, Sussex, in 1930, just before its closure, after more than a century as a parish poorhouse and then a workhouse. It must have been a cheerless place to end one's days.

Civil War cut off supplies of raw materials to the cotton industry. On a much smaller scale, usually, were the parish alms collected and distributed by the parson; we find the Revd Francis Kilvert visiting an old parishioner, one Edward Evans of Clyro in Powys, whom he found 'ill with cold from this vicious poisonous East wind, and sitting before the fire'.

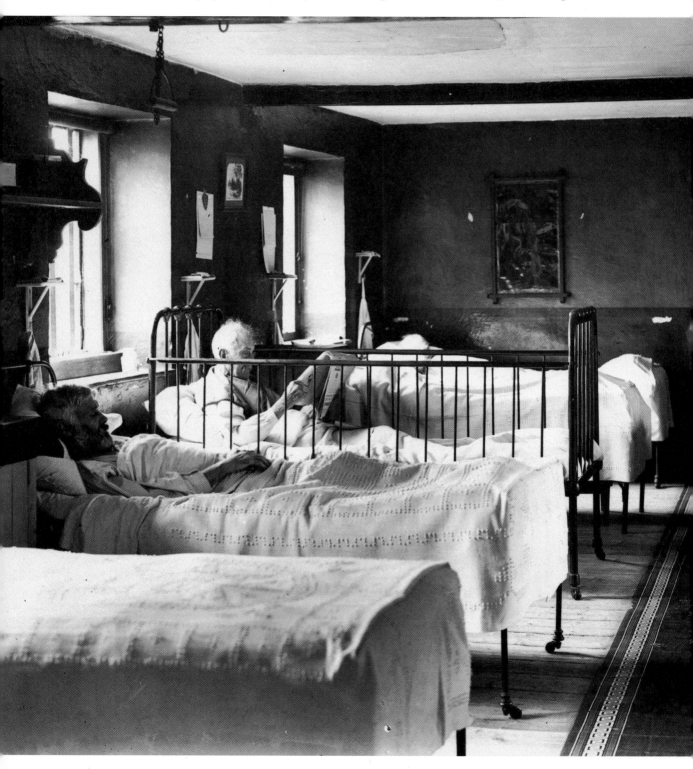

Kilvert was able to buy him bedding. But the most common and intrusive charity was that administered by the wives and daughters of the gentry or proprietor. They visited, almost by convention, the sick and needy, dispensing practical help by way of gifts of food, clothing, blankets and dressings. It was assumed by the landed classes that the deficiencies of Poor Relief would be made up by charity. Such gifts were gratefully received, no doubt, but the system was at its core demoralizing for the poor and open to resentment. The establishment (employers, the Church, the Boards of Guardians) regularly urged thrift and self-reliance. But meanwhile employers paid wages so low that they had to be augmented by charity and poor relief. That charity, granted to the 'deserving poor', was thus a potent instrument of social subordination.

The gentry were very keen on what came to be called 'cottage economy'. That was the means, theoretically, by which a ten-shilling wage could be stretched to provide the living for a family. The term was popularized by William Cobbett, who published a book under that title in 1821. However, the main lesson to be drawn from Cobbett's work is that popular and literary images of cottage life have a history of their own. They have rarely coincided with reality. Cobbett saw cottage economy as a noble endeavour which gave back to smallholders the independence they had had before enclosure. He offered the poor all kinds of impractical suggestions, such as a return to the domestic keeping of cows; cottagers generally had neither grazing nor shelter for them. Some of his ideas were frankly risible, particularly his notion that labouring families might solve their money problems by a sideline in straw bonnet-making. A later generation of country writers was to perpetuate the note of nostalgia. Flora Thompson, Richard Jeffries and Thomas Hardy all tended to look back to times before the Agricultural Depression, when life had not seemed quite so hard, and the village had been full of 'diamond-paned windows winking under the eaves' and 'a rustic porch smothered in honeysuckle'. Our twentieth-century vision has stylized and romanticized cottage life even further, into a world of chintz curtains, Aga cookers and little gardens riotous with colour. Those images (made reality by urban refugees and second-homers) have their own charm, but little to do with the practical economy of a labourer's household.

In reality the Victorian village family needed little encouragement in thrift; bare necessity demanded it. The burden was borne by the cottager's wife. She controlled the family budget. He simply earned it, and handed it over (minus a shilling's beer money). Flora Thompson recalled that

Many husbands boasted that they never asked their wives what they did with the money. As long as there was food enough, clothes to cover everybody, and a roof over their heads, they were satisfied, they said, and they seemed to make a virtue of this and think what generous, trusting, fine-hearted fellows they

ABOVE *Cottage life around the range, in* Answering the Emigrant's Letter *by James Collinson, 1850. This family is faring better than many, with everyone well dressed, a fire in the grate and children able to write.*

were. If a wife got into debt or complained, she was told 'You must larn to cut your coat accordin' to your cloth, my gal.'

It was the wife's skill in the kitchen, in making do and mending, and in drawing on domestic traditions of some antiquity that pulled the family through.

Activity at home focused on the kitchen fire. There was nothing new in that, but the technology of the fireplace was developing rapidly in the Victorian age, and had its effect on domestic routines. Coal had replaced wood as the main fuel; unlike wood or turf,

LEFT *Cast-iron range in a cottage at Little Barrington, Gloucestershire. Notice the oven and the toasting fork, the squares for lifting hot pans and the clothes-drier near the ceiling.*

it burns best in a basket. Eighteenth-century blacksmiths made rectangular iron fire baskets to stand in the old, wide fireplaces. Some years later stone hobs were being installed at either side of the fire, making useful perches for posts and pans. Around 1800 the stone was replaced by cast iron. When in time a door was added to one hob, and a lid to the other, a primitive oven and boiler were formed, and the Victorian range had been born.

The range was popular, indeed considered indispensable, because it provided in one appliance most of the requirements of a household. A single fire could warm the family, as well as boil and bake. It heated the smoothing-irons and brought to ordinary families their first experience of hot water regularly on tap from the boiler. For roasting, the cottager's wife could position a tinplate 'dutch oven' before the fire; inside, on a clockwork spit (the bottle-jack), the joint of meat would turn. Or she might use the ancient device of a dangle-spit, a twist of worsted thread which suspended and turned the meat in front of the fire. For toasting small pieces of food – bacon, kippers or a chop – there was a variety of ingenious devices to attach to the fire bars or to stand close to the coals.

Ranges became more and more complex, and by the end of the century incorporated hotplates, warming shelves, potstands and cranes, dampers, sometimes an additional oven, and a drying rail on the mantlepiece for socks and stockings. At the same time they were dreadfully inefficient in some respects. They burned coal all too well (there being little or no control of the airflow) and gave out a prodigious heat. That was welcome in winter, no doubt, but wearisome in summer when the fire was still needed for cooking and hot water. Only the well-insulated Aga cookers, which were used in some numbers in the 1920s and 1930s, began to overcome the problems. Considerable effort went into the range's upkeep. Flues had to be swept regularly. Spilt grease was wiped away with hot water and soda, the oven shelves scraped with an old knife and then washed in vinegar and water. The bright steelwork of the hinges and handles needed to be rubbed with emery, brass fittings polished with a paste and leather, and the boiler washed out once a week, any scale being scraped away. But, despite its deficiencies, the range was admired by all classes. Pride in a well-blacked and polished range is perfectly evident in early photographs. It was liked for its apparently free cooking and hot water, and gained a sort of respect as the universal provider. Above all it was a companionable thing to sit by.

The diet of the poor became a subject of concern and debate in polite circles. William Cobbett bemoaned the fact that cottagers had ceased to bake their own bread, arguing that the home-made loaf was both more wholesome and more economic than baker's bread. His hopes of a revivial were entirely misplaced. Few cottagers could afford the fuel or had access to a large brick oven suitable for baking. It is doubtful, in fact, whether there had ever been a popular tradition of oven-baked bread in Britain, for those reasons. Cobbett's advocacy of home brewing was similarly futile, for the cost of vessels and firing were beyond the labouring classes. Tea, sugar, potatoes, baker's bread and beer bought from the public house, which made up fully three-quarters of the cottager's food budget, were not, as Cobbett would have it, marks of indolence and poor home management. They were practical choices – the inescapable choices – for a hard-pressed household. Another critic of cottage cookery, the celebrated chef of the Reform Club, Alexis Soyer, compiled a *Shilling Cookery for the People* after a tour of asylums, hospitals, mines and ordinary homes in the 1850s. In it he portrayed the poor as ignorant of nutrition, and exhorted them to abandon roasting in favour of the traditional iron pot. That single vessel could produce stews, broths, soups, pottages, puddings and 'the

immortal pot-luck' (containing meat and whatever happened to be in the pantry) – all without losing any of the nourishing juices. The advice was undoubtedly sound in a nutritional sense, but it missed the point for the labouring poor. They did not want their small cut of meat dissipated in a stew; they wanted the man of the house, on whose labour their income depended, to have his fill. Middle-class advice of this kind generally foundered, because it failed to understand the strength of such traditions and conventions, which were quite alien to the world of the vicarage and drawing room.

Home produce made a difference, of course. A garden plot of potatoes helped the family through the leanest months. Cobbett once again carped, regretting the switch to potato-growing from corn, but it

Two young men taking the job of lifting potatoes rather seriously, but then the success of the crop on the cottage plot could make the difference between eating and going hungry.

was only when potatoes became a staple crop (in the eighteenth century in the north, the nineteenth in the south) that the population's chronic deficiency of vitamin C was overcome and scurvy began to retreat. Almost every cottage had a sty, and a good, fat pig – the fatter the better; there were no phobias about cholesterol then. The growing porker was the family's visible insurance against the winter, as Flora Thompson recalled:

During its lifetime the pig was an important member of the family, and its health and condition were regularly reported in letters to children away from home, together with news of their brothers and sisters. Men callers on Sunday afternoons came, not to see the family, but the pig, and would lounge with its owner against the pigsty for an hour, scratching piggy's back and praising his points or turning up their noses in criticism.

The pig was a hungry guest, too, devouring potato parings, windfall apples, grasses and dandelions collected by the children, and some expensive barley meal. Costs, and sometimes the meat, were shared between two families. Or part of the pig was mortgaged in advance with the butcher or baker for ready cash.

Cold weather, when the harvest glut was over, ushered in the pig-killing. Martinmas, 11 November, was the traditional start of the season; there was even an old saying: 'His Martinmas will come, as it does to every hog.' The spectacle, though bloody and barbarous, attracted a crowd, and could engender quite a carnival atmosphere as months of hard work came to a profitable end. The deed was done by a travelling butcher or pig-sticker , who cut the beast's throat to bleed the carcass dry. A Yorkshire labourer recalled how 'At Rosedale, uncle Willie Page used to go round, he was slaughterer there. . . . You used to have to take a jug when they cut t'pig's throat and get a jug of blood, and then you made black puddings with that.' Nothing of the pig was wasted except, as the saying went, the grunt. Cutting the carcass was a man's job, after the bristles had been singed or scalded and scraped away. Then the housewife took over, salting the cut-up joints in brine, and later hanging them to dry in the fireplace or attic. The offal was prepared for early use and the fat melted down and stored as lard; toast and dripping was a favourite cottage treat. The following Sunday the extended family would gather for its pig feast when, for once, the table groaned and there was no stint to roast pork and puddings. Even then the pig's contribution to the household economy was not finished. When the family could not afford candles, they would dip rushes into bacon fat, and burn them in a rushlight

The cottager's pig: this young man is pleased enough with his pig to arrange a portrait, and has dressed in Sunday best for the photograph.

holder. A portion of the meat would be sold for cash, and that would pay for the purchase of the next piglet in the spring.

Concern about the diet of the poor was coupled with fears of disease, particularly as a consequence of poor sanitation. In this respect conditions in the cities were undoubtedly worst, for village dwellers were spared the gross overcrowding, and the lethal water supply, polluted by inadequate sewers, which spread cholera and other contagious diseases. They endured, none the less, primitive conditions, which persisted in many instances long after sanitation in urban areas had been taken in hand. Some years ago, a lady who had been brought up on a farm in the little South Yorkshire village of Owston in the 1890s, Miss Edith Bradbury, told me that her family's privy was 'right down the garden, a long way from the house. We always kept it very nice though. It had to be emptied once a week, and new chemicals put in.' The chemical pail closet was, in fact, a major advance on the privies of earlier years, which were really no more than a hole in the ground over which a wooden seat was fixed. Another arrangement found in the country was the earth closet, which by means of a pull on a handle would send a shower of earth or sand into the closet.

Miss Bradbury remembered Friday night as bath night.

A fire was lit under the copper in the scullery to heat the water and a long zinc bath was put down on a rug in front of it. There were no fancy soaps then. The gentry had Pears Soap with no soda in it, but ordinary folks didn't have that. Bath towels weren't as nice as the towels today either; they were a rougher kind, though the people in the big house had nice ones. A bath was a luxury, though. You can keep clean by sponging yourself. I was the eldest and every night I used to sit my sisters on the table and wipe their hands and knees from a bowl at the sink. The water came from the boiler in a lading tin.

The bath in front of the fire sounds cosy enough but, in draughty and generally underheated houses, the

Hand-pump at Pembridge, Hereford and Worcester. An alternative to taking water to the house was to bring the work to the pump.

business of ablution could be a penance, as the Revd Francis Kilvert testified. In one of his more eccentric moments, on Christmas Day 1870, he 'sat down in [the] bath upon a sheet of ice which broke in the middle into large pieces [with] sharp points and jagged edges ... not particularly comforting to the naked thighs and loins'.

The securing and disposing of water, which hardly merits a thought today, was a daily chore for Victorian cottagers and all their predecessors. Medieval villagers had taken it from the local stream, or from a hole dug nearby, which after several emptyings would yield reasonably clean water. In the nineteenth century a piped supply in the house was still the exception, but matters had progressed to the point where some farms had boreholes headed by a hand pump, and many villages had access to deep wells. Water still had to be carried with pails and a yoke, though – a heavy and time-consuming labour. It was brought to the back kitchen or scullery where, if necessary, it would stand in large pancheons (earthenware bowls) while the sediment settled. Sinks were very shallow – almost flat slabs of stone or buff earthenware with drain holes. On this 'slop-stone' all manner of work proceeded, either in a bucket or directly on the surface. (Its front edge doubled as an ideal knife-sharpener.) It was the end of the nineteenth century before deep sinks took over. Plumbed drainage was by no means universal, and at best led to a soakaway just outside the walls of the house. At worst, the waste flowed into a tub, which was rolled outside for emptying in the garden or at the roadside.

Such arrangements helped to make laundry the heaviest of all the housewife's tasks. Not that clothes were changed frequently; expectations of personal hygiene were low. But the wash took the best part of a week to complete, with the washing, heavy with water, heaved about the house and even around the village. The traditional process began with 'bucking' – the soaking of the clothes in a bucket. In the absence of soap – prohibitively taxed until the 1850s – a lye was added to the water; lye was the alkaline product of burning plants such as ferns or soapwort. Alternatively, urine was used as a source of ammonia. Then there was rubbing and rinsing, best done in running water; hence the trip to the riverside where the family's dirty linen could be washed in public. Next the drying: for preference the washing was laid out on grass or on a hedge where the sun would bleach as well as dry. In poor weather a clothes-horse or 'winter-hedge' did service before the range. The more particular housewife still had her pressing to do, either with a heavy iron or in an old-fashioned linen press.

Washing day, 1871. These women had every reason to look miserable: laundry was a lengthy chore. While one is rubbing clothes by hand, the other is using a 'posser' in a tub of hot water.

Hard work, poor diet and doubtful sanitation took their toll. Edwin Chadwick's report on the *Sanitary Conditions of the Labouring Population* calculated a life expectancy for an agricultural labourer of thirty-three years. The medical profession contributed little. It is clear from payments entered in the vestry and churchwarden's accounts that a doctor was sometimes called from the town. But more often villagers relied on home-made remedies and probably fared no worse, and possibly rather better, than had they taken the doctor's 'physic'. At least home doctoring refrained from surgery, which was highly perilous in the absence of both anaesthetics and antiseptics; the amateurs merely treated the surface of the body with poultices and compresses, mostly of a herbal nature. Or they administered potions and infusions of common flowers and seeds which probably did little harm. However, against the many catastrophic diseases and debilities, which particularly affected the young and aged, all villagers from squire to labourer were defenceless. Kilvert's diary records in April 1874: 'Poor Lizzie Powell, a wreck and a shadow of the fine blooming girl she was when I last saw her, was crouching up in the sunny window opposite the Vicarage, pale, wasted, shrunken, hollow-eyed and hollow-cheeked, dying of consumption.'

All such diseases, diphtheria, smallpox and scarlet fever among them, thrived on undernourished and ill-cleansed bodies, especially little ones. The sufferings of the old, captured in this description of grandfather in *Lark Rise*, were perhaps more severe still:

... [his] daily visits had ceased, for the chronic rheumatism against which he had fought was getting the better of him. First the Church was too far for him; then the end house; then his own garden across the road and at last his world narrowed down to the bed upon which he was lying... the plain white bed beneath the sloping ceiling in the little whitewashed room under the roof.... Gradually his limbs became so locked he could not turn over in bed without help.

Possibly the gravest peril of all was childbirth, and at such times villagers would turn to a local midwife. She was probably untrained in a formal sense, but had practical experience. When Jane, the wife of a farm labourer, Richard Hodges, gave birth to her fourth child at Butleigh, Somerset, the confinement was supervised by such a woman for a fee of two shillings and sixpence. She arrived at the cottage, in March 1828, with a white apron, a needle and cotton, a basket of cotton rugs and some boracic powder. Mrs Hodges' sister-in-law assisted by carrying jugs of hot water up the narrow stairs to the bedroom. The baby, John, was one of the fortunates who survived, and he was baptized a few days later in the parish church, wearing a bonnet and christening robes lent by the Vicar.

It seems that as a child John Hodges, in common with many of his contemporaries, did not attend school – or at least not regularly enough to learn to write. At his wedding at the age of twenty-three he could only manage a very shaky mark in the marriage register. The village had a dame school at that time, run by a Mrs Cornish, the wife of a labourer. A little later it gained a National School (sponsored by an Anglican Society) and the Butleigh Infants' School. The failure of children of the period to learn a great deal at school may partly be put down to the teachers, whose own education, pay and status was usually rather poor, and partly to the parents. Without compunction they would keep a child away from school if there were potatoes to lift or errands to run. The cost of education was significant to a poor family – John Hodges was one of six children, and twopence a week per child was possibly more than they could regularly afford. As soon as a boy or girl was capable of earning a living, parents were most reluctant to continue with an education which, for all they could tell, did nothing to improve the child's earning potential. So school attendance was notoriously patchy. John Hodges' grandchildren in the 1870s

one or two 'monitors' – girls of twelve and thirteen, recently out of school themselves. Pupils spent much time entering letters and then words in a rounded script into a copybook that was frequently blotted. They recited parrot-fashion from 'readers', and rehearsed multiplication tables by rote. The vicar and his wife were regular visitors, to tell Bible stories and to hear the children recite their cathechism. Older children received an anecdotal version of British history and learned the repertoire of patriotic songs, while the girls practiced their stitches and buttonholes. Learning was certainly very formal; perhaps it had to be when teaching resources were so thinly stretched.

Armed with that panoply of wisdom, children of ten or eleven left school to seek work. John Hodges appears to have stayed in the village, and would have started as a farmboy. It was not his first taste of work by any means, as he would have helped on the land with such jobs as bird-scaring and picking stones from the field. This was the beginning of full-time employment, however. It was a hard apprenticeship. For three shillings a week he would work up to twelve hours a day. He would help the older men by harnessing and tending the heavy horses, cleaning the stables and possibly leading the plough teams out to the fields. At other times he would clear ditches or repair hedges, gradually learning a range of skills.

Boys of an adventurous mind took off to the annual mop fair in the town. There farmers looked for workers, and workers stood about in groups according to their trades – cowmen, shepherds, carters and so on. Servants and their prospective masters would bargain over wages, hours of work and accommodation and, if both were agreeable, struck a deal, sealed by the payment of a 'fasten penny', which was binding for a year's service. For the youngsters the contract would allow boarding in the master's farmhouse.

Girls out of school also headed for employment, and in all probability out of the village. In earlier days, many young women passed the interval between puberty and marriage as a living-in servant-in-agriculture. That pattern was breaking up, especially in the second half of the nineteenth century, as farmers cut back on labour. But in any case girls and their parents were setting their sights higher. They wanted a position in a house of the gentry. Failing that, a place with a good family in the city would do. There was a finely drawn hierarchy within the larger households revealed, for instance, in the Servants' Wage Book kept by Lady Onslow at Clandon Park, Surrey, in the 1880s. A new girl started at the bottom and worked upwards. In her first year she occupied a 'petty place', but could rise by ability and seniority

ABOVE *School house and children at Sandford St Martin, Oxfordshire, about 1877. There are teachers in the group, but the well-dressed ladies in the centre are perhaps gentry on a gracious visit.*

were the first generation to have compulsory elementary schooling, at establishments where some minimum standards were imposed by Her Majesty's Inspectors. Even so, school holidays were likely to be prolonged if the harvest required it.

Village schools were presided over by a teacher (usually female) or governess. She would attempt to cover the whole syllabus, and instruct all age-groups. This she did single-handed unless she had the help of

LEFT A Dame's School (1845), *by Thomas Webster, where there are not even any tables on which to write or enough books to go round. The children – or at least a few of them – are trying to learn to read by reciting aloud.*

the end of the century. All these opportunities for a self-supporting existence encouraged a sizeable band of women to remain independent, pursuing a career rather than a family life. What is abundantly clear is that young women as a group had turned their backs on farming, and consequently on their villages of origin. Very few who had left for the town as girls came back as young women to marry childhood sweethearts.

One good reason, of course, was that those farming villages had lost many of their young men. There was simply not the work available to support them all. A stark choice had to be faced: either a precarious existence on the land, picking up seasonal work, parish relief and irksome charity, or a farewell to loved ones and a new life elsewhere. Thousands upon thousands were tempted by higher wages in town, or in the mines, or even at sea in Britain's vast merchant fleet. The other way was to join the flood tide of emigration to America and Australia. Between 1853 and 1880 almost 3 million people, predominantly young and male, left the United Kingdom in search of greener pastures. They did not come back.

ABOVE *Children setting up stooks in a wheat field, about 1900. Children's work included cleaning lifted potatoes, gleaning for grain, clearing stones from the fields and scaring away birds.*

from housemaid to head housemaid, and thence to cook and finally housekeeper. There she might command a salary as high as £50 per annum and enjoy the status and power of a respected position. Not all households were so grand, however. Everyone with the slightest pretension to social standing kept a maid, so that a country girl might well find herself as house servant to a clerk or shopkeeper. In return she would receive board and lodging, and around £7 a year, much of which she would remit to her parents.

The scale of domestic service in Victorian Britain was quite staggering. The 1881 census figures showed 1,269,000 female indoor servants, with another 276,00 classed as washerwomen, charwomen and the like. We must add to that the growing number of jobs available to women in retail shops, in milliners' and tailors' workshops, as well as in textile factories (where 745,000 women were employed in 1881). We can even see the beginnings of the vast modern army of secretaries and typists in the form of Victorian book-keepers and female clerks, whose numbers, though still small, were beginning to grow towards

ABOVE *Domestic service was seen as a desirable alternative to farmwork, and attracted countless thousands of village girls to leave their roots to take positions in the 'big house' or in town.*

Celebrations

This story of village life seems to be ending on a sombre note. In fact there were many moments of conviviality despite all the hard work and disappointments. Communities thrown upon their own resources for entertainment value company and talk, songs and local festivals more, perhaps, than we do today.

Labourers had a nightly opportunity for a smoke and drink with their fellows at a village alehouse. It was an exclusively male gathering; a wife's place was at home with the children. (One cannot escape the conclusion that women, once married with a house and family to keep, led a relatively less sociable existence, both at work and at leisure). Patronage of the alehouse did not promote drunkenness. On wages of a few shillings a week, customers made a pint, or even half pint, last the entire evening. The enjoyment lay in the chance for wide-ranging conversation out of earshot of the squire. Down the centuries the alehouse was a political forum of a sort, there being none other available to villagers. All the petty grumbles and complaints against the parson, the farmer or the magistrates could be aired. As a result the village establishment remained wary of the alehouse. The clergy stayed aloof from it, and even denounced it as wasteful and a sin, perhaps sensing that its sociable and alcoholic fellowship was a rival for the allegiances of their flock. The vestry and the constable had an understandable prejudice that if unrest were to brew up in the village, it would begin in the alehouse. For the most part though, alehouse talk was only talk. As Richard Jeffries put it in *Hodge and his Masters* in 1880, 'in the affairs of life, in politics and social hopes, the labourer has no well-defined creed of race. He has no genuine programme for the future.'

Those alehouses – a village might have several – were small and unremarkable. We should not confuse them in our mind's eye with the inns which were far larger and grander, and provided food and accommodation for travellers. An alehouse was usually no more than a cottage, and much like any other in the parish. It differed only in that the family, or perhaps a widow, had thrown open the parlour in an effort to make a modest living. Such businesses could be quite ephemeral, and it is not easy for us now to identify which house or houses in a village were used in this way, unless there is documentary evidence. Possibly most old cottages in a village have been alehouses at some time in their past. The village authorities, too, had difficulty in knowing which were public houses ; in 1543 we find the manor court at Foxton in Cambridgeshire decreeing that all who sell beer should put out a sign. Then, and for another two centuries, the sign would not be a painted board but a green bush hung above the door – a symbol which seems to go back to taverns of the Roman era, which displayed branches of ivy or vine in honour of Bacchus. The alehouse thus identified was under the eye of the parish ale-taster, (an honorary but popular post); he checked on the price, measure and quality of the brew. Except for a prohibition on tippling during the hours of divine service, there was no general limit on opening times until 1872.

The passage of the farming year was marked by plenty of occasions for community celebrations, many of which undoubtedly had pagan roots. The more important festivities fell on or around the summer and winter solstices, the spring and autumn equinoxes and other important days of the Celtic year. The Celtic New Year's Eve, for instance, fell on 31 October, our Hallowe'en. The dates point to the obsession of ancient religion with the sun, the seasons, and the renewal of life each spring. Some ancient festivities implied contact with the spirit world; at Hallowe'en, for instance, the spirits of the dead were welcomed back to earth by the lighting of bonfires. Unsurprisingly, the Church was cool about relics of superstition, but as usual it assimilated the custom into its own rites by designating 2 November as the Feast of All (Christian) Saints. After the Reformation in England, the Church neatly diverted attention from Hallowe'en with Bonfire Night on 5 November. It thereby celebrated the failure of the Catholic Guy Fawkes' plot to destroy the king and the Protestant faith. The Puritan Church made every effort, in the seventeenth century particularly, to suppress revelries with superstitious overtones. As a result, many Victorian festivities were revivals rather than survivals, and they may not bear too close a resemblance to ancient practice.

On the first Monday after Twelfth Night (Midwinter's Day in the ancient calendar) farm labourers used to drag a plough around the parish, calling at each door to collect money. This Plough Monday marked their return to work in the fields, the beginning of the farming year. Festivities ensued; traditionally there was a mumming play and sword-dancing, which culminated in a ceremonial decapitation, and subsequent return to life, of one or other of the characters. The symbolism of the death of the old year and the birth of the new is anything but hidden. Victorian clergy, none the less, managed to tame the day a little by getting the plough brought into church for blessing.

The arrival of spring was greeted by dancing, merriment and, if the Puritan Philip Stubbs (c.1555–1610) is to be believed, by a degree of licence. On May

Eve young men and women went

some to the woods and groves, some to the hills and mountains, some to one place and some to another, where they spend all the night in pleasant pastimes, and in the morning they return, bringing with them birch boughs and branches of trees, to deck their assemblies withal.

On May Day, the maypole was set up

covered all over with flowers and herbs, bound about with strings from the top to the bottom and sometimes painted with variable colours ... and thus being reared up with handkerchiefs and flags streaming on the top, they straw the ground about, bind green boughs about it, set up summer halls, bowers, arbours hard by it; and then they fall to banquet and feast, to leap and dance about it, as the heathen people did at the dedication of their idols, whereof this is the perfect pattern, or rather the thing itself.

BELOW *Plough Stotts, a Yorkshire form of Plough Monday, from an early-19th-century watercolour. The participants are doing a sort of sword dance around the plough, while the village looks on.*

Maypole dancing on May Day. Maypole dancers are not usually children: in the past, as here at Ickwell, near Bedford, young men and women danced, and the fertility symbolism was unmistakable.

Stubbs's disapproval was shared by Parliament, which in 1644 ordered that all maypoles be taken down. The revival of May Day celebrations and maypoles fell to the Victorians, by which time the proceedings were innocent enough.

Some village festivals became, in time, excuses for the young men and women of the parish to let high spirits rip. Any householder who failed to give money on Plough Monday would receive a hail of stones at his door. Shrovetide began with a religious significance; it was a time to prepare for the penance and fasting of Lent. Part of the preparation, according to tradition, was the eating up of supplies of eggs, butter or lard in pancakes. In Olney in Buckinghamshire the bell summoning the faithful to 'shriving' or confession once rang out while a parishioner was cooking her pancake, and she dashed to church with it still in the frying pan. That at least was the story told to explain the pancake races held in the village each Shrove Tuesday. Elsewhere children went 'Shroving' from house to house, singing for food.

ABOVE *The celebration of Harvest Home, from an engraving of about 1770. With the last cartload of corn safely in, tables are set outside the inn and the music and dancing begin.*

I come Shroving, a Shroving, a Shroving
  For a piece of pancake
  For a piece of truffle cake
Of your own making.

Again, if the householder failed to comply, stones or pot shards were thrown at his door. A rowdy game of Shrove Tuesday football was a tradition in a number of villages, Ashbourne in Derbyshire being one. There the two teams drawn from those born north and south of the Henmore, the local stream, fought out a series of mauls around the ball in the attempt to score a goal through the millwheels at Clifton and Sturston, three miles apart. All the Shrovetide festivals were the prelude to the solemnity of Ash Wednesday.

A highlight of the year was a visit to the big fair in town. It combined the excitement of a modern sales day – the hunting out of bargains – with the chance to mix in a crowd, to laugh at the side-shows (dancing bears and human freaks) to ride the roundabout and swing-boats and to return home with gingerbread wrapped in gold foil and a 'fairing' or two – perhaps a pottery dog or a glass walking-stick. A fair, after all, was a holiday, as well as an opportunity for business.

Many villages had their own local fair on the feast day of the patron saint of the parish. (The original significance tended to be forgotten.) Gilbert White's village of Selborne revived its local celebration in 1681 when 'a set of jovial fellows' discovered in an old almanac that there had been a fair there in former days on the first day of August, and were 'desirous to revive so joyous a festival'. The vicar had set his face against it as 'the probable cause of much intemperance'. His fears were no doubt well-founded, as White records that 'most of the lower housekeepers brew beer against the holiday, . . . and their becoming victuallers for the day without a licence is overlooked'. At markets and fairs heavy drinking was an accepted part of the proceedings. 'Go but to the town's end where a fair is kept,' wrote a reproving preacher in 1638, 'and there they lie, as if some field had been fought; here lies one man, where another . . .' The village feast was a time for friends and relatives to return, and maybe for a few stalls and some entertainment in the pub or in a barn lent by a farmer. Someone might bring out a fiddle or a melodeon, and the dancing would continue while the drink lasted. Above all, a feast *was* a feast. When country people did eat, they spared nothing.

The other great day, the climax of the farming year, was the celebration of harvest home. Almost everyone was drawn into the team effort of the preceding weeks. The frantic activity on the land seemed to raise collective spirits to a fever. The 'King of the Mowers', elected from among the scythers, set a lively pace for the men who cut the broad swathes up and down the field. The farmer, knowing morale had to be high, sent out an encouraging supply of ale to refresh the workers. And when the last wagonload had been brought home, and stood in the rickyard, the village worked itself into a state of high excitement. It was then that the farmer would greet the workers with jugs of beer and an invitation to a harvest home dinner. Flora Thompson recalls:

And what a feast it was! Such a bustling in the farmhouse kitchen for days beforehand; such boiling of hams and roasting of sirloins; such a stacking of plum puddings, made by the Christmas recipe; such a tapping of eighteen-gallon casks and baking of plum loaves would astonish those accustomed to the appetites of today .... Long tables were laid out of doors in the shade of a barn, and soon after twelve o'clock the cottagers sat down to the good cheer, with the farmer carving at the principal table, his wife and her tea-urn at another, the daughters of the house and their friends circling the tables with vegetable dishes and beer jugs and the grand-children, in their stiff, white embroidered frocks, dashing hither and thither to see that everybody had what they required.

That one sumptuous meal, some might say, was the farmer's attempt to buy off the resentment of an otherwise ill-paid workforce. The one occasion on which he served his men was meant to balance the 364 days a year that they served his interests. And, by publicly treating his workers, as a father might indulge his children, he made them accomplices to a paternalistic system that was, at its roots, inequitable. Some might say it, and some did. Yet on that day such thoughts rested. The farmer and his men, their wives and children, all took the thing at face value; the village threw itself willingly into the simple festivities with an innocence that our own age has lost.

BELOW *Sleeping it off after Barrington Club Day in Somerset, 1907. Village folk might go in for a drinking bout on high days and holidays, but few could afford frequent drunkenness.*

The village of Corfe Castle, Dorset (see pp.164–5).

PART TWO

Village Histories:
A Gazetteer of
Selected Villages

Introduction

These profiles are deliberately confined to villages in which the National Trust has an interest or those mentioned in earlier chapters for their historical importance. It does not aim to be comprehensive, and many important villages are omitted because they do not satisfy these criteria. Properties owned by the National Trust are identified by an NT in brackets, and if individual buildings, gardens or nature reserves (but not shops, hotels, etc.) are open to the public, this is indicated by an asterisk: (NT*). Readers must, however, check this in the annual *National Trust Handbook*, which gives opening times and other practical information for visitors. Only in a few cases does the National Trust own the whole of a village, and some of these have been covered at greater length in the special historical features. More often the Trust owns one or two small buildings or, in the case of estate villages, the great house. In other cases it owns the adjoining land, and therefore can offer the village some protection.

I have omitted small hamlets in National Trust ownership, and other minor examples, as not of sufficient interest in their own right to warrant a visit. I have, however, included villages near an important National Trust house, in which the church is of particular relevance as it contains monuments relating to the owners of the great house. Often these villages also contain dower houses and other estate buildings which increase an understanding of life on the estate. If the church is locked, there is usually a notice in the porch giving the address of the keyholder. In the case of partially owned villages, the National Trust cannot be held responsible for unsightly later developments or for alterations to buildings over which it has no control.

I believe this to be the most comprehensive list of National Trust villages yet published. Other villages listed here, which may not have any National Trust connection, were included in earlier chapters for their historical interest. I have attempted, within the limited space available, to provide more detailed information in order to encourage readers to visit them. They have of course been included for many different reasons. An industrial village is not necessarily beautiful or rural, while a village containing sites of archaeological interest is not always visually attractive.

I should like to remind readers that villages are places in which people live. Even if the farms and cottages are owned by the Trust, they are tenanted; very few are open to the public. It is important that visitors should respect the privacy of villagers, and resist the temptation to park cars in inconvenient places and to peer into interesting interiors.

Finally, I hope that readers will feel, as I do, that villages and landscape are complementary; each gains from the other, and they should not be considered in isolation. The National Trust has pioneered the protection of our great landscapes and our outstanding country houses. Neither can exist in a vacuum. It is now time for some of our most important villages, and those which provide the setting for the great house or castle, to receive the degree of protection which only ownership by the National Trust can bring. In the scale of its possessions and the standards of care which it has set, the Trust is unique in the world; our villages also need its help.

Jane Fawcett

Village Histories

A

ALFRISTON
Sussex

A downland village, Alfriston was founded at the point where a prehistoric ridgeway crossed the River Cuckmere. The Old Clergy House (NT*), the first building acquired and saved by the National

Clovelly, Devon (see p.163), a dramatically sited 16th-century fishing village.

Trust, in 1896, is a rare fourteenth-century hall house, timber framed and thatched. Both the Star Inn and the George Inn date from the fifteenth century, and both are timber framed. The George has some interesting wall paintings. The Star was built as a pilgrims' hostel by the monks of Battle Abbey. It has medieval bargeboarding and carving, and the figure of a lion, reputedly a figurehead from a ship wrecked in the seventeenth century. St Andrew's Church, known as 'the Cathedral of the Downs', is a splendid flint cruciform building with a central

shingle spire. It stands commandingly on a circular mound overlooking both the river and the village green or Tye. An array of timber-framed or flint cottages, many now tearooms or shops, including Danny Cottage (NT), line the narrow village street. The timber-framed Smugglers' Inn is well named, for smuggling was actively carried on up the Cuckmere. There are also some eighteenth-century brick houses, and the bow windows of the eighteenth-century post office face the market cross, which is itself a rare survival.

ALLERFORD
Somerset
(Holnicote Estate – NT)

Allerford lies in the valley to the west of Selworthy which culminates in Hurleston Point, Bossington and the sea. It is typical of the area, with farms and thatched cottages, many dating from the seventeenth century. Some of the buildings have cream rendered walls and thatched roofs, while others are of stone, roofed with pantiles. Prominent circular chimneys and Gothic windows add to the picturesque effect. Behind lie North Hill with its magnificent trees planted by Thomas Acland in the 1830s, and Selworthy Beacon. Through the village runs the River Aller on its way to the sea at Bossington Beach. Allerford contains a working smithy and an ancient two-arched packhorse bridge, connecting with an old track crossing the moors to Minehead and beyond.

ATCHAM
Shropshire

This pretty estate village lies at the gates of Attingham Park (NT*), designed in 1782 by George Steuart. The original village was emparked and removed when Humphry Repton landscaped the park. The attractive colour-washed cottages were designed by John Nash who also carried out alterations to Attingham Park. There are two fine eighteenth-century bridges, one over the Severn by John Gwynn, the other over the Tern by Robert Mylne. The impressive eighteenth-century brick coaching inn, the Mermaid and Mytton, overlooks the river. Behind is the church, St Eata, of local red sandstone, containing some monuments to the Berwick family of Attingham. Traffic on the A5 pounds past continually. John Nash also designed the delightful villa, Cronkhill (NT), which stands outside the village on its own in the fields.

B

BAINBRIDGE
North Yorkshire

A traditional stone village in Wensleydale, Bainbridge is intersected by the River Bain, with

Avebury (NT), Wiltshire

The monumental stone circle at Avebury is one of the foremost prehistoric sites in Europe, notable for its great open air ceremonial gatherings to which people came from Spain and France. It was in use for about 2000 years from *c.* 2500 BC. The nearby Ridgeway, reputedly one of the oldest roads in Europe, provided a long distance network of communication to the Bristol Channel and the English Channel.

With the arrival of the first Christian chapel at Avebury in *c.* AD 700 a conflict developed which came to a head in the early Middle Ages with attempts by the villagers to bury the enormous pagan stones in their midst. By the eighteenth century the village was growing and the stones were cannibalized to construct new buildings. When William Stukeley carried out a detailed survey of Avebury many of the stones had already vanished and there were 13 houses standing inside the circle. In 1724 he wrote, 'And this stupendous fabric, which for some thousands of years had braved the assaults of weather ... [has] fallen a sacrifice to the wretched ignorance and avarice of a little village unluckily placed within it.' In the nineteenth century a large part of the Neolithic site was sold as building land and was only saved by the intervention of Sir John Lubbock, later Lord Avebury, who bought it. Then in 1934 Alexander Keiller bought Avebury Manor and carried out the first excavations of the site with Professor Stuart Piggott. He lived in the Manor until his death in 1955. In 1937 a public appeal was launched to save Avebury in perpetuity and by 1943 the purchase price of £11,000 had been raised; the site and much of the village came to the National Trust. But in 1961, when the manorial aisled thatched barn, which intrudes into the site, had become derelict, its demolition and that of parts of the village lying within the stone circle was seriously debated by the National Trust. The site and the village have had, over the years, an uneasy partnership both visually and ideologically. Of the 600 sarsen stones which crowned the original site, only 76 have survived.

Today it is the juxtaposition of the pretty village with the stark grandeur of the Neolithic circle that gives Avebury its special character. All attempts to destroy either the village or the site have now lapsed. A truce has been reached and each is accepted as part of history: only the traffic pouring relentlessly past on the main Devizes to Swindon road still threatens the integrity of the site.

High Street, were it not for the presence of the great circle through which it straggles, looks much like other downland villages. There are houses of brick, of flint and of cob, some timber-framed, many thatched. There is also widespread use of sarsen stone plundered from the site. The old school, early Victorian, is of sarsen stone and brick; the Old Rectory and Manor Farm are handsome eighteenth-century brick buildings. Also to be seen are whitewashed thatched cottages; a group of Victorian labourers' cottages of brick with bargeboarding, which intersect the outer circle; eighteenth-century gate piers and an avenue to Avebury Manor, which also cuts through the Neolithic bank; The Lodge, an early nineteenth-century stucco villa, once the home of Lord Avebury; and The Red Lion, thatched and timber-framed, also intruding into the great bank and overshadowed by massive monolithic sarsens.

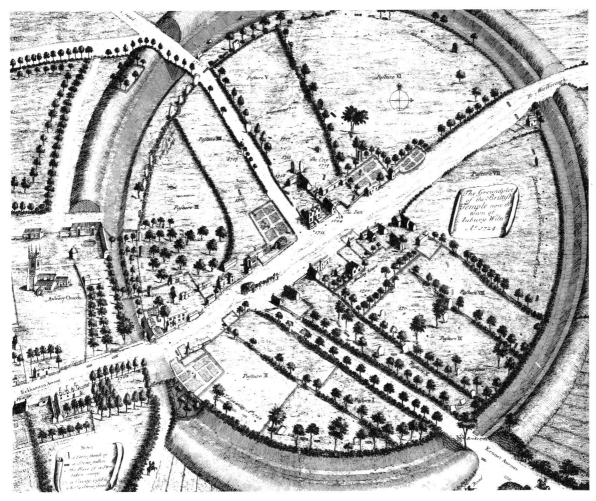

Avebury in 1724 by William Stukeley, showing the village within the circle and the thatched barn cutting through it, as well as the positions of the stones.

Beyond, leading the eye up to the downs and the Ridgeway, is Green Street, originally the Herepath (Saxon for 'a green road'). Silbury House and the Methodist chapel, both constructed of plundered sarsens, more thatched cottages and a farm lead to the original exit from the site. All the four prehistoric entrances to the great circle are still in use today, but the use has changed and intensified.

At the heart of the village lie the remarkable church of St James and, beside it, Avebury Manor, framed romantically by great trees. Some parts of the church, including the circular clerestory windows, survive from the Saxon period. The fine south doorway with zig-zag decoration, and the remarkable font bearing a figure of a bishop with crosier and cassock threatened by two serpents, are both Norman. Could this symbolize the pagan threat to the authority of the Church? The rare and beautiful painted rood screen decorated with friezes of leaves and grapes is partly Perpendicular, restored by Bodley in the late nineteenth century. The arcade of Tuscan columns, inserted by Mr Button a local builder in 1812, is a surprising

feature. The tall Perpendicular west tower, of flint and ashlar with battlements and pinnacles, proclaims the Christian message on the fringe of the pagan site.

Avebury Manor, approached by a lime avenue and surrounded by ancient topiary gardens, was acquired by Sir William Sharington of Lacock after the Reformation. This many-gabled stone house, was built in 1557 on the site of a small twelfth-century Benedictine priory and incorporates some medieval stone fragments. It has an impressive south front of 1601 with large mullioned and transomed windows. The great hall, drawing room and great chamber were altered in 1730 and have good plaster ceilings and original fireplaces. The old stables (now a museum), the circular stone dovecote, the old cowshed (now a restaurant), a small barn (now a National Trust shop) and the great thatched aisled barn (now an agricultural museum) are grouped round the old manor farmyard and its pond.

Trusloe Manor, approached across the water meadows over the four-arched Old Bridge, is a large seventeenth-century stone house with a hipped roof and impressive mullioned and transomed windows, recently altered and extended. Beyond, down Bray Street, is Bannings, a handsome Georgian farmhouse of chequered brick, and Westbrook Farm, thatched, with stone mullions.

Bainbridge, North Yorkshire, with the river Bain and the fells beyond.

spectacular waterfalls and the fine Bain Bridge at the north-east entrance to the village. Eighteenth- and nineteenth-century stone cottages are grouped round a large green, on which the old stocks still stand. A seventeenth-century inn (the Rose and Crown), a converted watermill and the Methodist Chapel face the green. Below there is a fine bridge over the River Ure. There is the site of a Roman fort on Brough Hill, from which the Roman road runs over Cam Fell.

BEARE
Devon
(Killerton Estate – NT)
see Broadclyst

BELTON
Lincolnshire

A small estate village largely built of ironstone, Belton is contemporary with Belton House (NT*), built in 1685–6 in the Wren tradition with a hipped roof, dormers and a cupola, standing in a landscape park. Bedehouses, the post office and the forge are seventeenth century. Anthony Salvin enlarged the village in the nineteenth century. The church of St Peter and St Paul, which stands charmingly in the grounds, has been altered over the years, and in 1816 Sir Jeffry Wyatville added a chapel to it. Inside are many interesting monuments to the

Brownlow family, owners of Belton for three hundred years. The tall fourteenth-century limestone tower is a landmark.

BERWICK WHARF
Shropshire

A small estate village on the Attingham Park Estate (NT*), Berwick Wharf consists of timber-framed rendered cottages built in 1810 to rehouse the occupants of Berwick village, who were moved to make room for the landscape park laid out by Repton at Attingham. Pairs of cottages are either rendered under heavy eaves or half-timbered.

BEWDLEY
Hereford and Worcester

Bewdley was once an important river port, and Telford's graceful three-arched bridge, built in 1795, crosses the Severn here. An impressive array of Georgian buildings, in brick with pantiles, faces the river from Severn Side, originally called Coles Quay. Above lies the old town, really an enlarged village, and beyond, the Wyre Forest. Although there are many black-and-white timber-framed houses typical of this area, the predominant character of Bewdley is Georgian. River trading is reflected in the street names: Load Street refers to a ship's cargo, Lax Lane to the Norse word for a

salmon. The name Flooding is a reminder of the habitual behaviour of the Severn. Ribbesford House (1820) is surrounded by a landscape park in which stands the parish church, approached by a lime avenue. The Norman tympanum represents a leaping salmon shot by an arrow. The timber south arcade and the Burne-Jones window are both noteworthy.

BIBURY
Gloucestershire

Called by William Morris 'the loveliest village in England', Bibury has changed little since. Arlington Row (NT), a remarkable group of stone-slated cottages with irregular gables and dormers, was once a fourteenth-century sheephouse, converted for weavers in the seventeenth century. Arlington Mill, now a museum, faces across the water meadows to Rack Isle, once used for drying wool on racks. The River Colne flows gently through the village, with ducks and a trout farm. The fine Saxon church of St Mary, which stands above the village, was restored by Sir George Gilbert Scott; its churchyard was described by Alec Clifton-Taylor as 'perhaps the most enchanting churchyard in England'. There are many table tombs to local wool merchants. Bibury Court, now a hotel, was built after the Reformation on an ancient Roman site, and faces the river with water gardens.

BLAISE HAMLET (NT)
Avon

A deliberately picturesque estate village grouped round a small green with a village pump in the centre, Blaise Hamlet was designed in 1810–11 by John Nash, favourite architect of George IV, for the wealthy and philanthropic Bristol banker John Scandrett Harford. Blaise was intended to complement Harford's Blaise Castle estate and landscape park. Like Selworthy, designed by his old friend Sir Thomas Acland, it provided comfortable accommodation for his aged retainers. Nikolaus Pevsner says of Blaise that it is the '*ne plus ultra* of picturesque layout and design.... Its progeny is legion and includes Christmas cards and teapots.'

Nevertheless, a contemporary account said that the rooms were comfortable and well arranged, and that each tenant was convinced that his cottage was the prettiest on the green. The deliberate artifice of high chimneys, exaggerated eaves and the wide variety of materials and styles used – thatch, stone slates, brick and timber – were in line with current thinking by the Picturesque school. Each cottage has a small garden and an outside seat on which the occupants could take their ease.

BLAKENEY
Norfolk

An important medieval port before the sea receded, leaving a shingle spit with sand dunes, Blakeney is now a nature reserve (NT*). A good natural harbour on the creek is surrounded by a pretty quayside village, containing a medieval guildhall with a fifteenth-century vaulted undercroft. The Red House, a distinguished eighteenth-century brick house with a pediment, stands by the quay. The flint church of St Nicholas has two towers, a large Perpendicular west tower and a smaller one by the chancel which may have been a beacon for the harbour. The Friary contains the remains of a Carmelite friary of 1296. There is a picturesque brick-and-flint windmill.

BLICKLING
Norfolk

This was an estate hamlet for Blickling Hall (NT*), the great Jacobean mansion built between 1616 and 1624 for Sir Henry Hobart. The cottages are mostly early nineteenth-century; the Buckinghamshire Arms (NT), a school, recently closed, and Blickling Lodge complete the scattered village. Weaver's Way runs through the village and into the park.

BODIAM
East Sussex

The castle (NT*) was built in 1385–7 to counter threats of French invasion, the French having burnt Rye in 1377 and Winchelsea in 1380. It is an example of an early fortified house contained within a curtain wall. It was restored in 1919 and given to the National Trust in 1926

by Lord Curzon of Kedleston. The village contains the Castle Inn (NT); a museum; Lord Curzon's former home Bodiam Manor, now a school; council houses, many of which were built for hop-pickers by Guinness, who owned the estate; and the station, shortly to be reopened, on a private line to Tenterden.

BOHETHERICK
Cornwall

A group of granite and slate-hung cottages overlooks a dramatic stretch of the River Tamar, close to Cotehele (NT*), the great medieval courtyard house built between 1485 and 1627. Many other estate buildings include the manorial water mill, in existence since the fifteenth century; the blacksmith's, carpenter's, wheelwright's and sadler's shops; and the cider mill. By the quayside are a group of warehouses, limekilns and a Gothic lodge to Cotehele.

BOSCASTLE
Cornwall

One of the few harbours on the treacherous north Cornish coast, Boscastle winds dramatically through a natural cleft of the precipitous cliffs at the mouth of the River Valency (NT). The inner jetty was rebuilt by Sir Richard Grenville in 1584; the outer jetty of c. 1820 was reconstructed in 1982 by the National Trust after damage by a wartime mine. In the eighteenth and nineteenth centuries the harbour supplied the area with slate, coal and wheat. Pretty quayside cottages and an old mill form the lower village. Steep terraces of old stone and whitewashed cottages with leaning stepped chimneys and crooked roofs climb to the upper village. Here stands Bottreaux Castle, with magnificent views of the cliffs, the harbour and Forrabury church on the clifftop.

BOSSINGTON
Somerset
(Holnicote Estate – NT)

The River Aller flows behind the village, but the leat to Porlock Marsh runs through it. The charming cottages, mostly cream-washed and thatched, are grouped along this channel. There is a pretty eighteenth-century farmhouse with a thatched

barn. It is an estate village at its best, and must be visited on foot to appreciate its special qualities. Above towers Bossington Hill, and below lies Bossington Beach.

BRADENHAM (NT)
Buckinghamshire

A 'green' village, Bradenham is backed by fine beech woods. The small, partly Norman flint church has an elaborately carved south door with dog-tooth moulding. The fine brick manor of 1670 with a hipped roof and formal gardens was once the home of Disraeli's father. Pretty flint and tile-hung cottages are grouped round the large green.

BRANDISH STREET
Somerset
see Holnicote Estate (NT)

BRANSCOMBE
Devon

Branscombe lies within the East Devon Heritage Coast and near the South Devon Coast Path, inland from Branscombe Mouth (NT) with its fine beach and superb views from the cliffs. One of Devon's largest villages, it contains an interesting farm, Great Seaside, with a massive chimney, and two medieval houses: Edge Barton, home of the Wadham family, founders of Wadham College, Oxford; and Church Living, of the sixteenth century and earlier, possibly a summer residence for Benedictine canons from Exeter, who founded the important church of St Winifred, one of the best in Devon. The large tower and the name are Norman. The fine east window was inserted by Bishop Neville in the mid-fifteenth century at the same time as the wagon roof. There are also a rare eighteenth-century three-decker pulpit, some box pews, and a Jacobean west gallery and screen. The village contains a thatched smithy (NT) and a bakery (NT), both working; many thatched cottages and farms; and Hole, a late-sixteenth-century house. Bovey House, now a hotel, also dates from the sixteenth century.

BREDON
Hereford and Worcester

Standing above the River Avon, the village is dominated by the delicate spire of St Giles. The church, partly Norman, contains splendid monuments. Bredon is also notable for the medieval tithe barn (NT*); one of the finest stone barns in England, it has porches and an upper room. The roof was recently restored after a fire. There are many timber-framed thatched cottages. The seventeenth-century brick Old Mansion, and the Manor House of the eighteenth century, are impressive. There are some unfortunate later additions.

BRETFORTON
Hereford and Worcester

The Fleece (NT) dates from the fourteenth century, a remarkable black-and-white timber-framed building with a heavy Cotswold stone slated roof. It has excellently preserved interiors. Several other black-and-white houses give a Worcestershire flavour to the village. There is a fine Jacobean Manor House. The church of St Leonard, once owned by Evesham Abbey, has unusual capitals. Some regrettable recent developments mar the village.

BROADCLYST
Devon
(Killerton Estate – NT)

The parish church of St John the Baptist is approached through a double lych gate. The tower, which forms a romantic feature in the Killerton landscape, has battlements and pinnacles, as do the aisles. The interior is high and light with tall piers, wagon roofs , and a fine monument to Sir John Acland, owner of the original Tudor house at Killerton, later rebuilt. The Acland almshouses group prettily with the old water conduit on the green; beyond lies the Red Lion (NT), and everywhere are whitewashed thatched cottages. Budlake, Beare and Westwood, also on the Killerton Estate, are small agricultural hamlets, consisting predominantly of cob and thatched cottages, with one or two substantial farmhouses.

BUCKLAND MONACHORUM
Devon

Buckland Abbey (NT*) nearby was founded by the Cistercians in 1278, acquired after the Reformation by Sir

Brownsea, with the castle pier on the right, and some of the embattled and gabled Gothick cottages of the attractive quayside village.

Brownsea (NT), Dorset

The densely wooded island of Brownsea, indented with white sandy beaches, lies dramatically in the middle of Poole harbour, commanding the entrance to the port. As one approaches by sea, the castle comes into view, surrounded by lawns and fine cedar trees, and beside it stretches the charming quayside village. The cottages, originally built for coastguards, are decorated with battlements, crow-stepped gables and armorial shields. Even the boat sheds are embellished, while the Gothick landing stage and pier, surmounted with octagonal battlemented turrets, form part of an architectural composition that never fails to delight. The castle is approached through a tiny battlemented gatehouse topped by a clock tower and cupola. Beyond lie the church, the peacocks, the nature reserve and the Scout Camp.

In about the sixth century AD the monks of Cerne Abbey founded a chapel on Brownsea dedicated to the patron saint of fishermen, St Andrew. Despite the Viking invasions, Brownsea continued in the ownership of Cerne Abbey, and a small religious community existed there until the reign of Henry VIII. Brownsea Island was fortified by Henry VIII to defend the entrance to the port of Poole from possible invasion by the French. A blockhouse, which forms the core of the present castle, was constructed in 1545 and extended in Elizabeth's reign to counter the Spanish threat.

During the following centuries Brownsea continued to control the movement of shipping in and out of Poole harbour, and the castle was garrisoned during the Civil War. The intrepid traveller Celia Fiennes paid a visit in the late seventeenth century: 'From thence by boate we went to a little Isle called Brownsea where there is ... only one house, which is the Governours, besides little fishermens houses, they being all taken up about the Copperice workes [copperas was obtained from stones and used for dyeing, tanning and making ink] ... This is a noted place for lobsters and crabs and shrimps, there I eate some very good.'

The castle itself was substantially rebuilt by Sir Humphrey Sturt of More Crichel, who bought the island in 1765. He heightened the central blockhouse to four storeys, built projecting wings with Venetian windows, brought much of the island into cultivation, laid out formal gardens with glasshouses, and formed two lakes. When in 1818 the Prince Regent visited the island, which by then was owned by Charles Sturt's son Henry, he declared that he 'had no idea there had been such a delightful spot in the kingdom'. By this time, deer were grazing on the lawns, and the castle was surrounded by a landscape park.

More serious work was also undertaken. In the late eighteenth century the island defences were improved to protect Poole from the unwelcome attentions of privateers and smugglers who infested the area. In addition the Preventive Service, later to become the Coastguard, established a station on the island, and built a Custom House near the castle. As the station grew, the existing village was built along the quayside to house the coastguards. By 1842 it was complete. The Chief Officer had a large house with a ten-gun battery in front of it. There was also an inn.

The island changed hands several times before being bought in 1852 by Colonel Waugh of the Indian Army. He employed Philip Brown, a local architect, to extend the castle. He built the gatehouse and the delightful family pier,

battlemented and pierced with arrow slits, and embellished the cottages to create an estate village in a picturesque style. He partly rebuilt the church, St Mary's, in 1853, adding to the existing thirteenth-century nave and chancel, and decorating the interior. Colonel Waugh also established a china clay works with a new pier at the west end of the island, served by a model village called Maryland after his wife Mary. The village was built in a crescent above the pottery. Waugh also developed a model farm complex. Unfortunately Brownsea clay turned out to be inadequate for the intended production of porcelain; Colonel Waugh became bankrupt, closed the works and sold the island. Only the castle and the quayside village survive as a record of this colourful history.

The next owner of Brownsea was George Cavendish-Bentinck, who bought the island in 1870. He and his wife lived in the vicarage which they named *The Villa*. He decorated the castle and the pier with marble armorial panels taken from Venetian palaces and imported several Italian wellheads, under one of which he and his wife are buried in the churchyard.

After another change of owner and a fire in the castle the island was bought in 1901 by Charles van Raalte and his wife, a colourful couple who furnished the castel lavishly. They employed a staff of thirty, with ten gardeners and a private band who played on the castle lawns in summer and in the great hall in winter. In 1907 Lord Baden-Powell established his Scout Camp behind the castle grounds.

Mrs Bonham-Christie acquired Brownsea in 1927, and refused permission to any visitor to land on the island. On one occasion she reputedly threw an unwelcome intruder into the sea! During her occupation the island became overgrown and the village ruinous and neglected. Only the birds and wild animals flourished; Brownsea is the only place in southern Britain where the red squirrel survives. Mrs Bonham-Christie's desire for solitude preserved Brownsea from the developments which would otherwise have occurred. When she died in 1961 the island came to the National Trust, accepted by the Treasury in lieu of death duties.

Brownsea in 1774, showing the castle enlarged to protect the busy approaches to Poole harbour. The Customs House and other buildings can be seen on the quayside.

Richard Grenville, and later bought by Sir Francis Drake in 1581; the monumental monastic tithe barn survives. Buckland Monachorum ('of the monks') lies in a wooded landscape, with stone cottages straddling the village street. The church has a high battlemented tower with pinnacles. Inside, the Drake aisle contains remarkable family monuments.

BUDLAKE
Devon
(Killerton Estate – NT)
see Broadclyst

BURNHAM OVERY
Norfolk

Once called Overy Town, Burnham Overy was a small port before the sea receded, and Overy Staithe was built. There is a well-preserved windmill with sails (NT).

BURWASH
East Sussex

Bateman's (NT*), Kipling's house, was built by a Sussex ironmaster of local stone in 1634. It has big mullioned-and-transomed windows, and gables with finials. The fine village street contains Rampydene, 1699, timber-framed with brick infill and a hipped roof; many attractive tile-hung and weatherboarded cottages; and the church of St Bartholomew, proudly placed with a Norman west tower. Here are a fourteenth-century iron tomb slab to John Collins, one of the many ironfounders in this area which was famous for its firebacks in the sixteenth century, and other tombs to local ironmasters.

BUSCOT (NT)
Oxfordshire

Buscot is a scattered village, the main street running down to a lock and weir on the Thames. The former lock-keeper's cottage (NT), dating from the seventeenth century, stands dramatically on the edge of the weir. The fine medieval church, with glass by Burne-Jones, has a graveyard surrounded on three sides by the river. Beside it stands the Old Parsonage (NT*) of 1700, a splendid William and Mary manor with a hipped roof. The Manor Farm of 1690 and several of the farms and cottages pre-date the building of neo-classical Buscot Park (NT*) in 1780. The estate passed in 1859 to an Australian, Robert Campbell, who industrialized the farm in an attempt to produce sugar beet and alcohol. A narrow-gauge railway ringed the estate, an extensive lake was dug in order to drain and irrigate the fields, a distillery and a gasworks were built, and in 1870 several pioneering concrete farm buildings were erected, one of which survives in the village. Steam engines pulled enormous six-furrow ploughs. The project failed, and when Campbell died in 1887, the estate was bought by Alexander Henderson MP, later Baron Faringdon. He commissioned Sir Ernest George, the distinguished country house architect, to extend and formalize the estate village. A group of semi-detached neo-Tudor cottages surround a village hall topped with a clock tower and cupola, and a charming little well house, all of local stone. Beyond, the earlier brick cottages line the village street. Harold Peto, George's partner, laid out the Italianate water gardens at Buscot Park in a formal Renaissance style and landscaped the lake.

C

CADGWITH,
Cornwall

In a dramatic valley setting, this classic Cornish fishing village has an active fishing fleet, the boats drawn up on a tiny beach, and fish cellars. Several stone and thatched fishermen's cottages line the Todden, the steep village street.

CAMBO
Northumberland

Developed as an estate village by the Blackett and Trevelyan families of Wallington (NT*) from 1740 onwards, and replacing the medieval village, Cambo stands on a hill above the house, with fine views over the surrounding moors and close to the site of the battle of Chevy Chase, immortalized in the famous Border Ballad. The post office occupies a much altered tower house. At the little school Lancelot (Capability) Brown, the landscape gardener, was educated. Front Row is a two-storey stone terrace, with charming gardens. There are two houses with porticos; one of these, a coaching inn, The Two Queens, was closed down by Sir Walter Trevelyan, a strict teetotaller. Front Row was built for estate workers in the 1740s by Sir Walter Calverley Blackett, who transformed the plain seventeenth-century house at Wallington into the Georgian mansion we see today. He employed Capability Brown to lay out the ornamental lake, and James Paine to design the bridge. He replanned the estate; enclosed fields; planted woods; and built roads, bridges and follies as well as the village school and smithy. The church, which overlooks the village, was designed for him in 1842 by J. and B. Green. He and his wife Pauline also commissioned John Dobson, the Newcastle architect, to roof over the central courtyard at Wallington, and Bell-Scott to decorate it. Sir Walter Trevelyan was succeeded by Sir Charles Edward Trevelyan, brother-in-law of Lord Macaulay, who in the late nineteenth century built North Row – a group of gabled houses overlooking the village green – the dolphin fountain, and the imposing church tower of 1883, which was intended to 'conform with the scale of Wallington'. He lies buried in the churchyard.

CANONS ASHBY
Northamptonshire

A flourishing medieval village of forty-one houses existed here in 1343, but by 1535 the Black Death and Tudor enclosures had reduced the village to nine tenants, much the same size as today. The manor house (NT*) was built in the 1550s, and was for many years home of the Dryden family. A fine medieval church (NT*) formerly belonged to the priory. Cottages of local ironstone flank the road.

CARTMEL
Cumbria

The old village is dominated by the great priory church of St Mary and St Michael, founded in 1190 by the Earl of Pembroke. The massive Norman columns are complemented by a magnificent fifteenth-century east window and a remarkable carved wooden screen and choir stalls. The church, and the priory gatehouse (NT*) of 1330, are all that remain of the Augustinian priory, dissolved at the Reformation. The gatehouse was used as a lock-up, then as a grammar school from 1624 to 1790, and is now a craft shop. The charming old village of traditional stone and roughcast houses is built around a small cobbled square, with a market cross in the centre. Many of the gardens back onto the Ea Brook running through the village. A milestone in the village records the distance to Ulverstone and Lancaster by the dangerous oversands route across Morecambe Bay, which was generally used until the arrival of the railway. Many lives were lost in the notorious quicksands. Cartmel racecourse lies just outside the village, and beyond is Holker Hall, home of the Cavendish family, dating from the sixteenth century but substantially and delightfully enlarged by Paley & Austin in the nineteenth century. There is an eighteenth-century landscape park, and formal gardens laid out by Joseph Paxton.

CHIDDINGSTONE
Kent

Anne Boleyn's family, who lived at Hever Castle nearby, also owned the village in the sixteenth century. An untouched group of sixteenth- and seventeenth-century timber-framed, jettied houses (NT) with bargeboarded gables and cat-slide roofs behind, includes the Castle Inn, with wood mullion windows and intricately-carved bargeboards and pendants. Opposite, making a perfect group, is the church of St Mary, much of it dating from the 1628 rebuilding after a fire. It has a fine Jacobean pulpit and font cover. The churchyard has cedars and a mausoleum of 1736 to the Streatfield family, originally local ironmasters. The Chiding Stone (NT), from which the village took its name, is a reminder that scolding wives received a sharp punishment there. There is a perfect early-eighteenth-century vicarage. On a hill stands the Gothick castle, rebuilt and castellated in 1805 by Atkinson.

CLARE
Suffolk

The remains of a Norman motte, erected to protect the Icknield Way on which the village stands, and a thirteenth-century shell keep survive. St Paul is a rich flint Suffolk wool church of the thirteenth, fourteenth and fifteenth centuries. The infirmary of the former priory still exists, and further monastic remains have been built into a seventeenth-century house. Some of the cob houses are decorated with pargeting. Priest's House, now a museum, is particularly fine. There are two interesting inns, the Globe and the Swan, and many attractive Georgian houses. Clare is a large village with an important history, and should be visited on foot.

CLOVELLY
Devon

Many of the Devon and Cornish fishing villages grew up in the sixteenth century, when fishing became a profitable pursuit. Clovelly is one of the most picturesque, owing to its position in a steep wooded cleft. Cobbled steps descend 400 feet to the sea, and many of the villagers transport their provisions on sledges or donkeys up this precipitous street. The little harbour at the bottom, surrounded by tiny slate-hung cottages, is unusually attractive. So are the clusters of old houses clinging to the steep hillside. The National Trust owns much of the surrounding land and the coastal footpath.

COLESHILL (NT)
Oxfordshire

The Manor of Coleshill was created by Edward the Confessor and given in 1086 to Winchester Abbey. Coleshill is an estate village of linear shape, sited on a hill near an ancient river crossing. Apart from the medieval church, post office and inn – the Radnor Arms – the whole village was rebuilt in stone between 1838 and 1860; and the gabled, semi-detached cottages with gardens surrounded by mature box hedges, are all neo-Tudor, with stone mullions, hood moulds and lattice windows. The great Renaissance house that once stood above the village, surrounded by a landscape park, was built in 1650 by Roger Pratt, but was demolished in 1956 after a disastrous fire; only the gate piers, the park, the Old Laundry and the dovecot survive as a poignant reminder of the house which still haunts the village by its absence. The model farm, built in 1852 by George Lamb for the Earl of Radnor, still exists and now contains workshops.

Coleshill, Oxfordshire. The great house once stood behind the trees on the right of the picture.

Corfe Castle, Dorset

The village of Corfe Castle, set in the rolling Purbeck hills, is dominated by the castle ruins (NT*), which are visible from every part of the village. Originally known as Corfe Gate, the village was already important in Saxon times, and became most prosperous in the thirteenth century with the demand for Purbeck 'marble', a dark limestone which could be polished. The 'marblers', or quarry owners, lived, and many had their stoneyards, in the village. Both Purbeck marble and the ordinary limestone were important products in the Middle Ages, and the marble industry and the royal castle made Corfe a prosperous place. Only one medieval house survives, in East Street, built in the late fifteenth century as a hall house, altered in the seventeenth century and with one room converted for use as a smithy in the nineteenth. Of the rest, the cottages date from the sixteenth and seventeenth centuries, reflecting a period of growth when Corfe Castle was made a borough in 1576. The small Georgian Town Hall (in West Street) is a survival from the era of parliamentary importance.

Most of the houses are, like the castle, built of Purbeck stone and form long terraces, punctuated by small passageways. The effect is largely medieval, an impression intensified by the survival of many stone mullions, reused Tudor arched doors, and worked stones incorporated as building material. Although few of the cottages in West Street deserve individual mention, the survival of thatch makes an interesting contrast to the undulations of the almost continuous roofline of large stone slates, enlivened by innumerable small dormers. West Street forms part of an estate village, whose preservation is very important.

The Fox Inn, although dated 1568, was rebuilt in the eighteenth century. It has a small panelled parlour, and

Corfe Castle: a view of the castle ruins, some village houses and their inhabitants in 1774.

none of the vulgarity that has ruined many historic inns.

East Street contains more individual buildings of interest, though it is less picturesque. The Bankes Arms Hotel of the 1920s is undistinguished, but has the traditional slate hanging and a columned porch extending over the pavement; Uvedale's House is Elizabethan, with mullion windows and hood moulds; Morton's House is an early seventeenth-century E-plan manor, with chamfered mullion windows; the almshouses are of the eighteenth century; and the school and schoolhouse are partly of 1834, the upper schoolroom now being used as a parish room.

The Market Square, overshadowed by the castle, is also notable for the market cross, some attractive stone cottages and the parish church of St Edward, King and Martyr. This stands prettily on a raised mound and is largely by T. H. Wyatt, 1860, although the fine west tower dates from the fifteenth century, and is an important feature in the townscape. The interior is surprisingly spacious, with tall, rather emaciated piers and severe detailing.

Opposite stands the Greyhound Hotel, adapted from two seventeenth-century cottages with additions including two columned porches, one with Tuscan columns, of 1733. The Greyhound now belongs to the National Trust.

The late-eighteenth-century ashlar Town House opposite has an unusual slate-hung bow with a round-headed window. It has also been acquired with much of Market Square by the National Trust.

The castle is sited strategically in a strongly defensive position, holding the defile through the steep Purbeck hills. The site first enters recorded history in 876 when King Alfred, in one of his many heroic actions against the Danish invaders, used it as a base. During the tenth century King Edgar enlarged and strengthened the position as his home, and from this time Corfe was interwoven with the royal history of England. The royal Norman castle at Corfe, on the site of the earlier Saxon building, was built to the orders of William the Conqueror. The walls enclosing the inner ward on the crown of the hill, and part of a hall with

*Corfe Castle today, with The Greyhound Hotel and its
1733 porch of Tuscan columns in the foreground.*

herringbone masonry date from this, the earliest surviving
period, when a wooden palisade would have surrounded
the outer bailey. The great keep, or King's Tower, perhaps
built by 1105, made the castle with its natural fortifications
virtually impregnable. King John, from 1201 onwards,
carried out a series of improvements to this, his favourite
residence. The gloriette was built, providing a courtyard
house with a hall, solar and undercroft, the vast outer ditch
excavated, the inner and outer bailey with gateways, walls
and a series of great towers were all constructed, and with
these additions the castle was finally fortified.

By 1572, after many changes of ownership, Queen
Elizabeth sold the castle to Sir Christopher Hatton, later
Lord Chancellor, for £4761, and in 1635 it was acquired by
Sir John Bankes, who as Attorney General frequently had
to be in attendance upon the king. During the Civil War
Lady Mary Bankes defended the castle alone for three
heroic years before being forced to surrender. Her son, Sir
Ralph, repossessed the family estates at the Restoration and
built Kingston Lacy House in 1663.

Before that, however, the Cromwellians had ordered the
total destruction of the castle; the contents were plundered
and removed, the foundations undermined and the entire
building blown up, hurling huge sections of the structure
into the valley below, where they still remain. Nevertheless,
Corfe Castle still overwhelms by its stupendous outline,
visible from miles away. In 1982 the National Trust
received Corfe Castle Estate, including the castle and fifty
cottages in the village, and Kingston Lacy Estate and house
from Mr H. J. R. Bankes, whose family had owned Corfe
for nearly 350 years. It was one of the richest bequests ever
made to the Trust.

COLTHOUSE
Cumbria

An important Quaker community
containing a famous seventeenth-
century Friends' Meeting House
(NT), Colthouse is a hamlet of
exceptionally unspoilt whitewashed
seventeenth- and eighteenth-century
farmhouses. The Wordsworth
brothers lodged here with Ann
Tyson and her family, while
attending Hawkshead Grammar
School; Wordsworth refers to this
happy period in *The Prelude*.

COUNTISBURY
Devon

This pretty village with farms and a
church overlooks the Lynmouth
valley, which descends dramatically
in a wooded gorge to the sea. Above,
on Wind Hill, lies Countisbury
Camp (NT), an Iron Age
earthwork. Much of the surrounding
land and cliffs is owned by the
National Trust.

CUSHENDUN
County Antrim

Cushendun means 'the end of the
brown river'. It is beautifully placed
in a wide bay at the foot of Glendun,
one of the most lovely of the
spectacular Glens of Antrim.
Although the plans for a new
harbour by John Rennie never
materialized, the little port is well
worth a visit. Until the building of
the Royal Military Road in 1833
Cushendun and the adjacent villages
were virtually inaccessible except by
sea, and maintained strong local
traditions. From the mid-nineteenth
century it became popular as a small
holiday resort; hence the group of
hotels. It contains two attractive
early-Victorian churches: St Patrick's
Roman Catholic church of 1865,
roughcast and cream-washed,
surrounded by old yew trees; and the
parish church of 1839, set in another
pretty churchyard. The architectural
interest of Cushendun stems from
Lord and Lady Glendun, who from
1912 commissioned Clough
Williams-Ellis to design first the
Square, laid out round a courtyard
garden; then Glenmona House, neo-
Regency, for themselves, and finally
Maud Cottages, a slate-hung row of
arcaded cottages. The views towards
the Mull of Kintyre are spectacular.

Glendun viaduct by Charles Lanyon, the Belfast architect, and the remarkable caves add a touch of drama. Much of the village was acquired by the National Trust in 1954.

D

DENT
Cumbria

Dent became a Statesman's village in 1429, when its affairs were run by twenty-four Statesmen, or owner-farmers, whose pews are still visible in the church. The old Grammar School in the churchyard was founded under James I. The cobbled streets lined by terraces of small stone cottages, many backing directly on to the churchyard, are amazingly picturesque. Known originally as Dent Town, it had a self-supporting community of 2000 in the eighteenth century, with workshops, knitting galleries and marble quarrying. It is also famous as the home of Adam Sedgwick, the great geologist, born in the Old Vicarage in 1785. The contrast between the tightly packed village and the wild fells beyond give it a special character. The River Dee is crossed by two eighteenth-century bridges.

DINTON
Wiltshire

This downland village contains St Mary, a substantial Decorated church, and Philipps House (NT*), built by Sir Jeffry Wyatville in 1814–17, a handsome nine-bay ashlar house with a giant portico and an interesting stair, set in a landscape park. Hyde's House (NT), the former rectory, is a pedimented five-bay house with fluted columns, the main front eighteenth-century, the rear and the dovecote sixteenth-century or earlier. Lawes Cottage (NT) of the seventeenth century was once the home of the composer Henry Lawes (1596–1662). There are several more houses of interest, some with stone mullions. Wick Ball Camp, an Iron Age hill fort, is half a mile from the village.

Dunster, Somerset. The priory church of St George was originally part of the Benedictine Abbey.

DUNSTER
Somerset

Dunster Castle (NT*), home of the Luttrell family for six hundred years, was remodelled by Anthony Salvin in the nineteenth century, and given to the National Trust in 1976. Superbly sited on a wooded hill overlooking the village and sea, it is set in gardens filled with semi-tropical plants. The ancient village, with stone and timber-framed cottages lining the main street, is dominated by the castle and by Exmoor beyond. In the centre of the market square is the Yarn Market, an octagonal building dating from 1589 with a stone-slated roof and dormers, the structure supported by columns. The Luttrell Arms, opposite, was originally the residence of the abbots of Cleeve. A timber-framed wing dates from c. 1500; the main front was altered in 1622; it has been an inn since 1651. The Nunnery, a fourteenth-century timber-framed and slate-hung house, stands near the churchyard. The large church of St George was built as the priory church of the Benedictine abbey of Dunster in the eleventh century, of red sandstone, and was restored by G. E. Street in 1875. It has an interesting interior with magnificent screens and some fine Luttrell monuments. Of the priory, only a circular dovecote and a sixteenth-century barn remain. On the outskirts of the village are a working mill (NT) and Grabbist Hill (NT) above the village, with magnificent views to the Quantocks and Exmoor.

DURGAN
Cornwall

A beautiful little port with views over the Helford River, Durgan lies below Glendurgan Garden (NT*). An old school, whitewashed fishermen's cottages and boat-building sheds cluster in this steep valley. An old packhorse track leads up the hill.

E

ELMLEY CASTLE
Hereford and Worcester

Lying under Bredon Hill, the village was named after the medieval castle, now disappeared. The wide streets of black-and-white timber-framed houses are handsome, and a good example of this regional style. They are interspersed with a few brick houses and several inns, particularly the Queen Elizabeth. The fine church contains some early pews and an outstanding alabaster monument to the Savage family.

F

FELBRIGG
Norfolk

Where in medieval times the village once stood, there now remains only a fine fifteenth-century church, isolated amid ploughed fields on one hand and the parkland of Felbrigg Hall (NT*) on the other. The Weavers' Way leads through the churchyard and forms the one link with the modern hamlet half a mile away, clustered round a small green. The church displays Norfolk flint or 'flush' work at its best. Inside there are fine brasses, inscribed in Norman French, of the original Felbrigg ancestors and more recent memorials to the Windhams who lived at the Hall. One of these is carved by Grinling Gibbons and another by Nollekens. Humphry Repton lived at nearby Sustead but did not work in the park, his only contact with the Windhams being the borrowing of books from their exceptional library.

FLATFORD
Suffolk

Flatford Mill (NT), immortalized in Constable paintings, belonged to John Constable's father. The mill, a rambling brick building dating from the fifteenth century, makes a beautiful group with adjoining mill houses reflected in the mill pool. They, with Willy Lott's Cottage (NT) of the seventeenth century, also painted by Constable, and the Valley Farm (NT), a half-timbered fifteenth-century building, are let to the Field Studies Council.

FOXTON
Cambridgeshire

The village was made famous by Rowland Parker's *The Common Stream*. The stream has retreated to a trickle. The cottages lining the village street are typical of many East Anglian villages. Much of it was rebuilt in the sixteenth century. The fourteenth-century church was built by Thomas de Foxton.

G

GANLLWYD
Gwynedd

This is an attractive village of stone cottages, with a chapel and a hotel (NT), environmentally damaged by road widening. It is surrounded by spectacular mountain scenery, with Rhaiadr Ddu (NT), one of the grandest waterfalls in Wales, a quarter of a mile west of the village hall.

GOUDHURST
Kent

A famous hilltop village in the high weald, Goudhurst has clusters of tile-hung and weatherboarded houses in picturesque groups, crowned by the large aisled church of St Mary. With its tower and chancel of 1638, the church is a mixture of Gothic and classical. It contains the important seventeenth-century tomb of Culpeper, the famous herbalist. Church House is a fine sixteenth-century timber-framed house with an overhang and hipped roof; and among many others of interest, the Star and Eagle is a fifteenth-century timber-framed inn.

GRASMERE
Cumbria

Grasmere is famous as the home of Wordsworth, who lived in Dove Cottage for the most creative years of his life, and as his resting place in death. He lies with his wife Mary, his beloved sister Dorothy and his daughter Dora in the churchyard of St Oswald, on the banks of the River Rothay. Opposite is Church Stile (NT), an ancient sixteenth-century building, once an inn. Allan Bank (NT) was also for a time Wordsworth's home. The setting of

Grasmere, dominated by Helm Crag and backed by Grasmere Tarn and Rydal Water, is very beautiful; Wordsworth described it as 'the loveliest spot that man has ever found'. Despite many later additions and much tourist activity, the village, mostly built of local stone, still retains much character. The Swan Inn, an old coaching inn on the road to Dunmail Raise, remains little changed. Behind Dove Cottage is an excellent Wordsworth Museum.

GREAT TEW
Oxfordshire

This estate village became notorious for the dilapidated condition of many of the cottages, now being restored. Lord Falkland built the original cottages in the seventeenth century, and the Falkland Arms is a reminder of this period. J. C. Loudon developed the village, the great house and the park in 1808 to demonstrate his theories on agriculture and planning, maintaining that well-kept cottages with pretty gardens were an enhancement to the big house. In 1820 Thomas Rickman added porches and rustic features for Matthew Boulton, the new owner. The fine fourteenth-century church stands above the village, and contains some interesting monuments. This is a rare place.

GROOMBRIDGE
Kent

This neat, estate village contains the Dower House, a seventeenth-century, brick, hipped-roof building, a triangular green and The Walks, a row of eighteenth-century red-and-blue brick tile-hung cottages lying behind pollarded limes. Ashurst Hill has further rows of cottages and Court Lodge, a half-timbered building removed here from Udimore, Sussex, and rebuilt with additions in 1912. Hillside, up the hill, is a small, brick, tile-hung house with half-timbered gables built in 1871 by Norman Shaw in his vernacular-revival style. The church of St John the Evangelist was enlarged in 1818 from a brick chapel built by John Packer in 1625 and contains monuments to the Packer family who lived in the big house, Groombridge Place. This was built some time between 1652 and 1674 by

Philip Packer and is one of the best and least altered houses of this date in the country. Surrounded by an earlier moat, it is an 'H'-plan, hipped-roof brick house with a sandstone loggia of Ionic columns. John Evelyn advised on the garden layout.

H

HAMBLEDON
Surrey

The scattered village includes Glebe House (NT), an imposing gabled manor built in 1710 of local stone, and seven traditional cottages belonging to the National Trust. The church of St Peter, mainly rebuilt in 1846, has a wooden-shingled bell cote. It makes an attractive group with the Old Granary and Court Farm. Malthouse Farm and its cottage, and School Cottage, are probably of the seventeenth century. Hydon's Ball (NT) stands prominently on the summit of Hydon Heath, at an altitude of 593 feet, with distant views to the North and South Downs. It was acquired as a fitting memorial to Octavia Hill, co-founder of the National Trust, who fought so hard to save the viewpoints on the North Downs.

HARDWICK IN CLUMBER (NT)
Nottinghamshire

Clumber Park (NT*) was landscaped in the late eighteenth century by the Duke of Newcastle on heath land bordering Sherwood Forest. The house, designed by Stephen Wright in the eighteenth century, was demolished, but his classical bridge and two temples survive, with the stables, the ornamental lake and the pleasure gardens. The village of terraced brick cottages lies within the park. The choir school for the private church is now closed. The late-nineteenth-century Gothic church, designed by G. F. Bodley, is an important example of his work and contains some outstanding late Victorian furnishings and decoration.

HAWKSHEAD
Cumbria

Hawkshead owes its present fame to William Wordsworth, for it was here, as he describes in *The Prelude*,

that his poetic imagination was fired. The school he attended from 1779 remains substantially unaltered. He and his three brothers boarded with Ann Tyson, whose cottage can still be seen. St Michael's, the parish church, which Wordsworth described as 'snow white, like a throned lady', dates from the sixteenth to the mid-seventeenth century. Roughly inscribed Bible quotations decorate the whitewashed walls of the nave. The sixteenth-century Courthouse (NT*) is the only surviving fragment of Hawkshead Hall, formerly owned by Furness Abbey, whose estates were managed from the Hall. Furness, on Morecambe Bay, was rich in iron ore, much of which was transported by the monks into the heavily wooded area of Hawkshead to be smelted. Charcoal-burners lived in huts and worked in the woods until the last gunpowder works in the area was closed in 1937. Hawkshead owed much of its prosperity to the wool trade which flourished, with Kendal as its centre, from the fourteenth to the early nineteenth century. During the seventeenth and eighteenth centuries, the jettied galleries were used for spinning and the display of yarn and cloth on market days. The market place is still the centre of the village, dominated by the arcaded Market House or Town Hall of 1790, built on the site of the Shambles, where butchers once

had their stalls. In the seventeenth century many of the houses had spinning galleries. Of these only the reconstructed gallery at Pillar Cottage exists today. A number of houses are jettied, indicating a timber-framed construction, rare in the Lake District. Despite the many tourists, much of the original character remains: the flagged yards, the clustered cottages, the cylindrical chimneys topped by slates, even Tabitha Twitchett's house. The Beatrix Potter gallery in the square shows some of her original drawings.

HEBDEN BRIDGE
West Yorkshire

As water-powered machines came in, the home-based weaving industry of Heptonstall, above Hebden Bridge, was replaced here by mills spinning cotton and wool, powered by Hebden Water. Steam power arrived in Hebden Bridge around 1800, and new mills grew up beside the Rochdale Canal nearby and alongside the railway. Beside the mills stand terraces of workers' housing, stepped dramatically up the steep hillside. Once there were rows of chimneys belching black smoke into the soot-laden air; today, many of the mills stand deserted.

HEMINGFORD GREY
Cambridgeshire

Hemingford Grey's two main claims

Hawkshead, Cumbria: one of the many enclosed yards in the village.

to fame are that it contains reputedly the earliest inhabited house in England, of 1160, and that the top half of the spire of the church blew off in a storm in 1741 and still lies in the River Ouse below. The octagonal stump was topped with eight stone balls to finish it off. The Norman manor, one of the finest medieval houses in England, is built of Northamptonshire limestone and has two storeys, a ground-floor store and two upper rooms, originally approached by an outside stair. Much of the village overlooks the river and its water meadows, and contains both beautiful timber-framed houses, and pretty eighteenth-century brick ones. There is an attractive mill (NT) nearby. This is a lovely spot.

HEPTONSTALL
West Yorkshire

The village, largely built of local gritstone, stands dramatically above the Calder valley. It was settled in the medieval period by weavers, the wool being brought across the moors on packhorses. Most of the existing weavers' houses are of the eighteenth century and contain long mullioned windows to light the weaving attics. Buttress Path is a steep paved packhorse track leading down to Hebden Bridge in the valley. The old bridge across the Hebden Water was built *c.* 1510.

HIDCOTE BARTRIM
Gloucestershire

This village is grouped round a seventeenth-century stone manor with famous gardens (NT*) created over forty years by Major Lawrence Johnston, who gave it to the National Trust in 1948. It is a pretty hamlet of Cotswold stone cottages, thatched, with small cottage gardens and ancient cedars. A duckpond completes the picture.

THE HOLNICOTE ESTATE (NT)
Somerset

The Holnicote Estate includes nine villages, which, together with 12,443 acres encompassing Dunkery and Selworthy Beacons and over 6000 acres of Exmoor, were given to the National Trust by Sir Richard Acland in 1944. The protection of the Acland family and of the National Trust has preserved the traditional character of the villages, which have changed very little over the past one hundred years. The various groupings of houses along river valleys, with packhorse bridges, farms and the wild moorland beyond, make them exceptionally picturesque, and the sea and cliffs, which are never far away, add a further dimension. Brandish Street, Tivington and West Luccombe have delightful groups of cream-washed thatched cottages, while Horner contains small stone cottages with prominent chimneys, and two packhorse bridges; it also has magnificent views of Dunkery Beacon. Near Brandish Street is Piles Mill (NT), a working cornmill and museum. The other villages in the estate – Allerford, Bossington, Luccombe, Lynch and Selworthy – are covered in separate entries.

HOLY ISLAND
Northumberland

The outline of Lindisfarne, the castle (NT*) perched on its precipitous rock, is visible for many miles along the Northumbrian coast. It is only when approaching across the causeway, exposed at low tide, that Holy Island itself becomes visible, and still later, the superb priory ruins. It was from Lindisfarne that St Aidan brought Christianity to northern England, here that St Cuthbert lived and died, and here that the Lindisfarne Gospels, one of the glories of Celtic art, were inscribed. Today the fishermen's cottages, small and stone-built, many with single storeys and red pantile roofs, and some grouped round a small green, give the village its character, though some intrusive bungalows are making their appearance. There are two small hotels, inns frequented by local fishermen, a lifeboat station and some old stone fish stores, now converted, near the little harbour. Upturned boats used as fishermen's huts are grouped around the bay. Fishing is still the local industry. The castle of Lindisfarne, built as a blockhouse during the reign of Henry VIII, was bought in a ruinous state by Edward Hudson in 1902, and brilliantly adapted by Edwin Lutyens. Few concessions were made to comfort, but the building is

Luccombe, Somerset (see p.171) a typical Holnicote estate village.

handled with Lutyens' usual skill and eye for detail. To experience the isolation of Holy Island one has to wait for the high tide to expel the tourists. Then the sound of the sea birds and the roar of the wind takes over.

HORNER
Somerset
see (Holnicote Estate – NT)

I

IGHTHAM
Kent

Fine timber-framed medieval houses, including the gabled Town House of 1555, cluster round the square, with the sixteenth-century George and Dragon and Skynners House nearby. The Rusty stream runs through the village, which has modest brick and tile-hung cottages. The church has a monument to Sir Thomas Cawne, 1374, builder of Ightham Mote (NT*), and monuments to the Selby family, who lived there from the seventeenth to the twentieth century.

Ightham Mote, one of the least altered moated manors in the country, seems almost too good to be true, nestling in the valley, sheltered by great trees. The great hall, solar and chapel are spectacular. Oldbury Hill, an Iron Age camp, lies outside the village.

ILAM
Staffordshire

The village was built from 1821 by a wealthy industrialist, Jesse Watts-Russell. It is picturesquely sited on the banks of the Manifold River. The Hall (NT) of 1821 is now a Youth Hostel and a National Trust shop. The model cottages were built in the form of *cottages ornés*, half-timbered and tile-hung with decorative bargeboards. Russell placed an Eleanor Cross in the village center in memory of his wife. A model school and a chapel restored by Sir George Gilbert Scott complete the estate village, which is now surrounded by a country park.

K

KEARNEY
County Down

The position of Kearney, on the furthest point of the Ards peninsula, is magnificent: a cluster of whitewashed cottages dotted along the rocky shore, surrounded on three sides by the sea, with one of the most remarkable views in the British Isles. Kearney today looks well cared for, but it was not always so. Together with Knockinelder Bay to the south it was bought by the National Trust in 1965, thus saving two miles of this wonderful coast. At its peak in 1836 Kearney had three windmills, a school and 236 acres of land divided between eleven farming families. The main occupation for the villagers besides farming was fishing, gathering kelp and spinning yarn. An illicit trade was also carried on plundering wrecks on a coast that was described as the most dangerous on the east coast of Ireland. One of the largest, longest-lived and most colourful of Kearney's inhabitants was Big Mary Ann Donnan, born in 1841; her house still stands. She was 6 feet tall and the skipper of a boat known as the *She Cruiser*, crewed entirely by women, and used mainly

for fishing, although it also acted as a lifeboat when there were wrecks. Mary Ann also served as the village midwife, prepared corpses for burial and told endless stories, becoming a legend in her own lifetime. There were 1160 inhabitants when she was born, but in 1940 when she died aged 99, the village was almost deserted and many of the houses were semi-derelict.

KELD
Cumbria

A remote limestone hamlet near Shap summit, not far from Shap Abbey, Keld has a cluster of seventeenth-century farmhouses and a tiny sixteenth-century chapel (NT*), remarkable for its unrestored condition. Beyond stretch the wild moors. This is a bleak spot.

L

LACOCK
Wiltshire
see pp. 172–173

LAVENHAM
Suffolk

Lavenham was settled by Flemish weavers in the fourteenth century. As wool technology developed in the fifteenth century, the entire village was gradually rebuilt in a style more appropriate to its new prosperity: fine timbered cloth halls, the Woolstaplers and Swan Inn, both of the fifteenth century, the magnificent houses of the merchant clothiers, the splendid church, the Guildhall of Corpus Christi of 1535 (NT*), and even the weavers' cottages have remained virtually intact to this day. The Spring family, rich clothiers, and the Earl of Oxford subsidized the magnificent church, St Peter and St Paul, built in 1495 of limestone and flint, and the unusually tall west tower of knapped flint. With other master clothiers the Spring family controlled the cloth trade from the Guildhall. When Lavenham's prosperity declined it reverted to agriculture and was spared the rebuilding of many wool towns which became industrialized. An astonishing number of leaning gables, jetties, and Tudor shop fronts survive.

LODE
Cambridgeshire

A Fenland estate village for Anglesey Abbey (NT*), Lode has white brick and thatched cottages and a water mill (NT*) on the Lode, or canal, with an ancient wooden sluice gate. There is direct access by canal to Wicken Fen (NT*).

LONG CRENDON
Buckinghamshire

Long Crendon's medieval prosperity was based on wool. Lace-and needle-making begun in 1558, and continued as cottage industries until the nineteenth century. The fourteenth-century Courthouse (NT*) is a very early acquisition by the National Trust made in 1900, four years after the first, the Alfriston Clergy House. A jettied timber-framed building with brick cladding, the Courthouse was probably built as a wool store, then known as a staple hall. The huge single space above was used for manorial courts by stewards of Queen Catherine, wife of Henry V, who owned the Manor. It later became a meeting place for scholars of All Souls College, Oxford. Today the lower rooms are let. The Manor House, built round a courtyard in the fifteenth century, is remarkable: stone and timber-framed with a stone gatehouse. The church of St Mary has a big Perpendicular tower added by John Cannon, whose monument lies inside. Otherwise, Long Crendon has a notable series of early thatched and timber-framed cottages which are well worth a visit. The ruins of Notley Abbey, with the abbot's lodging and a fourteenth-century dovecot, lie just outside the village.

LONG MELFORD
Suffolk

A wool village, Long Melford was settled by Flemish weavers in the fourteenth century. A Roman road runs through it and has become the long main street, off which the large green opens and also the grounds of Melford Hall (NT*). As well as the Trinity Hospital, originally the almshouses, and the Bull Inn of 1450, containing remarkable carvings, there are delightful eighteenth-century houses lining the road. Melford Hall was built as a Tudor

Long Melford, Suffolk. Trinity Hospital stands before the fine flint tower of Holy Trinity Church.

courtyard house with prominent corner turrets and large mullion windows, by William Cordell, later Speaker of the House of Commons, whose important monument is in the church. The gardens contain a rare Tudor pavilion. Melford Manor, also owned by William Cordell, was originally built and owned by the abbots of Bury St Edmunds Abbey. The Cloptons, a wealthy wool family, owned the moated Kentwell Hall, also turreted like Melford Hall, and endowed the superb church of Holy Trinity, which is filled with their monuments and is a fine example of knapped flint work.

LOW NEWTON-BY-THE-SEA
Northumberland

This is a planned Northumbrian fishing village built in the early nineteenth century, with an earlier group of former coastguards' cottages and extensive farm buildings. Small whitewashed stone cottages with slate roofs group prettily round a square (NT), with an inn and a slipway to the sandy beach. There is an attractive bay with fishing boats.

LUCCOMBE
Somerset
(Holnicote Estate – NT)

Luccombe, through which a

tributary of the Aller flows, is one of the prettiest villages on the Holnicote Estate. Its cottages are mostly of cream-washed cob with uneven thatched roofs and wide eaves; one contains the little post office. They cluster round the large churchyard, dominated by the church of St Mary on the hill, with its Perpendicular, battlemented west tower. The interior is high and light with tall piers topped with bands of finely carved foliage, a wagon roof decorated with large bosses, and carved wall plates. The village cross stands in the churchyard, and the ancient rectory lies concealed within its garden walls. Beyond is Exmoor.

LYNCH
Somerset
(Holnicote Estate – NT)

Lynch is tiny, tucked in below North Hill with its great trees. Scattered up the steep village street are some interesting farm buildings, thatched cottages and a large stone manor. In a field below lies a small sixteenth-century chapel, used for years as a barn and restored in 1885. The unusually large east window with three lights, a wagon roof and panelled dado and the seventeenth-century balusters along the west gallery give it much charm, and its isolated position is delightful.

M

MALHAM
North Yorkshire

Once important as the site of two monastic granges owned by Fountains and Bolton Abbeys, from which their sheep runs were managed, Malham still contains relics of this period. Moon's Bridge, an ancient clapper bridge (constructed of limestone slabs), is named after Prior Moon, who was the last prior of Bolton Abbey before the Dissolution and was responsible for much of the abbey's rebuilding in the sixteenth century. Malham was important during the droving period, when sales of Scottish cattle were held there, and Great Close (NT) above was used for grazing to fatten the animals after their long journey. Today the village contains a National Park Information Centre, a number of fine seventeenth- and eighteenth-century farmhouses, the seventeenth-century Reading Room on the site of a monastic grange and, above, a remarkable network of dry-stone walls, some of Saxon and Norman origin, some even earlier. The Pennine Way intersects the village, heading north over Malham Cove, a spectacular limestone circle. Above the Cove lie the 4168 acres of the Malham Tarn Estate (NT), including the Tarn itself, Tarn House (let to the Field Studies Council), and several traditional farmsteads.

MARPLE
Greater Manchester

Once a rural textile community, this site of cottage industry was overtaken by mechanization with the arrival of the canals. The Peak Forest and the Macclesfield Canals meet in Marple, and it takes its character from these. Like Samuel Greg at Styal (see p. 182) Samuel Oldknow, a cotton magnate, built large mills; he also developed the Peak Forest Canal to provide transport for his works. At Marple a rare snake bridge, designed to enable horses towing canal boats to cross the canal from side to side without untying the towrope, and a horse tunnel to take the horses under the road, are both preserved. So is the splendid aqueduct, opened in 1800, which

A photograph of Lacock in c.1842 by Fox Talbot, showing High Street unmade up, with the Red Lion on the left and the medieval Chamberlain's House on the right.

Lacock (NT), Wiltshire

Lacock, whose name comes from *lacuc*, Anglo-Saxon for 'little river', has been occupied for over two thousand years. An Iron Age fort and a Roman road close-by testify to its early settlement. The Saxons settled along the banks of the Bide, or Bye, Brook and laid the bones of the present village, but Lacock first became important after the Norman Conquest, when the church of St Cyriac, a rare Norman dedication, was first built. Domesday Book records that the manor, with mills, a vineyard and woods, belonged to Edward of Salisbury, the son of one of William the Conqueror's knights, and King William visited Lacock with his court in 1086, shortly before his final return to France.

Lacock village is a planned medieval estate village built by the Abbey of Lacock for its employees. Although many of the cottages have been considerably altered, the layout and character has remained little changed since the fifteenth century. Of the two rivers that border it, the Avon is crossed by the remarkable medieval Lacock Bridge and a raised stone causeway, and the Bide Brook by the double-arched Town or Ladd's Bridge and by Dummer's Bridge, a small eighteenth-century packhorse bridge, partially rebuilt after a flood.

The village is laid out on a grid plan, with uneven terraces of cottages, each on its narrow medieval plot, topped with stone-slated roofs and irregular dormers. Early timber-framed houses, often jettied to accommodate the looms of the weavers on the first floor, are mixed with a remarkable assortment of stone cottages, many with mullioned windows, hood moulds and medieval carving. Of the timber-framed houses, the medieval Chamberlain's House in East Street, dating back to the monastic period, and the Angel Inn in Church Street, built in 1480 and named after a contemporary gold coin, are the most distinguished. The Angel has a fine medieval doorway, a horse passage to enable visitors to stable their horses in the yard behind, some medieval panelling and early fireplaces. Nearby is an early fourteenth-century cruck house.

Church Street, the original site of the market, also contains the thirteenth-century King John's Hunting Lodge, with a cruck frame and a fourteenth-century traceried window, and No. 8 has an early-fourteenth-century doorway. Both East and West Streets have delightful rows of seventeenth-century stone cottages, some with fragments of earlier buildings incorporated. The great fourteenth-century monastic tithe barn in East Street, one of the most distinguished buildings in Lacock, has eight bays with cruck trusses. The other sixteenth-century barn at the abbey gates now houses a museum commemorating William Henry Fox Talbot, one of the pioneers of photography, who lived at the abbey and carried out much of his research there, leaving a unique photographic record of the village at that date. Cantax House and the Red Lion Hotel, both of brick, date from the eighteenth century, as does the Congregational Church of 1783. A raised walk-way, The Brash, rounds the corner of Church Street, lined with a curved terrace of early stone houses. It was once the site of the village pump. Many of the houses have retained their wrought-iron lamp holders and foot scrapers.

The Old Smithy in West Street is now the bus shelter, while the George Inn next door still has a dog-powered spit and some early panelling. High Street contains several important timber-framed buildings, some attractive stone cottages and the school, partly of 1824, with later additions by John Prichard. In front stands the nineteenth-century village cross on a medieval base. This was the site of the market after its removal from Church Street.

The church of St Cyriac, built largely in the fifteenth century, is remarkably grand, as befits a prosperous wool church; both north and south aisles were paid for by local clothiers. Its graceful sixteenth-century spire dominates the village. Battlements, pinnacles and gargoyles embellish the north aisle, while built into the south transept is a three-storeyed seventeenth-century house, now the vestry. This is a rare survival in England, although common enough on the Continent. The splendid interior, tall and light, has clerestory windows and a wagon roof. The north-east chapel of 1430 is dominated by Sir William Sharington's magnificent Renaissance monument of 1566.

The abbey (NT*) stands in its own landscape park beside the Avon. It was founded in 1232 by Ela, Countess of Salisbury, who also founded a weekly market and a fair at St Thomas's Tide, which continues to this day. This, and the quality of the wool produced by the downland sheep, made Lacock both rich and famous. The Cloth Road, on which Lacock lies, linked the centres of the wool trade in the West Country for over six hundred years. The inns, with their horse passages and stables, are a survival from this period.

The abbey itself was rich enough to escape the 1536 Act for the Suppression of Small Monasteries, but in 1539 it became one of the 800 monasteries and nunneries to be dissolved by Henry VIII. The consequent destruction was only curtailed when, as in the case of Lacock, a purchaser could be found for the monastic buildings. If a new owner could be found he had, as a condition of sale, to destroy all those buildings he did not require for his own use, to prevent the homeless monks from returning.

Sir William Sharington bought the abbey buildings and land in 1539 for £783. Subsequently he was arrested for suspected dishonesty while Vice-Treasurer of the Bristol Mint, but was released. His property was confiscated, but he was later able to buy it back again on payment of £8000. He set about transforming the abbey buildings. The church was demolished, only the north wall surviving to form the south wall of the house. The cloister, sacristy, chapter house and monastic living quarters were incorporated into the new house. Sharington added the beautiful octagonal tower and the fine range of stables, and a brewery. Sharington's great hall was again transformed in 1754 by Sanderson Miller. To Sharington we owe the survival of much of the original fabric, with the addition of his own early Renaissance detailing; to Sanderson Miller we owe the embellishment of the Gothic facade with some delightful Gothick ornament. Sharington's niece married a Talbot, and the abbey has descended through the Talbot family since then.

In 1713 the Cloth Road had become turnpiked, and in 1745 a new road was opened which by-passed Lacock. This led to the gradual decline of the village. At this time, too, the centre of the wool trade moved from the West Country to the north. Lacock saw a brief period of relative prosperity when a branch of the Kennet and Avon Canal was opened in 1810. Constructed to transport stone from the Corsham quarries to London, it passed through the village, and for a short time created employment. It was abandoned in 1914 and has since been filled in

The Tanyard and drying loft, founded in the early nineteenth century, continued to be used for drying skins until this century, but the great days of Lacock were over. The workhouse built in the 1830s, and the lock-up dating from the eighteenth century, are reminders that life in Lacock was not always peaceful. However, the inns, of which the Angel and the George are the oldest, still thrive and the school, founded by the Talbot family in 1824, is still open.

Church Street, Lacock. The Sign of the Angel Inn on the right dates from 1480 and the cruck house at the end of the street, is 14th-century.

takes the canal over the valley of the River Goyt and on towards Manchester, and the flight of locks that leads to it. Oldknow also built the set of limekilns near the junction of the canals.

MELLOR
Greater Manchester

An upland farming community supported by an active domestic textile industry, Mellor has continued as a scattered rural community and avoided the expansion and mechanization that overtook its neighbour Marple. As Marple expanded, so the weaving activity in Mellor declined.

MONTACUTE
Somerset

The name derives from *mons acutus*, – the 'pointed hill', known as St Michael's Hill, which dominates the village. The honey-coloured Ham stone with which most of the village is built comes from Ham Hill nearby. Montacute House (NT*), begun in 1588 by William Arnold for Sir Edward Phelips, Speaker of the House of Commons, and twenty-four cottages were given to the National Trust in 1931 by Ernest Cook through the Society for the Protection of Ancient Buildings. The great Elizabethan H-shaped house is secluded from the village, hidden by high walls and yew hedges. Abbey Farm contains the gatehouse of the Cluniac priory of Montacute, founded by the half-brother of William the Conqueror in 1102. Much of the surviving fabric was built in 1514. The Chantry in the Borough contains the arms of Robert Sherborne, prior in 1532. By the fourteenth century Montacute had an important market, a fair, a guildhall and a shambles (a row of covered stalls), and was a centre for textiles and leather goods, quarrying, and a staging post on the route to Devon and Cornwall. Bishopton, Middle and South Street, and the Borough all contain seventeenth-century houses of Ham stone with stone mullions, some with stone slated roofs, some with thatch. St Catherine's church, also of Ham stone, has a magnificent Somerset west tower; inside are some splendid Phelips monuments. This is a

remarkably homogeneous estate village, with a good inn and few later intrusions.

MORWENSTOW
Cornwall

A small agricultural village in a wooded coombe near the clifftop, Morwenstow has a superb Norman church richly decorated with zig-zag designs and crude heads on the south porch, and remarkable Norman capitals, arches and spandrels inside, all carved in crisp Cornish granite. The graveyard contains a ship's figurehead, and graves of sailors lost on the *Caledonia*, wrecked here in 1843. The vicarage was built by Robert Hawker, the vicar-poet, in the nineteenth century, the chimneys imitating the towers of churches with which he had been connected. A hut (NT*), in which he wrote, sits on the cliff edge.

MOTTISFONT
Hampshire

This is the estate village to Mottisfont Abbey (NT*), a twelfth-century Augustinian priory, adapted after the Reformation to domestic use and extended during the eighteenth century in brick. There is a fine park with great trees and a chalk stream. The village contains attractive cob and thatch cottages and the church of St Andrew, with a weatherboarded bell turret and some fifteenth-century stained glass.

MOTTISTONE
Isle of Wight, Hampshire

The small village, of ancient origin, is set around a green, and has an interesting church. The romantic stone manor house (NT), dated 1559, lay buried for two hundred years by a landslide. It was dug out and restored in 1926 by Lord Mottistone. A fine house, with a classical façade, it is attractively tucked under Mottistone Down.

MUCHELNEY
Somerset

The Priest's House (NT*), originally used by priests serving the parish church, is an unusual two-storey thatched cottage dating from the fourteenth century. It was once a hall house, and has a large Gothic four-

light mullion-and-transom window. Muchelney Abbey, of which a surprising amount survives, was a Benedictine foundation sited on an eminence above the surrounding marsh; Muchelney means 'the big island'. The abbey was founded by Athelstan in 939. Much of the surviving fabric is of the early sixteenth century. Next to it is the parish church, embattled, with a prominent tower and pinnacles. The wagon roof of the nave has rustic seventeenth-century paintings of angels. In the village many of the cottages have stone mullioned windows with hood moulds and fragments salvaged from the abbey ruins.

N

NEAR SAWREY
Cumbria

The names of the two adjacent villages, Near and Far Sawrey, refer to their distance from Hawkshead. They owe their existence to the old ferry road linking Kendal with Hawkshead, via Ferry Nab on Lake Windermere. This ferry reputedly dates back to the Roman occupation. Near Sawrey is a typical lakeland sheep-farming village, situated on a small rolling plateau with distant views of the Coniston fells. The cottages and farms date predominantly from the seventeenth and eighteenth centuries, with some nineteenth-century additions. All are built of local stone, some roughcast, generally limewashed, and roofed with Coniston slate. Set among small hilly fields with outcrops of rock, Sawrey is distinguished in its setting, but without Beatrix Potter it would not be famous. She called it 'as nearly perfect a little place as I ever lived in, and such nice old-fashioned people in the village'. For their summer holidays her parents, leaving their rigid middle-class life in London, took houses in the Lake District. Beatrix developed an abiding love of the Lakes; in 1905 she bought a house in Near Sawrey, Hill Top (NT*). This was a small seventeenth-century farmhouse, with the long stair window, flagged floors and slate porch traditional to the Lakes. The wrought-iron gates she added are illustrated in *Jemima Puddle-Duck*, which also contains the Hill Top farmyard and the nearby Tower Bank Arms (NT). *The Tale of Tom Kitten* shows the garden and staircase at Hill Top. *The Pie and the Patty Pan*, more than any other of her books, paints a recognizable picture of the village, with its post office, white cottages and gardens, village pump and farmyards. *Ginger and Pickles*, the last book to illustrate Sawrey, shows the village shop. In 1913 Beatrix Potter married William Heelis, a solicitor from Hawkshead, and moved to Castle Cottage (NT), within sight of Hill Top. She gave up writing, and devoted herself to serious farming, specializing in Herdwick sheep. On her death in 1943, she and her husband bequeathed 4000 acres and fourteen farms to the National Trust, including her property at Near Sawrey.

NETHER ALDERLEY
Cheshire

The village is remarkable for the splendid fifteenth-century watermill (NT*), with wooden water wheels and machinery, recently restored. Its magnificent roof has four dormer windows. From here a lane winds past old brick and half-timbered cottages, some fine beech trees and the Georgian rectory to the church of St Mary, largely of the fourteenth century. The Stanley family from Alderley Park owned the village, and there are some interesting Stanley monuments in the church, as well as a font which was buried during the Civil War and only rediscovered in 1821. There are two inns, the Eagle and Child and the Wizard of the Edge (NT).

NEWTOWN
Isle of Wight, Hampshire

A failed medieval village founded in 1256 by the Bishops of Winchester, Newtown, originally called Franchville, was destroyed by the French in 1377. Newton became a 'rotten borough' with a right, like Old Sarum, to return a Member of Parliament despite its tiny population. The ancient borough was laid out on a grid plan: High Street, Gold and Silver Streets all peter out into fields in which the ancient house sites are still visible.

Below lie the oyster beds, reputedly developed by the Romans. The Old Town Hall (NT*), now standing oddly on its own, is a handsome Georgian brick building with stone quoins, a hipped roof, a classical portico and Gothick windows. Noah's Ark, an attractive stone building formerly an inn, the Franchville Arms, dates from *c.* 1700. There are two stone cottages, a council house, a tiny range of pretty single-storey almshouses and Causeway Cottage, stucco with an eighteenth-century portico. Marsh Farm is an interesting *cottage orné* of stone, with double corbelled chimneys on the gable end, bargeboarding and oriel windows. The church of the Holy Spirit, standing on an earlier site, has a bellcote, severe early nineteenth-century lancet windows, and eighteenth-century gravestones. The cushion pointing is unfortunate. Lamb Cottage, early nineteenth-century stucco, and Anchor Cottage complete this ghost village, which has a distinctive character unlike any other. Below lies Newtown Creek with its quays and a fine stone bridge. Much of the surrounding land, including the estuary of the Newtown River with its quays, is owned by the National Trust.

O

OLD WARDEN
Bedfordshire

In the Middle Ages Warden, or Old Warden as it became in 1500, was known for its pears, grown by monks from Warden Abbey, a Cistercian foundation connected with Rievaulx and founded in 1135. Nothing now remains of this. The Icknield Way was joined to Old Warden by an Iron Age bank running from the top of Old Warden Hill (Warden means 'watch hill'), and this has a wide view over the Bedfordshire flats. Lord Ongley, whose family arrived as linen drapers in the late seventeenth century, rebuilt Old Warden as an estate village in the 1830s. Terraces of thatched cottages are embellished with dormers, neo-Tudor brick chimneys, bargeboards, Gothick windows, trellis porches and some delightful planting. The inhabitants

wore red cloaks, as at Selworthy. In 1841 Lord Ongley fitted up the church with an astonishing profusion of Belgian and French wood carving, including fragments from Anne of Cleves' chapel in Bruges. There are also monuments to the Ongley family. Old Warden Park was built in 1872 by Henry Clutton for the Shuttleworths and now houses an agricultural college, while a world-famous aircraft museum founded in memory of Richard Shuttleworth, a pioneer aircraft collector who was killed in 1940, flourishes next door to the house.

P

PAMPHILL
Dorset
(Kingston Lacy Estate – NT)

A small plain church by Ponting, 1907, is prettily sited in a field, with an avenue of mature oaks running from this point across a large green. The Manor (NT*), a little gem of the late seventeenth century, is of brick and stone with a stone-slated hipped roof and dormers. Beyond, before the road descends to the Wareham marshes, stands Gillingham's school and almshouses, an imposing brick building of 1698 with a big segmental pediment. A small brick inn and some pretty thatched cottages complete the village.

PENBERTH
Cornwall

This is a fishing village, the cottages of granite and thatch. It is a rare spot: picturesque but still a working community, with boats drawn up on a slip, scattered cottages and tiny hillside fields given over to flower production, principally daffodils and violets. In appearance it is the most purely pre-war community in Cornwall. Both Penberth Cove and Cribba Head above the village are owned by the National Trust.

PENSHURST
Kent

The Sidney family have owned Penshurst Place, one of the most important fourteenth- and fifteenth-century houses in England, since they were given it by King Edward VI in the sixteenth century. Sir Philip

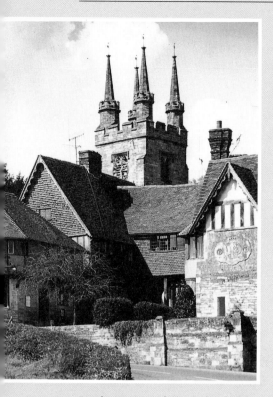

Penshurst, Kent, showing the church and some estate cottages.

Sidney lived here when not campaigning in Holland. The famous great hall, still retaining its central fire and louvred chimney, was built in the mid-fourteenth century. The romantic estate village contains the first Leicester Square, named after Lord Leicester, Queen Elizabeth's favourite. Until recently, with its rich mixture of old ragstone tile-hung and timber-framed cottages, it was thought to be largely original. It is now known that George Devey carried out such skilful additions and pastiches in the mid-nineteenth century that it is difficult to tell the original from the Devey. It is sufficient to say that the whole ensemble, including the thirteenth-century church, partly rebuilt by Sir George Gilbert Scott in the nineteenth century, full of splendid Sidney monuments, is enchanting. Clipped yew hedges and tall brick neo-Tudor chimneys complete the composition of one of the most satisfying and coherent villages in England.

PORT GAVERN
Cornwall

Only the fish cellars remain as a reminder that this was once a small port. It is now a pretty tourist hamlet, with a small shingle beach (NT). In the nineteenth century it was a busy port used to ship Delabole slate.

PORTQUIN
Cornwall

This is a picturesque fishing village with stone and slate cottages and ruined fish cellars lying at the head of an inlet, with an old quay and, on Doyden Point, the red-brick folly Doyden Castle (NT), built c. 1830. Abandoned as a port reputedly when the male population were all lost at sea, and for many years a deserted village, it now consists largely of holiday cottages.

PUMPSAINT
Dyfed

Gold was found at Dolaucothi in Wales before the coming of the Romans; its importance was rapidly recognized and by AD 75 mines (NT*) were being developed by the Romans, who also built a fort. These are the only goldmines known to have been worked by the Romans. After the abandonment of the fort in AD140, the settlement for mineworkers continued until the Romans withdrew and it became the site of the present village of Pumpsaint. Subsequent attempts to reopen the mines in the late nineteenth and early twentieth centuries failed because on each occasion the cost of extracting and refining the ore was found to be uneconomic, and since 1938 the mines have remained closed. The Dolaucothi Estate, including the Dolaucothi Arms Hotel and part of the village, was given to the National Trust in memory of the Johnes family of Croft Castel and Hafod, owners of the estate since the time of Henry VII.

Q

QUATT
Shropshire

A village on the Dudmaston Estate (NT), which has remained in the ownership of the same family since the twelfth century, Quatt contains cottages built partly of local sandstone and partly of brick, designed in 1890 by William Woolryche-Whitmore. A fine church sits on a dramatic site overlooking the River Severn, and an interesting seventeenth-century dower house lies nearby. Dudmaston Hall, a large eighteenth-century house, stands in a landscape park with a lake.

R

ROBIN HOOD'S BAY
North Yorkshire

One of the most dramatically placed fishing villages in the country, Robin Hood's Bay marred only by the usual tourist clutter and some unfortunate Victorian developments at the upper end. The small terraces of stone cottages with red pantile roofs, clinging precariously to the cliff's edge along a network of incredibly steep cobbled alleys and steps, cluster amid some of the grandest scenery in Yorkshire. The great sweep of Robin Hood's Bay (NT) provides an incomparable setting. Formerly known as Bay Town, it had in the nineteenth century a fleet of 100 boats involved in fishing and trading. Smuggling was notorious; in 1800 every resident was said to be involved, and many of the houses are connected by passages and cellars to enable smuggled goods to pass invisibly from one end of the village to the other. Sailors were press-ganged into the navy from here, and The Bolts, a terrace built in 1709, was used as an escape route from arrest. The sea is encroaching at an alarming rate, despite the vast retaining wall which helps to prevent the Bay Hotel from following its predecessor into the sea. (A ship's bowsprit once came through the window of the old Bay Hotel in a storm.) Possibly as many as 200 houses have subsided into the sea, and in 1780 a large part of King Street collapsed. In the churchyard of St Stephen's many shipwrecked sailors are buried. The village expanded from 1885 with the arrival of the railway, to its detriment. The Victorian villas of Mount Pleasant were developed near the station.

Robin Hoods' Bay, Yorkshire, showing tightly packed cottages – some with pantile roofs – and the bay below.

RODMELL
East Sussex

Beautifully placed between the Downs and the River Ouse, Rodmell has outstanding views. The houses, mostly of flint, are grouped unevenly along the single street. The Rectory is a pretty early Victorian Gothic building. Lower down the village street stands Monk's House (NT*), home of Virginia and Leonard Woolf. Built of flint, with white weatherboarding and many additions to the original cottage, including a large conservatory, the house contains decoration by Vanessa Bell (Virginia's sister) and Duncan Grant, who lived at Charleston Manor near Lewes. Beyond lies the tiny downland flint church of St Peter. Its pyramid spire is unusual and may have acted as a landmark for ships navigating the river, as did the spires at Piddinghoe and Southease nearby. The church, of Norman origin, was restored in the nineteenth century. It contains fragments from Lewes Priory.

ROSTHWAITE, SEATHWAITE, STONETHWAITE
Cumbria

With Stonethwaite and Seathwaite, Rosthwaite (NT) lies among National Trust land in the magnificent Borrowdale landscape. Rosthwaite is a small nucleated village with a core of seventeenth-century farmhouses and later buildings, and a hotel nearby. Stonethwaite is an agricultural village with a good collection of seventeenth- and eighteenth-century farms and cottages, mostly owned by the National Trust. Seathwaite (NT) is a hamlet laying below the dramatic Sty Head Pass and contains one seventeenth-century farmstead, Rain Gauge Cottage, (formerly owned by the Bankes family) and other buildings. Stockley Bridge and Taylor Gill waterfall are nearby.

S

ST MICHAEL'S MOUNT (NT)
Cornwall
see pp. 178–9

SELBORNE
Hampshire

The village is best known for the Reverend Gilbert White's *Natural History and Antiquities of Selborne*, published in 1789, a best-seller even in his lifetime and one of the earliest works of its kind. His home, Wakes, is now a museum and his garden is carefully restored and cherished; it has an early ha-ha. The zig-zag path leading to Selborne Hanger (NT) was much loved and well recorded by White at all times of the year. The view of the South Downs from the top is extensive and grand. There are flint and sandstone cottages, some thatched; a village green; and a Norman church, St Mary, with an impressive arcade. The interior was much restored by William White, great-nephew of Gilbert White, in 1856. An enormous yew stands in the churchyard, its branches supported by posts. Alfred Waterhouse designed the great house for the Selborne family in uncompromising High Victorian Gothic. The Selbornes and the National Trust have wisely kept the village's traditional and unspoilt character.

SELWORTHY (NT)
Somerset
see pp. 180–181

SHAPWICK
Dorset
(Kingston Lacy Estate – NT)

A large flint church, St Bartholomew, stands near some thatched cottages in this straggling agricultural village on the edge of Wareham Marsh. White Mill Bridge, downstream, has eight arches with cutwaters and refuges. Beside it stands White Mill of 1776, making a romantic group. Badbury Rings (NT), an Iron Age fort, and several barrows are within a mile of Shapwick.

SHERBORNE
Gloucestershire

The village is beautifully sited near the Sherborne brook, and is part of the estate of Sherborne House. It is divided into two parts, east and west, separated by Sherborne Park. There are traditional stone cottages of the seventeenth and eighteenth centuries at the west end. The east end was rebuilt in the early nineteenth

St Michael's Mount (NT), Cornwall

The dramatic outline of the Mount, towering above the rollers of Mount's Bay, suggests defence. But the castle (NT*) is only 300 years old, much of it less, whereas the monastery existed as an important pilgrimage site for a thousand years before that, and the port, as a link between Britain and the Mediterranean, since before 3000 BC, exporting Irish gold and copper and Cornish tin to Bronze Age Europe. The Mount's significance has been on an international scale since the earliest records began.

The quayside village was first developed by the monks of the Benedictine Priory of St Michael in the early thirteenth century; the quay was constructed in 1385, and the causeway connecting the island with the mainland at low tide was built by the monks in 1425. The first lighthouse in Cornwall was built on the Mount in 1433, a small beacon set on one of the turrets of the monastery and still visible today. The harbour was extended and the pier strengthened during the fifteenth century, allowing 200 ships to anchor safely.

Throughout the fifteenth century many pilgrims sailed from St Michael's Mount to Santiago de Compostela. As the shrine of St Michael, the Mount was itself an important pilgrimage centre (it had been a Christian site since AD 495, when St Michael the Archangel was reputedly seen standing on the rock by a group of fishermen). The Pilgrims' Banqueting House, which lay to the east of the port catered for the needs of pilgrims, and can be seen in early engravings. But the monastery was dissolved in 1535, and all the valuables were removed. Only the church and the fifteenth-century refectory, transformed into a great hall, now the Chevy Chase room, survived.

The strategic importance of the Mount had always been recognized, and after the Dissolution it was held for the Crown by a series of governors and fortified. It was from the Mount in 1588 that the Armada was sighted, and the beacon on the church tower signalled the approaching fleet

The Mount in 1734 by Buck. Note the bare rock, and the ruins of the Pilgrims' Banqueting House on the left.

of 130 ships. During the Civil War it became an important Royalist centre, but was finally overcome by the Parliamentarian army. Colonel John St Aubyn, an ancestor of the present owner, was appointed in 1647 as Captain of the Mount, and the family has been there ever since.

In 1727 the St Aubyns improved the harbour and the export of Cornish tin and copper increased. By 1811 there were fifty-three houses, four streets, three schools, three inns, a Wesleyan Chapel, a Customs House and 300 inhabitants. The prosperity of the harbour continued until the mid-nineteenth century, when Penzance harbour was developed. Now only thirty people live on the island.

Everything in the port today is in miniature. The Change House, once the Sugarloaf Inn, built in 1801, stands at the end of the breakwater. Beside it stands the Steward's House also of 1801, a pretty classical building, and adjoining it the Bird and Fish Museum, built in 1820. Beyond are the old riding stables, where the family coach was kept; the mounting block can still be seen. The old laundry, a gaunt gabled building, is now a café.

The lych gate leads to the graveyard, used by the St Aubyn family since 1870, and also containing the graves of shipwrecked sailors and countless others; the Mount, as a holy site, has been used for burials from its earliest history. Close by is the bowling green, on which stands a family barge of 1770.

The two rows of harbour cottages, partly of stone and partly whitewashed, are sheltered from the gales by the rock towering behind them, and by the breakwaters enclosing the harbour. The Harbour Front row contains the former St Aubyn Arms Inn, built in the late seventeenth century, and distinguished by a small bay window, and a pole, which originally carried the inn sign. The old barge house, built in 1700 and once used as a cow house, now contains the NT ticket office. Behind lies Elizabeth Terrace, late-Victorian stone-gabled houses designed by Piers St Aubyn.

At the west end lie the NT shop, formerly the carpenter's shop, the NT restaurant, in the old sail loft, and, beyond,

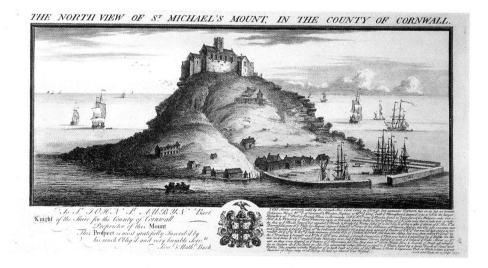

THE NORTH VIEW OF St MICHAEL'S MOUNT, IN THE COUNTY OF CORNWALL.

The Mount today, with the quayside houses, and Elizabeth Terrace and the wooded gardens behind.

the main entrance to the castle, a fifteenth-century archway with the St Aubyn arms above. The miniature fire engine of 1900 stands nearby.

Lying behind the village are small fields, once grazed by cattle driven over from the mainland. Here stands the dairy, designed by Piers St Aubyn in 1870. It is octagonal, buttressed, with stone mullion and transom windows, and a stone-slated conical roof, topped with a louvred Gothic lantern for ventilation.

From this point the climb begins and the castle is approached through spectacular gardens: owing to the mild climate, many sub-tropical plants thrive here. Much of this planting is quite recent; before the nineteenth century, the rock was virtually bare.

An underground railway constructed during the 1870s takes provisions up to the castle, cutting through the rock and emerging under the castle kitchens. Piers St Aubyn extended the castle by adding the south-east wing, which clings dramatically to the vertical rockface, thus turning the seventeenth-century castle into a habitable house without destroying the overall impact of one of the most famous outlines in Europe. The Mount was given to the National Trust in 1954 by the 3rd Lord St Levan.

century as a model village, with pairs of neo-Tudor cottages. Cottage No. 88 contains stones from a Norman church, including a carved tympanum with zig-zag ornament. The church of St Mary Magdalene is joined to the great house by a corridor, as at Dyrham. It was substantially altered in 1820, although the tower and spire survive from the fourteenth century. Inside are many distinguished monuments to the Dutton family, who built Sherborne House in 1551. Some rebuilding of Sherborne House took place in 1651, and again in the nineteenth century, but the form of this fine early classical house remains. The stables, coach house and dovecote are all eighteenth century. Lodge Park (NT) was originally built within the deer park in the mid-seventeenth century as a pavilion from which to watch the coursing of deer by greyhounds. It was turned into a house in 1890 by Lady Sherborne. There are several late eighteenth-century farmhouses, including Woeful Lake Farm, lying outside the village.

SISSINGHURST
Kent

The castle gatehouse (NT*) is a survival from a moated Elizabethan courtyard house of 1558. The famous castle gardens (NT*) designed by Vita Sackville-West and Sir Harold Nicolson contain two sixteenth-century cottages, the South House and the Priest's House, and the original entrance range of the Elizabethan house. The village, originally called Milkhouse Street, contains many white weatherboarded Wealden houses, some built by weavers in the sixteenth century or earlier. Sissinghurst Court, which is also of the sixteenth century, and Sissinghurst Place have interesting gardens open to the public.

SLINDON
West Sussex

The Slindon Estate (NT) of over 3500 acres includes much of the village and protects the magnificent hills of Bignor and Coldharbour, Gatting Beacon, the Neolithic causewayed enclosure Barkhale, and the famous beech woods, tragically

decimated by the hurricane of 1987.
The views from the village
encompass the whole of the plain
below, edged by the sea, with the
spire of Chichester Cathedral visible
on a clear day. The village was
owned by the Archbishops of
Canterbury; the ruins of their
thirteenth-century palace survive in
the garden of Slindon House, a
rambling flint mansion, which was
once an Elizabethan house, and was
much altered and extended in 1921
by Mervyn Macartney. The church
of St Mary which stands close to it,
was skilfully restored in 1866 by the
eminent Oxford architect Sir T.G.
Jackson. The village was planned in
a square, and has four roads lined
with attractive flint and brick
cottages, some thatched, some
whitewashed, interspersed with
larger houses. The smithy is still in
use, and so is the duckpond.

SMALLHYTHE
Kent

Now on the edge of Romney Marsh,
Smallhythe was a port in the Middle
Ages, before the sea receded.
Smallhythe Place (NT*), 1480, dates
from this period and was once the
Port House. It became the home of
Ellen Terry and is now a theatre
museum dedicated to her memory.
This and the adjoining Priest's House
(NT) are fine timber-framed houses,
jettied, with a barn theatre; other
ancient cottages are nearby. The
church of St John the Baptist was
rebuilt in brick in 1516.

SNOWSHILL
Gloucestershire

This is one of the most beautifully
placed villages in the Cotswolds.
Groups of limestone cottages cluster
round a large green, with a Victorian
church, rebuilt in 1864, and a good
inn providing a focus. The land falls
away beyond in a series of small
valleys. Snowshill Manor (NT*) is a
remarkably untouched Tudor manor
with a fine façade of *c.* 1700, stone
mullions and a big hipped roof all of
Cotswold limestone. It contains
Charles Wade's eccentric collection,
and is set in beautiful walled and
terraced gardens. Opposite is a
charming row of traditional stone
cottages (NT) probably
contemporary with the house.

Selworthy (NT), Somerset

Selworthy is a planned village, rebuilt in 1828 on the
Holnicote estate by Sir Thomas Acland (1787–1871), the
10th Baronet, to house his pensioners in a picturesque
setting. The cream-washed thatched cottages, informally
grouped in a steep valley below Exmoor and sheltered by
mature trees, look much like the cottages in the neighbour-
ing villages, many of which date from the seventeenth
century. They were, however, planned and laid out round a
green by Sir Thomas Acland himself. The picturesque effect

*Selworthy – the Aclands' 'happy valley' – with Exmoor
beyond. The woods were originally planted by Sir
Thomas Acland.*

of the village was enhanced by the red cloaks provided for the pensioners to wear on Sundays.

Holnicote House, the Aclands' holiday house, recently rebuilt after a fire, lies at the bottom of the valley, and the fine fifteenth-century church of All Saints half-way up the hill. Between stands the medieval stone tithe-barn dating from the fourteenth century. The Aclands acquired the estate in 1745 through the marriage of the 7th Baronet to Elizabeth Duke, a local heiress whose family owned much of Exmoor. In 1944 it was given to the National Trust by their descendant Sir Richard Acland, together with the Killerton Estate in Devon, which had been in the family for four hundred years.

The rebuilding of Selworthy was probably suggested to Sir Thomas Acland by his friend John Harford, a successful banker from Bristol, who in 1810 commissioned John Nash, then at the beginning of his career, to design Blaise

Hamlet to complement his Blaise Castle Estate. The Blaise cottages are deliberately asymmetrical, and the variety of materials and styles employed by Nash give a sense of artifice entirely lacking at Selworthy.

Both Harford and Acland were inspired by social concern, and also by the cult of the picturesque promoted by Richard Payne Knight and Uvedale Price. Harford and Acland took a keen interest in religion, education and anti-slavery, and both did much to improve life for their workers. Acland carried his interests beyond his estates and had a distinguished career in Parliament, as well as being a dedicated churchman and a friend of Wilberforce, Hannah Moore and Alexander Knox, all in the forefront of religious and evangelical thinking.

Acland was also influenced by the publication in 1823 of P. F. Robinson's *Rural Architecture*, which recommended that: 'in making provision for the aged . . . it is pleasing to render their cottages . . . objects of interest, as picturesque features in the landscape.' Acland's cottages at Selworthy, loosely grouped around a sloping green, have high chimneys and thatched roofs with wide eaves and dormers, and are deliberately vernacular. The scene is highly picturesque, the cottage gardens merging with the green and with the steep wooded valley behind, while beyond the eye is led to the stark moors, crowned by Dunkery Beacon. Acland had begun planting trees along the 'happy valley', as Selworthy was known by his family, in 1809. Belts of trees on the hill above Selworthy were then planted to celebrate the births of successive children, and also provided shelter belts for the village. They were intersected with delightful walks and seats placed at viewpoints. Paths lead through the woods to Allerford and Bossington and along North Hill as far as Hurleston Point. Their total length was once forty miles.

A typical Sunday at the Aclands would begin with a stroll up through the village to the morning service, then lunch with Joshua Stephenson, the rector of Selworthy and a close friend of Sir Thomas Acland's. This was followed by a second service, and then a walk through the woods, which gave Thomas a chance to discuss the sermon and to declaim hymns and poems to his children. From seats on the way a magnificent view was revealed of Exmoor or of the cliffs and the sea far below.

All Saints Church crowns the village, and its lime-washed walls and tower can be seen for many miles. From it one can see across to Dunkery Beacon. In the churchyard grow two yew trees, planted in 1860 by Thomas to celebrate the rector's ninetieth and his own seventy-third birthday. Stephenson lies buried beneath his tree and inside the church is a memorial to Thomas, who was buried at Killerton. The interior of the church, entered from a two-storeyed porch, is high, elegant and light, its glory being the south aisle, dated 1539 on one of the capitals and, according to Nikolaus Pevsner, 'unsurpassed in the county . . . . The tracery of the large transomed windows is of that exquisite, elegant, yet by no means exuberant design worked out probably at Dunster . . . and used at Luccombe.' The wagon roofs are original, richly decorated with angels and large bosses. The Squire's Pew, 'a delicious little Gothic pavilion within the parvise chamber of the porch', is early nineteenth century. Could it have been inspired by Thomas Acland himself? One is certainly reminded of him at every turn. Even the road descending from the church is lined with holly trees, many of his planting.

Styal (NT), Cheshire

Styal is an early and unusually picturesque rural mill complex, complete with the mill owner's house, workers' cottages, the chapel, school, shops and home farm all intact and little altered since the day that they were built. The village lies on an upland, and gives no hint of the existence of the mills, which are hidden in a dramatic river gorge far below. The complex arose from the vision of Samuel Greg, who founded the mill estate in 1784 and made one of the largest fortunes of the early cotton industry.

Styal was planned at a time when new spinning inventions were encouraging the establishment of small mechanized mills. The early mills were often located in remote rural areas near rivers, where water power could be used, but this isolation created problems. In order to attract a labour force it was necessary to build suitable accommodation and to recruit workers. These communities, wholly dependent upon their employers for housing, work and entertainment, also gave enlightened mill owners a unique opportunity to educate and encourage their workers, an opportunity made full use of by Samuel Greg and his wife Hannah, and the sons who succeeded him. The system could also lead to exploitation, particularly since the workforce tended to be largely made up of orphaned children.

The first mill building (NT*) was constructed in 1784, and has Greg's name and date over the door. Others followed as the business expanded. The simple, symmetrical buildings are iron-framed, clad in brick, with slate roofs, large

Farm Fold Cottages, Styal, in c.1900 with the Methodist Chapel, a converted cornstore, behind. Note the Yorkshire horizontal sliding sash windows.

windows, many with fixed lights and their original cast-iron glazing bars, and stone stairs. The headrace which drove the great water wheel, installed by 1819, went out through a tunnel from the mill to Giant's Castle, three-quarters of a mile downstream.

The next development was the Apprentice House (NT*), a brick building built in 1790 on the hill above the mills. The children, mostly orphans, were recruited from local workhouses. Eventually, when the local supply became scarce, they came from as far away as Liverpool and even London. By 1800 one hundred children were living in the Apprentice House, sleeping two in a bed in long dormitories, separated by sex. Their welfare was carefully supervised: they went to church on Sundays, they had their own doctor and schoolmaster, and they were provided with adequate food and clothing. Hannah Greg was deeply involved in the teaching of the apprentice children. and she also set up the Sick Club, the Women's Club and Infants' School.

In 1799 the Greg family built Quarry Bank House beside the mills, an elegant white stucco Georgian house, with a portico and bow windows, and surrounded by an extensive garden. Hannah Greg loved to escape there from their town house in King Street, Manchester, and found it 'truly a renovation of life... to change the long confinement among brickhouses for ... this lively scenery – this incomparable seclusion'. On the other side of the mill was the Mill Manager's House, built in 1810 and also white stucco.

During the early nineteenth century the mill expanded, and with it the workforce. Oak Cottages were built in the 1820s to house the growing population and comprised groups of small two-storey brick cottages with slate roofs, laid out in back-to-back terraces with privvies, allotments and cobbled paths. A list of household goods and chattels from a Styal cottage indicates that the interiors were adequately furnished with beds, chairs, a clock, an iron, pictures, a table, cooking implements, bowls, pots and

FARM·FOLD·STYAL·

Oak Cottages, Styal, built in the 1820s, with the former entrance to the school at the end.

mugs, rugs, bedclothes, a cupboard and a copper 'kettel'. By 1841 sixty-six cottages had been constructed.

The small village school was built around 1820, and Norcliffe Chapel, a severe Early English rectangular building, followed in 1823; it was altered and extended in 1867, and again in 1905. The chapel became the centre for community activities, including lectures and meetings, which were promoted by the Gregs.

Oak Farm was run by the Gregs as a home farm, to provide fresh dairy produce for the community. A sixteenth-century timber-framed building, it was extended between 1855 and 1865. Samuel Greg's shop was another important addition to the village. After 1831 it was taken over by the mill workers and run as a co-operative venture by worker committees. To discourage drunkenness, Henry Philips Greg acquired the Old Ship Inn in 1894 and limited each customer to two glasses of alcoholic drink. Four of Samuel's sons went into the business. In 1731 Robert Hyde Greg, the eldest, built Norcliffe Hall, a large neo-Elizabethan house with a substantial clock tower, also on the Oak Farm Estate.

Since Alec Greg gave the mill complex and the village to the National Trust in 1939, many of the cottages have been modernized. The paths have been cobbled and paved, and the green, once the site of the allotments, landscaped. The whole estate is designated as a Country Park. But throughout all these changes, Styal village continues as an integrated community. The chapel, school and inn are still in use, and the descendants of many of the original families, including the Gregs, still live there.

STEVENTON
Oxfordshire

A remarkably early and unspoilt group of leaning, gabled, timber-framed houses flanks the ancient raised paved causeway in this otherwise unattractive village. No. 39 The Causeway (NT) is a small house of *c*. 1350 containing a cruck-trussed hall and a single cross wing. No. 103 The Causeway (NT) is another medieval timber-framed house with a central hall and projecting wings, partly thirteenth-century, partly fifteenth-century, altered in the seventeenth century, and restored in this century. No. 81 was also restored in this century by Walter Godfrey as his home, and inherited by his son Emil. It is considerably altered inside, but retains a most interesting medieval timber-framed exterior. Even more surprising are Priory Cottages (NT*) on the corner of The Causeway and Mill Street, containing the great hall of the former priory. Beyond lie the water meadows, an attractive farm and mill house and the old station, now closed.

STOKE-BY-NAYLAND
Suffolk

Like Lavenham (see p. 170) this is a predominantly Tudor village, owing its prosperity and its great flint church of St Mary to medieval merchants. Immortalized by Constable, the village has changed very little since he painted it. It has been preserved by the National Trust, which have covenants over the sixteenth-century timber-framed Guildhall, the Old Maltings of *c*. 1620, and the Tendring Hall Estate, and own Thorington Hall (NT*), a timber-framed, plastered and gabled house of *c*.1600 extended in 1700. The ancient timber-framed houses with tall brick chimneys, the old almshouses, the ancient inns – the Crown and the Black Horse – and Giffords Hall beyond the village, all give an impression of a place that time has overlooked.

STOKE SUB HAMDON
Somerset

It lies under Ham Hill, source of most of the building stone. The priory buildings (NT*) date from the fourteenth and fifteenth centuries and were formerly the residence of the priests of the chantry of St Nicholas in the Beauchamp manor house which once stood nearby; the great hall, a fine barn and a dovecote survive. There is an interesting church, St Mary, partly Norman with a Perpendicular tower and Jacobean furnishings. Some attractive cottages are to be seen in East and West Stoke.

STONETHWAITE
Cumbria
see Rosthwaite

STOURTON (NT)
Wiltshire

Henry Hoare created at Stourhead (NT*) from 1741 onwards the most important landscape park of his generation. In 1764 he acquired the outstanding fourteenth-century Bristol Cross, removed from Cathedral Green, Bristol, and set it up beside the lake to act as a foil to his classical temples. In 1791 Richard Colt Hoare formed a new entrance to the park from this point. He removed some cottages and landscaped the village of Stourton to form part of the picturesque composition. Gothick parapets were added to the fine medieval church and to the cottages to create a romantic outline. They were encircled with lawns, and the steep banks behind were planted with trees, to make the village worthy of the park. The Spread Eagle Inn with its stables (NT*) was built shortly after the public opening of the gardens in the late eighteenth century to cater for the ever-increasing number of visitors.

STUDLAND
Dorset
(Corfe Castle Estate – NT)

A large village, with one or two late-nineteenth-century Queen Anne-revival villas and some infill, adjoins a wonderful coastline. Hill Close, built for Sutro the Edwardian playwright in 1896 by Voysey, is roughcast with stone-slated roof dormers and wide eaves, but is unfortunately much altered. The pretty Gothick Manor House Hotel (NT) of 1825, formerly George Bankes's Marine Villa, overlooks the sea. The Knowl House Hotel and the

Bankes Arms are also owned by the National Trust. St Nicholas, hidden away in a churchyard sheltered by mature yews with the sea beyond, is a rare, almost complete Norman church: only one or two later windows and the south porch detract from its unity. Externally its low nave and chancel, squat central tower and grotesque corbel table are remarkable. The dark interior is breathtaking: heavy rib vaults, tiny lancet windows, columns with scalloped cushion capitals, and rounded chancel arch dating from the eleventh and twelfth centuries. It is on the site of an even earlier church. A fine barn and farm buildings stand nearby.

STYAL
Cheshire
see pp. 182–183

SUDBURY
Derbyshire

This is an attractive estate village built by George Vernon, owner of Sudbury Hall (NT*) in the late seventeenth century, containing almshouses, a stableyard and an inn of 1671, the Vernon Arms. Sudbury Hall, a Jacobean E-shaped brick house, contains important ceilings painted by Laguerre and carving by Grinling Gibbons. Vernon demolished the cottages lying near the Hall to gain privacy and laid out the curving village street; some of the gabled cottages have diaper brickwork. It is an unusually complete example of an early planned village. The church contains a fine early monument to two women of the Montgomery family of Sudbury, who lived there for four hundred years before the Vernons, and monuments to the Vernon family itself.

T

TICKNALL
Derbyshire

Lying on the northern edge of Calke Park, and set astride the Melbourne-Swadlincote road, Ticknall is largely an estate village with a small general store and a fine nineteenth-century church, the building of which was funded by the Harpur-Crewes of

Calke Abbey (NT*). Some modern infill indicates the village's growing role as a dormitory for Derby, although a fair proportion of the inhabitants remain employed on the land. The estate brickyards in the village, and limepits linked by rail, just in the park, provided further employment until they ceased to function after the war. Brick is the main building material in the village, many of the buildings being timber-framed, although there are two splendid cottages with grand gabled façades faced in stone that must surely have belonged to the estate. There is an antique shop in a pleasant Georgian house near the park gates, and nineteenth-century cast-iron water hydrants in the streets. The National Trust owns three cottages in the village and the brick bridge which arches over the road near the park gates. It was constructed to carry the trucks to and from the brickyard. The Harpur-Crewe Estate retains ownership over some of the village; the majority, however, is now privately owned.

TIVINGTON
Somerset
see Holnicote Estate (NT)

TROUTBECK
Cumbria

A large village straggling along the side of a hill above Lake Windermere, Troutbeck has many large seventeenth-century farmhouses containing fine carved woodwork – a relic of the time when it was an important farming community of statesmen (or yeomen) – the farmsteads linked by steep paved tracks. Some seventeenth-century spinning galleries and oak mullion windows survive. There is infill housing built in the nineteenth century. The walls along the village lanes contain drinking troughs for horses making the ascent to Kirkstone Pass. The church, rebuilt in the eighteenth century, has a good east window by Burne-Jones, William Morris and Ford Madox Brown. Townend (NT*) is an important statesman's house built in about 1626 by the Browne family, who occupied it continuously for over 300 years. It has the massive cylindrical chimneys and rows of stone mullions typical of the area, and fine traditional interiors with exceptional wood carving, stone-slated floors and a large farm kitchen. Troutbeck Park Farm was bought by Beatrix Potter in 1928 and left to the National Trust. It is one of the most famous sheep farms in the Lake District, containing three peaks of over 2000 feet, and covering nearly 2000 acres. The Roman road from High Street ran through the land and down Scots Rake to Galava Fort at Ambleside.

U

UPPER SHERINGHAM
Norfolk

This is an important estate village designed by Humphry and John Adey Repton in 1812 to complement the great house and its landscape park ('my most favourite work'), and putting into effect many of Repton's theories on exploiting the picturesque qualities of a village (see pp. 113–115). The noise of the sea is never far away from this village which, by-passed by the railway and coast road, has remained small and secluded. The enormous churchyard, however, full of the gravestones of those lost at sea, is witness to Upper Sheringham's former importance. The robust flint cottages, most traditionally built with flushwork walls, are dominated by All Saints' Church, of typically Norfolk Perpendicular style and dating from c. 1450. It is notable for a handsome south porch with intricate flushwork and crocketed pinnacles. Inside, the fifteenth-century rood screen and loft remain, a very rare survival, with access through a small door behind the pulpit. At the west end of the long nave is a cambered tie-beam that carries the pulley and counterpoise for controlling the wooden font cover, again a rarity. The bench ends display some lively carvings and there are memorials to the Upchers of Sheringham Park (NT). The village square, beside the church, boasts an unusual fountain built in 1814 as a premature thanksgiving for victory over Napoleon. The Red Lion Inn remains a nucleus for the village, and in 1987 a small housing development beside the square earned a commendation for good design.

V

VERYAN
Cornwall

Approached down deep, narrow lanes, Veryan has a sheltered position in a fine wooded dell. There is an interesting church, St Symphonian – an unusual dedication – and, next to the churchyard, exotic water gardens with semi-tropical plants. Many whitewashed thatched cottages include several round houses with Gothic windows and conical thatched roofs topped by crosses, guarding the entrances to the village. Veryan Bay and the surrounding cliffs are owned by the National Trust.

W

WATENDLATH
Borrowdale, Cumbria

Beautifully sited on the edge of Watendlath Tarn, high above Derwentwater, this small, isolated hamlet of whitewashed farm buildings dates from the seventeenth century, but is reputedly of Norse origin. It is best approached on foot by track from Borrowdale to appreciate the impressive setting, cradled by mountains.

WEOBLEY
Hereford and Worcester

This is a typical black-and-white village. The ancient houses, some cruck-framed and some jettied, many dating from the early fourteenth century, group charmingly, while towering above them is the big stone fourteenth-century church with its prominent pinnacled spire. It has been called 'the capital of black and white'. Once a 'rotten borough', it returned two Members of Parliament until 1832. There are two interesting inns – the Red Lion and the Unicorn – an old grammar school, the old workhouse, and much else. It is also said that Herefordshire cattle originated here.

WEST CLANDON,
Surrey

Clandon Park (NT*) by Leoni, c. 1735, built for the second Earl of Onslow, stands in an extensive park designed by Capability Brown. The village, strung along the road, has many half-timbered cottages, tile-hung or with flint infilling, and the Onslow Arms inn. The church of St Peter and St Paul has a nineteenth-century wooden spire, and the fine Onslow family pew, which is of the seventeenth century.

Widecombe-in-the-Moor (see p.187), Devon, with the prominent tower of the 'Cathedral of the Moor' and, beyond, Dartmoor.

West Wycombe, Buckinghamshire

The church of St Lawrence, West Wycombe, on the hill above the village, engraved in 1822.

West Wycombe village is a product of the road on which it is built, linking London with Oxford, the Midlands, Wales and the West Country. Through it passed medieval foot, horse and wagon traffic, but this flow was small in comparison with the stage and mail coaches that clattered through in the eighteenth and early nineteenth centuries. Three of the eight coaching inns recorded in the eighteenth century still survive as inns: the George and Dragon, dating from 1720; the Swan of 1739, now shorn of its brewhouse and stables; and the Plough, with a date stone of 1727. The remainder are now private houses. At their height, the eight inns supplied a change of horses and had inner courtyards for carriages. On one evening 14 coaches and 30 horses were counted leaving the village for the west. The thunder of traffic continues today, somewhat alleviated by the by-pass effect of the M40 motorway.

The village street is lined with rows of small cottages, gabled, timber-framed, often jettied and many dating from the sixteenth century or earlier. Although the roofs are now tiled, the steep pitch indicates that many were originally thatched. Most of them face directly onto the road, giving little privacy in front, but the gardens behind, separated by small fences, are suprisingly secluded. The street pattern is varied by the occasional Georgian house, either of brick or faced with flint, by the Victorian Gothic Methodist chapel and school, and by the arched approaches to the inner courtyards of the coaching inns.

Crown Court, entered through an archway, contains a pretty group of remarkably unaltered cottages. At the western, opposite end of the street there is an eighteenth-century malthouse, its low, flint-built outline in strong contrast with the upright building pattern. The most distinguished eighteenth-century house in the street is Steps House, a fine Queen Anne brick house approached by a double stair, with a hipped roof and sash windows. The Dower House, designed by Nicholas Revett for Sir Francis Dashwood in the mid-eighteenth century, is faced in flint. Church Loft frames the entrance to Church Lane, a steep track lined with delightful eighteenth-century brick and flint houses, a nineteenth-century furniture factory and a Methodist chapel of 1781. The village pump stands prominently beside the Old Vicarage. The village clock has been attached to Church Loft from an early date, and the existence of the vicarage on Church Lane suggests that this and not the church on the hill was the centre of village life.

Church Loft, built in the fifteenth century as a rest house for pilgrims, is timber-framed and jettied, and in the eighteenth century a weather-boarded bell turret was added. The remains of the village lock-up and whipping post are still visible, but the stocks have disappeared. The staircase is a post-medieval addition, leading to a fine upper room with an open timber roof, queen posts, massive tie beams and trusses. The whole building, despite some remodelling, with its jettied upper storey supported on large moulded beams and its ancient doorways, is a remarkable survival.

The Dashwood family acquired the village (and estate) in 1698. But it was the second Sir Francis Dashwood, (1708–81), who was chiefly responsible for building the house (NT*) and creating the landscape park, Although notorious for his connection with the Hell Fire Club, he went on to become Chancellor of the Exchequer and Joint Postmaster General. In the mid-eighteenth century Sir Francis diverted the road in order to remove it from the park, and on Church Hill, dominating the village, he erected a hexagonal flint mausoleum, close to the medieval church which was also substantially rebuilt. All the alterations to the church reflect his Italian sympathies: classical columns, large Georgian windows, and a high tower adorned with a golden ball inspired by that on the Customs House in Venice. The exterior is all of flint, while inside marble floors and painted decoration by Giuseppe and Giovanni Borgnis complete the scheme.

Thomas Phillibrown, a London wine merchant who visited West Wycombe at the time, reported:

With some difficulty and a little fear, we at last arrived at the Church, which is situated on a very high chalk hill, the tower of which Sir Francis has (at his own expense) for the sake of a prospect to his house and gardens, raised to twice the height it was before, and on the top ... is building a spire of timber, on the top of which is built of wood a very large hollow globe.

The remodelled church contains no Christian symbolism, and it was in a chamber below the altar that the Hell Fire Club celebrated its rites. Sir Francis also built a mock ruin at the entrance to the caves, excavated by him and used by the Hell Fire Club. The landscaping of Church Hill may have been suggested by Nicholas Revett, who remodelled the house and designed the temples.

The village remained in the ownership of the Dashwood family until 1929, when Sir John Dashwood offered it for sale in sixty lots. This, for an estate village which had remained virtually unchanged since the seventeenth century, would have been a disaster. The Royal Society of Arts, fearing the consequences of such a sale, intervened and bought the whole village within a week of hearing of the impending sale, an unprecedented step for a learned society. It then had to undertake a major repair programme, but the survival of such a diverse collection of vernacular buildings, containing to an unusual extent so many of their original features, testifies to the restraint with which these repairs were carried out. In 1934 the Royal Society of Arts transferred the village to the National Trust, which also owns West Wycombe house and park.

Looking down Church Lane, West Wycombe, towards the medieval Church Loft, once a pilgrim's hospice, and, beyond, the village street.

WEST LUCCOMBE
Somerset
see Holnicote Estate (NT)

WESTWOOD
Devon
(Killerton Estate – NT)
see Broadclyst

WIDECOMBE-IN-THE-MOOR,
Devon

Famous for its fair, and the ballad of that name, the village contains the colonnaded Church House (NT*), a fifteenth-century granite building with a portico, which was once an almshouse but is now partly used as a village hall. Glebe House, 1575, and the seventeenth-century Old Inn are grouped round a square with the church of St Pancras, known as the 'Cathedral of the Moor'. It has an early-sixteenth-century screen with painted panels of saints, a sixteenth-century wagon roof, and one of the best towers in Devon, battlemented and pinnacled. It owes its opulence to rich tinners. The village lies in a fine wooded setting on Dartmoor. The village green was once known as Butte Park, and was used for archery.

WINCHELSEA
East Sussex

Much of the village, once a great port, is owned by the National Trust. Founded in 1191 and destroyed by a storm in 1288, it was refounded on its present site by King Edward I as a planned defensive port and as a centre for the wine trade with Gascony. Built on a grid plan, it stands dramatically high above the marshes, partly surrounded by defensive walls. Three of the original town gates, Strand Gate, Pipewell Gate and New Gate, all of the fourteenth century, guard the entrances. Many of the medieval wine vaults, including those beneath the New Inn and Salutation Inn, still exist and can be seen. Only the fourteenth-century chancel of St Thomas's Church, planned on a vast scale but never completed, survives; it contains interesting monuments. Several medieval houses, including the fourteenth-century Court House – now a museum – the Armoury and the ruins of a fourteenth-century Franciscan church remind one of Winchelsea's former importance before the sea receded.

Ysbyty Ifan, Gwynedd. The 18th-century bridge over the river Conwy was once the route of the ancient Chester road.

smithy, wheelwright's and carpenter's shops and two inns, in one of which, the Penrhyn Arms, the local courts were held. Today these are closed and this part of the village looks somewhat forlorn. But the Conwy valley, the river bank clothed with alders and willows, is beautiful, and the setting overshadowed by the high moors is wild and grand.

ZENNOR
Cornwall

The only village along miles of rugged coast west of St Ives, Zennor is set in an ancient granite landscape and well matches it. Beyond is Zennor Head (NT), a spectacular viewpoint. The church of St Senara dates from the twelfth century, and has many later additions and a prominent west tower. The Tinners' Arms is a good pub, and the Wayside Museum, housed in a disused mill, an excellent folk museum.

WINSTER
Derbyshire

An industrial leadmining village built on a steep slope, Winster has some fine Derbyshire stonework and gritstone slate roofs. The main street has some substantial eighteenth- and nineteenth-century houses. The Market House (NT*) had an arcaded, stone lower storey, now filled in, with a brick hall above, rebuilt in 1675.

Y

YSBYTY IFAN
Gwynedd

The name means 'the hospital of St John' and here on the River Conwy the Knights of St John established a hospice in 1189; it was closed at the Reformation in 1532. The parish church of St John the Baptist, built in 1861, stands on the site. Until Telford developed the road which is now the A5, the ancient Chester road from England to North Wales passed through the village, which provided an important refuge from the wild mountainous country surrounding it. The hospice was famous for its size and its hospitality. Indeed, the

sanctuary it offered was exploited by a number of criminals, who eventually had to be evicted in the mid-fifteenth century. A coat of mail found near the bridge may date from this period. The outstanding alabaster effigies in the church are of Rhys Meredydd, standard bearer to Henry Tudor at the battle of Bosworth Field in 1485, his wife Lowry and his son Robert, chaplain to Cardinal Wolsey. The Ysbyty Estate (NT), including the village and 25,000 acres, was bought in 1854 by the first Baron Penrhyn of Penrhyn Castle (NT*) as a sporting estate. He rebuilt the village, including the church, the Methodist chapel, the almshouses – which had originally been founded in the seventeenth century by the Vaughan family – the school, the parsonage, a drinking fountain inscribed 'Penrhyn' and the cottages lining the road on both sides of the River Conwy, turning Ysbyty into an estate village. The old hospice was demolished, and only a few structures including the fine double-arched eighteenth-century bridge remain from the earlier village. Ysbyty was then a self-supporting community with a watermill grinding corn for the district, a

Bibliography (to Part One)

A book covering so many centuries of history has to call heavily on the work of others. Many of the details, and much of the broader argument, too, have come from the work of specialist historians. I hope this bibliography serves to acknowledge my major debts but it is not a comprehensive list of sources. It may suggest some worthwhile further reading on particular aspects of the story.

The origins of village settlement before and after the Norman Conquest have been rethought substantially in recent years. P. H. Sawyer (ed.) *Medieval Settlement* (Edward Arnold, 1976) and C. Taylor *Village and Farmstead* (George Philip, 1983) summarize research and put forward many ideas to challenge past assumptions. G. Beresford *Medieval Clayland Village* (Society for Medieval Archaeology, 1975) investigates particular sites in detail, while R. Muir *A Traveller's History of Britain and Ireland* (Michael Joseph, 1983) is a well-illustrated guide to surviving early settlement sites.

The village community is very readably portrayed in the classic H. S. Bennett *Life on the English Manor* (Cambridge University Press, 1937, re-printed 1971), but there is more modern research in many works, such as H. Hallam's *Rural England 1066–1348* (Fontana, 1981), J. Z. Titow *English Rural Society 1200–1350* (Allen and Unwin, 1969) and R. Hilton *English Peasantry in the Later Middle Ages* (Oxford University Press, 1975). A. McFarlane's *Marriage and Love in England 1300–1840* (Basil Blackwell, 1986) poses some interesting questions about family life in early communites.

Open-field agriculture has attracted academic enquiry over a long period. The more recent work includes two articles by J. Thirsk and by J. Z. Titow in the journal *Past and Present*, Vols 29 and 32 (1962 and 1965), and T. Rowley (ed.) *The Origins of Open-Field Agriculture* (Croom Helm, 1981). See also C. Taylor *Fields in the English Landscape* (Dent, 1975) and the books on enclosure, cited below.

On early village houses, much of the evidence is assembled in M. Beresford and J. G. Hurst *Deserted Medieval Villages* (Lutterworth Press, 1971), while I. C. Peate *The Welsh House* (1940, 2nd rev. edn. Brython Press, 1944) has descriptions of very primitive houses which survived into the modern age.

Later village buildings have been studied extensively since the last war. M. W. Barley *English Farmhouse and Cottage* (Routledge and Kegan Paul, 1971), R. W. Brunskill *Illustrated Handbook of Vernacular Architecture* (Faber and Faber, 1971, 2nd rev. edn., 1978), A. Clifton-Taylor *The Pattern of English Building* (Faber and Faber, 1972), and R. B. Wood-Jones *Traditional Domestic Architecture in the Banbury Region* (University of Manchester, 1963) have each been important in my handling of the subject. W. G. Hoskins *The Midland Peasant* (Macmillan, 1957) and A. Quiney *House and Home* (BBC, 1986) help to put housing in its social context. M. Filbee *Dictionary of Country Furniture* ('Connoisseur', 1977) and J. Ayres *The Shell Book of the Home in Britain* (Faber and Faber, 1981) are useful on interiors.

On religion and superstition in village life K. Thomas *Religion and the Decline of Magic* (Weidenfeld and Nicolson, 1971) is particularly important. I have also found much of interest in C. Platt *Medieval England* (Routledge and Kegan Paul, 1978), R. Foster *Discovering English Churches* (BBC, 1981) and R. W. Malcomson *Life and Labour in England 1700–1780* (Hutchinson, 1981).

The advance of rural industry and commerce was chronicled in Daniel Defoe's *Tour through the Whole Island of Great Britain* (first published in 1724–6, but reprinted by Dent in 1962, and by Penguin in 1971) and in C. Morris (ed.) *The Illustrated Journeys of Celia Fiennes 1685–1712* (Macdonald, 1982). Much that is written on road and river transport is extremely speculative, but I have found help in W. G. Hoskins *Fieldwork in Local History* (Faber and Faber, 1967), in O. G. S. Crawford *Archaeology in the Field* (Phoenix House, 1953) and in A. E. and E. M. Dodd *Peakland Roads and Trackways* (Moorland, 1974).

On enclosure of the fields I cite Arthur Young, whose extensive writings include *The Farmer's Guide* (2 vols, 1770) and contributions to the volumes of the Board of Agriculture's *General View of Agriculture* (1793–1815). Good modern works include A. R. H. Baker and R. A. Butlin (eds.) *Studies of Field Systems in the British Isles* (Cambridge University Press, 1973), J. Thirsk (ed.) *The Agrarian History of England and Wales* (Vol. 5, Part II, Cambridge University Press, 1985), J. A. Yelling *Common Field and Enclosure in England, 1450–1850* (Macmillan, 1977), W. E. Tate, *The English Village Community and the Enclosure Movement* (Gollancz, 1967), and G. Darley *The National Trust Book of the Farm* (Weidenfeld and Nicolson, 1981).

Once into the nineteenth century we find some marvellous first-hand descriptions of village life. Among them are Flora Thompson's *Lark Rise to Candleford* (Oxford University Press, 1954), W. Plomer (ed.) *Kilvert's Diary* (Cape, 1973), and R. Jeffries *Hodge and his Masters* (Smith, Elder & Co., 1880). W. Cobbett's *Rural Rides* (1830, reprinted Macdonald and Jane, 1975) and *Cottage Economy* (1821, reprinted Chivers, 1975) give a trenchant if idiosyncratic critique of social conditions.

J. G. Jenkins *Life and Traditions in Rural Wales* (Dent, 1976) is good on village craftsmen and I have also cited a small book of oral history, S. Harrison *Yorkshire Farming Memories* (Castle Museum, York, 1981). The story of agricultural unrest is told by E. J. Hobsbawn and F. G. Rudé in *Captain Swing* (Lawrence and Wishart, 1969).

Victorian paternalism in action at Styal is described in an anonymous booklet *Mill Life at Styal* (Willow Publishing, 1986), while the life story of John Hodges is recounted in A. Heeley and M. Brown *Victorian Somerset:John Hodges – A Farm Labourer* (Friends of the Abbey Barn, Glastonbury, 1978). I have found the analysis of employment, population, migration, etc. in G. Best's *Mid-Victorian Britain* (Weidenfeld and Nicolson, 1971)

particularly illuminating.

Finally there are a number of excellent books covering a long period, among them the classic W. G. Hoskins *Making of the English Landscape* (1955, reprinted Hodder and Stoughton, 1977), R. Muir *The English Village* (Thames and Hudson, 1980) and R. Parker's *The Common Stream* (Collins, 1975) which traces the life of a single village through several centuries.

Index

Page numbers in *italics* refer to illustrations.